17

Mastering
ITALIAN
Grammar

Beatrice Rovere-Fenati

BARRON'S

Author: **Beatrice Rovere-Fenati**
English translation: **Kathleen Luft**

All inquiries should be addressed to:
Barron's Educational Series, Inc.
250 Wireless Boulevard
Hauppauge, NY 11788
http://www.barronseduc.com

ISBN-10: 0-7641-3656-9
ISBN-13: 978-0-7641-3656-6
Library of Congress Control Number: 2006929368

Printed in Canada
9 8 7 6 5 4 3 2 1

How to Use This Book

You're interested in improving your knowledge of Italian grammar. Maybe you want to review, practice, and add to what you've already learned—or even just look something up quickly. *Mastering Italian Grammar* will help you do all of that. This book presents and discusses all the essential features of Italian grammar, it provides **simple explanations**, arranged in a way that is clear and easy to understand, and helps the learning process by way of plenty of helpful exercises.

How the Chapters Are Structured

First, in an **introductory illustration** accompanied by mini-dialogues, we present a selected aspect of Italian grammar in an everyday context. Clear, easy-to-understand rules, **neatly arranged tables**, and detailed **sections on usage** provide a quick overview of the fundamentals. Ample numbers of **practical, real-life examples** show you the right way to use the grammatical element in question.

In the many **exercises** that follow, you have a chance to practice and apply what you have learned. Here the level of difficulty is indicated by asterisks:

* = easy exercise; ** = moderately difficult exercise; *** = difficult exercise. This way you can easily monitor your own progress as you go.

In the marginal notes, you will find many helpful **tips** and information concerning correct usage:
▶ Introductory explanations of the grammatical concept
▶ Tips to help you learn and additional hints
▶ Important exceptions and stumbling blocks
▶ References to other grammar chapters
▶ Vocabulary aids and help with translation

All the **grammatical terms** used in this book are listed and explained in the overview on page 4.
The **index** in the back of the book will help you find the right grammar information in a flash. To speed your search, important topics are shown in red.

We wish you great success as you use this book as a reference tool and a means to improve and practice your Italian!

Overview of Grammatical Terms

The terms used in this book are indicated in **bold**.

English	Italian
accusative object	oggetto diretto
adjective	aggettivo
adverb	avverbio
article	articolo
auxiliary verb	ausiliare
cardinal number	numero cardinale
comparative	comparativo
conditional	condizionale
conditional sentence	frase ipotetica
conjugation	coniugazione
conjunction	congiunzione
consonant	consonante
dative object	oggetto indiretto
demonstrative pronoun	pronome dimostrativo
direct object	oggetto diretto
feminine	femminile
future	futuro
future perfect	futuro anteriore
gender	genere
genitive	genitivo
imperative	imperativo
imperfect	**imperfetto**
indefinite pronoun	pronome indefinito
indicative	indicativo
indirect object	oggetto indiretto
infinitive	infinito
interrogative pronoun	pronome interrogativo
masculine	maschile
negation	negazione
noun	sostantivo / nome
number	numero
object	argomento
object pronoun	pronome personale complemento
ordinal number	numero ordinale
passive	passivo
past participle	participio passato
past perfect	**trapassato prossimo**
personal pronoun	pronome personale
plural	plurale
possessive pronoun	pronome possessivo
predicate	predicato
prefix	prefisso
preposition	preposizione
present	presente
present perfect	**passato prossimo**
preterit	**passato remoto**
pronoun	pronome
reflexive pronoun	pronome riflessivo
reflexive verb	verbo riflessivo
relative pronoun	pronome relativo
simple past	**passato remoto**
singular	singolare
stare + present participle	stare + gerundio
subject	soggetto
subject pronoun	pronome personale soggetto
subjunctive	**congiuntivo**
suffix	suffisso
superlative	superlativo
tense	tempo
verb	verbo
vowel	vocale

Table of Contents

Contents

Contents

The Article

The Definite Article

> Ho comprato **il** pane, **lo** zucchero, l'acqua e **la** carne al supermercato; **i** peperoni, **gli** spinaci e **le** melanzane invece al mercato.

> **Il, lo, l'**, or **la**?
> **I, gli**, or **le**?
> The form you need depends on the gender of the noun (masculine, feminine) and on its initial letter.

I bought the bread, the sugar, the water, and the meat at the supermarket, but the peppers, the spinach, and the eggplant at the street market.

Forms

1. Before Masculine Nouns

▶ **Masculine Nouns,** p. 18

Singular		Plural		With masculine nouns:
il	mese cane tè	**i**	mesi cani tè	Use **il** for the singular and **i** for the plural if the nouns begin with a consonant.
lo	studio specchio zio	**gli**	studi specchi zii	Use **lo** for the singular and **gli** for the plural if they begin with **s** + consonant or with **z**.
l'	amico elefante ufficio	**gli**	amici elefanti uffici	Use **l'** for the singular and **gli** for the plural if the nouns begin with **a, e, i, o**, or **u**.

The forms **lo** and **gli** are also used with words such as **lo ps**icologo, **lo y**acht, **lo x**enofobo, **gli gn**occhi: that is, with masculine nouns beginning with **ps, y, x**, or **gn**. You will not come across such words often, however.

lo specchio – *the mirror*
lo zio – *the uncle*
l'ufficio – *the office*
lo xenofobo –
the xenophobe

2. Before Feminine Nouns

▶ Feminine Nouns, p. 19

Singular		Plural		With feminine nouns:
la	casa madre bambina	le	case madri bambine	Use **la** for the singular if the noun begins with a consonant and
l'	amica idea ora	le	amiche idee ore	**l'** if it begins with a vowel (**a**, **e**, **i**, **o**, **u**). For the plural, always use **le**!

If an adjective appears between the article and the noun, the form of the article is determined by the gender of the noun and the first letter of the adjective:

il film – **lo st**esso film – **l'u**ltimo film
l'idea – **la st**essa idea

Use

There are instances when Italian uses the definite article and English does not:

Ieri ho visto **il** signor Busi e **la** signora Merli.
Sai dove abita **la** professoressa Marello?

Omit the article when you are speaking to the person: Buongiorno **professore Costa**, come sta?

▮ The article precedes **signor**, **signora**, **signorina** + name, as well as title + name, when you are speaking <u>about</u> the person

La mia macchina è rossa.
Stasera vado al cinema con **i** miei amici.

▶ Possessive Pronouns, p. 47

▮ Unlike English, Italian uses the article also in connection with the possessive pronoun.

Normalmente **la** domenica vado dai miei genitori.
Domenica prossima però vado al mare con alcuni amici.
La sera torno a casa tardi. **Ieri sera** invece ero a casa alle sette.

▮ If you want to say that you always do something at certain times of day and on certain days of the week, use the definite article. Otherwise, omit it.

~ Che ora è?   + Sono **le** quattro.
Se partiamo verso **l'**una arriviamo dopo **mezzanotte.**

When you state the time of day, use the definite article. Omit it only with **mezzanotte** and **mezzogiorno**!

Mi piacerebbe vedere **l'**America.
~ Ti piace **l'**Italia?   + Sì, soprattutto **la** Toscana e **la** Sicilia.

The definite article is used with continents, countries, regions, and larger islands.

Lea ha **i** capelli corti, **gli** occhi chiari e porta **gli** occhiali.
Fausto ha **le** spalle larghe e **le** braccia muscolose.

Use the definite article when describing body parts and other external characteristics of a person ...

Lea non porta mai **i** jeans.
Se vai dal direttore devi mettere **la** cravatta.

... as well as articles of clothing, when a type of clothing is referred to.

La frutta e **la** verdura fanno bene.
Ascolto volentieri **il** jazz e **la** musica leggera.
~ A te piace **l'**opera?   + Sì, ma preferisco **l'**operetta.

In addition, the definite article is used in generalizations and when a noun stands for an entire genre ...

Il rosso mi piace, **il** giallo no.
Leo sa **il** tedesco, **il** russo e **l'**inglese.
Chiara ha **il** raffreddore e **la** tosse; forse ha **l'**influenza.

... as well as with colors, languages, diseases ...

Il 1968 e **il** 1969 sono stati anni importanti.

... and year dates.

The article is omitted if the noun is preceded by **in**: Quando andate **in** Francia?

---

i capelli – *the hair*
gli occhi – *the eyes*
gli occhiali – *the (eye)glasses*
le spalle – *the shoulders*
largo – *wide, broad*
le braccia – *the arms*
il raffreddore – *the (bad) cold*
la tosse – *the cough*
l'influenza – *the flu*

▶ Prepositions,
  p. 218

Prepositions and the Definite Article

Dove sono le foto?

①

② Nell'armadio o **nel** cassetto **della** scrivania.

1. Where are the photos? 2. In the cupboard or in the drawer of the desk.

Forms

If the definite article is preceded by the preposition **a**, **da**, **di**, **in**, or **su**, the two are combined to form a single word.

+	il	lo	l'	la
a	al	allo	all'	alla
da	dal	dallo	dall'	dalla
di	del	dello	dell'	della
in	nel	nello	nell'	nella
su	sul	sullo	sull'	sulla

That applies also when the article is in the plural.

+	i	gli	le
a	ai	agli	alle
da	dai	dagli	dalle
di	dei	degli	delle
in	nei	negli	nelle
su	sui	sugli	sulle

At times the preposition **con** also is combined with the following definite article. Usually, however, the separated alternative is preferred, as in **con il treno**, **con i miei genitori**, rather than **col treno** and **coi miei genitori**.

il giornale –
the newspaper
la cartella –
the briefcase

Use

Il treno parte **alle** nove e arriva **all'**una.
~ Dov'è il giornale? + **Sul** tavolo o **nella** cartella.
~ Vieni anche tu **al** cinema stasera?
+ No, devo andare **dai** miei genitori.

■ The combination preposition + definite article is very common in Italian.

The Indefinite Article

> **Un** caffè, **una** birra, **un'**acqua minerale e **uno** spumante, per favore.

A coffee, a beer, a mineral water, and a sparkling wine, please.

There are only a few forms to memorize for the indefinite article: **un** and **uno** as masculine forms and **un'** and **una** as feminine forms.

Forms

1. Before Masculine Nouns

un	mese cane amico	**Un** is the masculine form used with nouns that begin with a consonant or a vowel (**a**, **e**, **i**, **o**, **u**).
uno	studente sciopero zio	Use uno if the nouns begin with **s** + consonant or with **z**.

Watch out! **Un** does not have an apostrophe when used with masculine nouns, even before a vowel!

The form **uno** of the indefinite article also precedes nouns whose initial letters are **gn**, **ps**, **y**, or **x**: **uno gn**occo, **uno ps**icologo, **uno y**ogurt, **uno x**enofobo.

2. Before Feminine Nouns

una	casa madre storia	**Una** is the feminine form used with nouns whose initial letter is a consonant.
un'	amica idea ora	**Un'** is used when the first letter is a vowel.

Remember that **un'** is written with an apostrophe when a feminine noun starts with a vowel.

Like the definite article, the indefinite article can also change its form if an adjective precedes the noun:
uno specchio - **un g**rande specchio
un'idea - **una b**ella idea

Use

Chi conosce **un** buon dentista?
Ho bevuto **un** ottimo vino e mangiato **una** bistecca eccellente.

Use the indefinite article when no particular person or thing is referred to ...

Ho **un** sonno!

... or when you want to intensify a statement.

Che sfortuna!
Che bella giornata!

Unlike English, Italian uses no indefinite article in exclamations ...

Mi dia **mezzo** chilo d'uva.
Il treno arriva fra **mezz'**ora.

... and before **mezzo.**

il dentista – *the dentist*
la bistecca – *the steak*
il sonno – *the sleep*
Ho un sonno! – *I'm really sleepy!*
la sfortuna – *the misfortune, bad luck*
l'uva – *the grapes*

The Partitive Article

① Vuoi **del** tè freddo?

② Ho già bevuto **dell**'acqua, grazie.

---

1. Do you want some iced tea? 2. I've already drunk some water, thanks.

Ho comprato **del** pane.	**di + il**	**= del**
Nel dessert c'è **dello** yogurt.	**di + lo**	**= dello**
Ho bevuto **dell'**acqua.	**di + l'**	**= dell'**
Ho mangiato **della** frutta.	**di + la**	**= della**
Ho visto **dei** bei film.	**di + i**	**= dei**
Ho comprato **degli** spaghetti.	**di + gli**	**= degli**
Oggi esco con **delle** amiche.	**di + le**	**= delle**

The partitive article consists of the preposition **di** and the definite article. It serves to indicate an indefinite amount or an indefinite number.

Omit the partitive article, however:

Marco <u>non</u> ha **amici**.	in negated sentences,	il condimento – *the dressing (food)*
Mia dia <u>un chilo di</u> **mele**, per favore.	with statements of quantity,	il pepe – *the pepper* il sale – *the salt* l'olio – *the oil*
Il condimento è fatto solo con **sale**, **pepe**, **olio** e **aceto**.	and in enumerations, when the amount is irrelevant.	l'aceto – *the vinegar*

The Definite and Indefinite Articles

un caffè

le uova

l'aceto

un'aranciata

la città

il gelato

lo zucchero

l'uva

i panini

un'insalata   una birra   le mele   gli spaghetti   uno spumante

1. In which column do the nouns belong? Pay attention to the article. *

	Masculine	Feminine
Singular	un caffè	
Plural		

2. Write down the prepositions that are combined with a definite article, and then write their components separately. *

a) Oggi vado al lavoro in bicicletta.   al   a + il

b) Alle dieci incontro dei clienti.   _____

c) Vado a pranzo con delle colleghe.   _____

d) Forse prendo il risotto alle vongole.   _____

e) All'una devo tornare in ufficio.   _____

f) Nel pomeriggio vado dal medico.   _____

g) Prima compro della frutta.   _____

h) Forse compro anche del vino.   _____

i) Stasera vado dalla mia amica Eva.   _____

The Definite and Indefinite Articles

3. Write down the nouns with their corresponding indefinite article, and then write them with the appropriate definite article.*

A Natale ho ricevuto un libro, uno scialle, una borsetta e un'agenda. Carlo invece ha ricevuto un pigiama, un abbonamento per il teatro, una sciarpa e una camicia.

Natale – *Christmas*
ricevere – *to receive, get*
uno scialle – a shawl
una borsetta –
a handbag
una sciarpa – *a scarf*
una camicia – *a shirt*

<u>un libro - il libro</u>

_____

_____

_____

4. Decide where you need to fill in the definite article, and where no article is needed. **

a) • Buonasera, _____ signora Cesari.

   ○ Buonasera.

b) • Che ore sono?

   ○ Sono _____ undici e mezza.

c) • Pronto?!

   ○ Buongiorno. Sono _____ signora Cecchi. Vorrei parlare con _____ signor Vilardo.

   • Mi dispiace, ma _____ signor Vilardo non c'è.

d) • Conosci Carlo Cesari?

   ○ Certo, è ____ nuovo ragazzo di Angela. È un bel ragazzo alto con

   _____ capelli neri e _____ occhi azzurri.

e) • Dov'è Simona?

   ○ È a letto con _____ tosse e _____ raffreddore.

   • Ha anche _____ febbre?

   ○ Certo.

f) • Tu sai se _____ direttore sa _____ inglese?

   ○ Ma certo! Sa anche _____ tedesco e _____ spagnolo.

The Noun

8. i fiori
6. la finestra
7. il vaso
5. il topo
4. il formaggio
3. il piatto
1. il tavolo
2. la sedia
9. il gatto

In Italian, nouns are either masculine or feminine. There are no neuter nouns.

---

1. the table 2. the chair 3. the plate 4. the cheese 5. the mouse 6. the window
7. the vase 8. the flowers 9. the cat

The Gender of Nouns

Tip! Always memorize nouns together with their associated articles!

Generally you can tell the gender of a noun by its ending. If not, then the article usually indicates its gender, as in these examples: **il bar** and **la notte**. However, if you encounter nouns like **l'estate**, where neither the ending nor the article gives a clue about gender, then the dictionary will supply the answer.

1. Masculine Nouns

lo specchio – *the mirror*
l'armadio – *the cupboard*
il cane – *the dog*
il tram – *the streetcar*

il lett**o**, lo specchi**o**, l'armadi**o**, il tavol**o**, il piatt**o**, il gatt**o**	Most masculine nouns end in **-o**,
il mes**e**, il bicchier**e**, il nom**e**, il can**e**, il padr**e**, lo student**e**	many end in **-e**,
il bar, il film, il fax, lo sport, l'autobus, il computer, il tram	some end in a consonant,
il programm**a**, il cinema, il sof**à**, il problem**a**, il dramm**a**	and a very few have the ending **-a**.

2. Feminine Nouns

la casa, l'ora, l'arancia, la porta, la moda, la pizza	Feminine nouns usually end in -**a**,
la notte, l'estate, la chiave	many end in -**e**,
la radio, la foto, la mano	some end in -**o**
l'analisi, la crisi, la metropoli	and a very few end in -**i**.

l'estate – *the summer*
la chiave – *the key*
la mano – *the hand*

3. Nouns That Sound Alike But Differ in Gender

There are a few nouns that are almost identical but differ in meaning, depending on whether they are masculine or feminine.

masculine		feminine	
il banco	*the bench, the bar counter*	**la** banca	*the bank*
il capitale	*the capital (financial)*	**la** capitale	*the capital (city)*
il fine	*the aim, object*	**la** fine	*the end*
il foglio	*the sheet (paper)*	**la** foglia	*the leaf (plant)*
il porto	*the port, harbor*	**la** porta	*the door*

Gender in Designations of Persons and Occupations

① Mio **figlio** vuole diventare **avvocato**, mia **figlia** invece **traduttrice**.

② Il **signor** Merlo è il nostro nuovo **vicino**.
È **professore** di filosofia.
Sua **moglie** è una **signora** molto gentile.
Lei è **casalinga**.

Nouns that denote a person or a profession are generally masculine when they refer to a man and feminine when they refer to a woman.

---

1. My son wants to become a lawyer, my daughter, a translator.
2. Mr. Merlo is our new neighbor. His wife is a very friendly lady. She is a housewife.

il **ragazzo**	la **ragazza**	In general, a masculine designation of person or occupation has a feminine equivalent, which is derived from the masculine form.
il **vicino**	la **vicina**	
il **traduttore**	la **traduttrice**	
il **dottore**	la **dottoressa**	
il **signore**	la **signora**	
il figl**io**	la figl**ia**	Numerous masculine designations of person or occupation that end in **-o** form the feminine by adding an **-a**.
l'impiegat**o**	l'impiegat**a**	
l'opera**io**	l'opera**ia**	
l'amic**o**	l'amic**a**	
lo z**io**	la z**ia**	
il camer**iere**	la camer**iera**	Masculine nouns ending in **-iere** and some ending in **-e** have a feminine equivalent ending in **-a**.
l'inferm**iere**	l'inferm**iera**	
il parrucch**iere**	la parrucch**iera**	
il signor**e**	la signor**a**	
il dott**ore**	la dottor**essa**	Some designations of occupation ending in **-e** add **-essa** for the feminine form.
il profess**ore**	la professor**essa**	
lo stud**ente**	la student**essa**	
l'at**tore**	l'at**trice**	If the masculine form ends in **-tore**, however, the feminine ending usually is **-trice**.
il diret**tore**	la diret**trice**	
il lavora**tore**	la lavora**trice**	
il pit**tore**	la pit**trice**	
l'insegn**ante**	l'insegn**ante**	Many designations have only one form for both genders. Usually they end in **-ante**, **-ente**, **-ese**, or **-ista**.
il cli**ente**	la cli**ente**	
il franc**ese**	la franc**ese**	
il giornal**ista**	la giornal**ista**	
il farmac**ista**	la farmac**ista**	
l'**uomo**	la **donna**	There are also cases where a different word is used for the feminine designation.
il **padre**	la **madre**	
il **marito**	la **moglie**	
il **genero**	la **nuora**	

l'impiegato –
the employee
l'operaio – *the laborer*
l'infermiere – *the nurse,*
medical attendant
il parrucchiere –
the hairdresser
l'attore – *the actor*
il lavoratore –
the worker
il pittore –
the painter (artist)
il genero –
the son-in-law
la nuora –
the daughter-in-law

For a number of designations of occupation, only a masculine term exists; then it must also be used for a woman.

il medico   l'ingegnere   l'avvocato   il ministro   l'architetto

Thus Italians say **ho un buon medico**, regardless of whether they are referring to a man or a woman.

The feminine designations **l'avvocatessa** and **l'architetta** also occur in rare instances.

The reverse case—use of a feminine form for both genders—also occurs.

la guida   la guardia   la recluta

Italians say **La guida è brava**, even if referring to a man.

la guida – *the leader, the guide*
la guardia – *the guard*
la recluta – *the recruit*

Singular and Plural of Nouns

① Nel centro ci sono poche **abitazioni**. Ci sono soprattutto **negozi** e **uffici**.

② Alcuni **bar** vendono anche **giornali** e **riviste**.

---

1. In the center of town there are few houses. There are mainly businesses and offices.
2. Some bars also sell newspapers and magazines.

1. Regular Formation of the Plural

Singular	Plural	
il lett**o** il mes**e**	i lett**i** i mes**i**	Generally, **masculine** nouns that end in **-o** or **-e** in the singular form the plural by adding **-i**.
la ser**a** la nott**e**	le ser**e** le nott**i**	Most **feminine** nouns ending in -**a** add an **-e**. If they end in **-e**, they add an **-i**.

2. Special Features of Forming the Plural

Nouns ending in *-co* **or** *-go*

il tedes**co** il par**co** il dialo**go** il catalo**go**	i tedes**chi** i par**chi** i dialo**ghi** i catalo**ghi**	If a noun ends in **-co** or **-go**, its plural ending is **-chi** or **-ghi**.
il medico lo psicologo l'austriaco	i medici gli psicologi gli austriaci	A number of nouns that are stressed on the third-from-last syllable, however, do not follow this rule.

l'austriaco – *the Austrian*

il nemico – *the enemy*
il greco – *the Greek*

l'amico	gli amici	Many nouns stressed on the
il nemico	i nemici	second-from-last syllable follow
il greco	i greci	this pattern.

Nouns ending in -*ca* or -*ga*

Forming the plural
is easier with nouns
ending in **-ca** or **-ga**.

l'amica	le amiche	Nouns whose singular ends in
la tedesca	le tedesche	**-ca** or **-ga** form the plural by
la psicologa	le psicologhe	adding **-che** or **-ghe** if they are
la collega	le colleghe	feminine.
il collega	i colleghi	If they are masculine, their
il patriarca	i patriarchi	plural ending usually is **-chi**
il monarca	i monarchi	or **-ghi**.

Nouns ending in -*cia* or -*gia*

la ciliegia –
the cherry
la provincia –
the province
il pendio –
the hillside, slope

la camicia	le camicie	Nouns with a vowel before the
la ciliegia	le ciliegie	ending **-cia** or **-gia** usually add
la farmacia	le farmacie	**-cie** or **-gie** in the plural.
la spiaggia	le spiagge	
l'arancia	le arance	If **-cia** or **-gia** is preceded by a
la provincia	le province	consonant, the plural is formed
		with **-ce** or **-ge**.

Nouns ending in -*io*

il figlio	i figli	If a noun ends in **-io**, it simply
il negozio	i negozi	loses the **-o** in the plural.
lo zio	gli zii	If the stress in the singular falls
il pendio	i pendii	on the **-i-** of the ending, the
		plural is **-ii**.

Masculine nouns ending in -*a*

il problema	i problemi	Many masculine nouns that end
il programma	i programmi	in **-a** in the singular have the
il farmacista	i farmacisti	ending **-i** in the plural.

Invariable nouns

		These are invariable:
il caffè	i caffè	Nouns that end in a stressed
la città	le città	vowel or in **-i**,
l'analisi	le analisi	
il film	i film	nouns that end in a consonant,
il fax	i fax	and
il cinema	i cinema	nouns that actually are short
la foto	le foto	forms, such as **cinema** for
la radio	le radio	**cinematografo.** Usually these
la moto	le moto	are feminine nouns ending
l'auto	le auto	in **-o**.

> The article tells you whether an invariable noun is singular or plural.

> **Tip!** It is advisable to memorize these nouns as exceptions.

3. Nouns with an Irregular Plural

l'uomo	gli uomini	Some nouns have an irregular
la mano	le mani	plural.
il paio (m)	le paia (f)	Some nouns even change their
il dito (m)	le dita (f)	gender in the plural.
l'uovo (m)	le uova (f)	

4. Nouns Used Only in Singular or Plural Form

la gente	the people	i dintorni	the surroundings
la roba	the things	le mutande	the underwear
l'uva	the grapes	gli occhiali	the (eye)glasses
		i pantaloni	the (pair of) pants
		i soldi	the money
		gli spiccioli	the (small) change

These nouns need to be memorized. They are used only in the singular or in the plural.

Compound Nouns and Their Plural

I **francobolli** si comprano dal tabaccaio.

①

Ho bisogno di una **camicia da notte**.

②

Con Internet si ha accesso a un'infinità di **banche dati**.

③

---

1. Stamps are bought from the tobacconist. 2. I need a nightgown.
3. With the Internet, you have access to many, many data banks.

Italian has various ways of forming compound nouns:

– as one word
– with a preposition
– or with two nouns written separately

1. Compound Nouns

il passaport**o**	i passaport**i**	If the nouns are written as one word, they often form the plural in the same way as simple nouns.
il pianofort**e**	i pianofort**i**	
il marciapied**e**	i marciapied**i**	
il capolavor**o**	i capolavor**i**	

il marciapiede –
the sidewalk
il capolavoro –
the masterpiece
il cavatappi –
the corkscrew
l'aspirapolvere –
the vacuum cleaner
il saliscendi –
the ups and downs
il senzatetto –
the homeless person
l'asciugamano –
the towel

Some nouns that are written as a single word, however, remain unchanged in the plural. These usually are nouns made up of:

il cavatappi	i cavatappi	verb + noun in the plural
l'aspirapolvere	gli aspirapolvere	verb + feminine noun in the singular
il saliscendi	i saliscendi	verb + verb
il senzatetto	i senzatetto	preposition + noun

Compounds created with verb + **mano**, however, form the plural by adding **-i**:
l'asciugaman**o**   gli asciugaman**i**

2. Two Nouns Written Separately

il	**vagone** letto	i	**vagoni** letto
il	**vagone** ristorante	i	**vagoni** ristorante
lo	**studente** modello	gli	**studenti** modello
la	**banca** dati	le	**banche** dati
la	**zona** disco	le	**zone** disco
l'**anno** record		gli	**anni** record

> **il fine settimana**
> *(the weekend),*
> however, remains
> unchanged in the
> plural: **I fine
> settimana.**

In modern Italian, there are a great many compound nouns made up of two nouns written as separate words. Here, in general, only the first noun is pluralized.

3. Noun + Preposition + Noun

la	**barca** a vela	le	**barche** a vela
il	**lavoro** a mano	i	**lavori** a mano
il	**succo** di frutta	i	**succhi** di frutta
il	**pacchetto** di sigarette	i	**pacchetti** di sigarette
il	**costume** da bagno	i	**costumi** da bagno
la	**sala** da pranzo	le	**sale** da pranzo

Many compounds are formed with the prepositions **a**, **da**, or **di**. Here, generally only the first noun is made plural.

il vagone letto –
the sleeping car
lo studente modello –
the model pupil
la zona disco – *the
zone in which parking
is allowed only with a
parking disk*
la barca a vela –
the sailboat
il lavoro a mano –
the handiwork
il succo di frutta –
the fruit juice

The Noun

valigia
vestito
radio
specchio
cinema
ufficio
ristorante
zio
stazione
arancia
città
caffè
sciopero
albergo
uovo
sport

1. Match the nouns with the appropriate article, and then put them in the plural, making sure to supply the article as well. *

il   lo

_____ _____   _____ _____

_____ _____   _____ _____

_____ _____   _____ _____

_____ _____   _____ _____

l'   la

_____ _____   la valigia –   le valigie _____

_____ _____   _____ _____

_____ _____   _____ _____

_____ _____   _____ _____

2. Fill in the blanks in the right-hand column with the feminine form of the nouns in bold in the text on the left, and add the appropriate article. *

a) Il mio nuovo **collega** si chiama Busi.

a) _____ mia nuova _____ si chiama Busi.

b) È sposato e ha due **figli**, Martino e Francesco.

b) È sposata e ha due _____ , Martina e Francesca.

c) Francesco è **un ragazzo** simpatico, ha molti **amici** e vuole diventare **medico** come suo **padre.**

c) Francesca è _____ simpatica, ha molte _____ e vuole diventare _____ come sua _____ .

d) Martino è ancora **un bambino.**

d) Martina è ancora _____ _____ .

e) Lui da grande vuole fare **l'attore.**

e) Lei da grande vuole fare _____ .

3. What are the plurals of these compound nouns? ***

a) l'ufficio informazioni _____

b) il marciapiede _____

c) la madre modello _____

d) il libro di cucina _____

e) la camera da letto _____

f) il pianoforte _____

g) l'asciugamano _____

h) l'anno record _____

4. Translate the following. **

a) the sheet (of paper) b) the bank   c) the end

_____   _____   _____

d) the capital (city)   e) the door   f) the capital (money)

_____   _____   _____

5. What is the feminine form of the following designations of persons and occupations?*

a) il professore   g) l'impiegato

b) l'autore   h) il farmacista

c) l'insegnante   i) il tedesco

d) il marito   j) lo studente

e) l'uomo   k) lo psicologo

f) il lavoratore   l) il parrucchiere

a) _____   g) _____

b) _____   h) _____

c) _____   i) _____

d) _____   j) _____

e) _____   k) _____

f) _____   l) _____

The Adjective

① Nora è una **bella** donna **alta** e **snella**. È ancora abbastanza **giovane**.

② Suo marito invece non è più tanto **giovane**. È anche piuttosto **piccolo** e **grassottello**.

1. Nora is a pretty, tall, and slender woman. 2. Her husband, however, is not so young anymore. He is also rather small and dumpy.

Adjective Endings

Remember that despite agreement, the adjective ending can differ from that of the noun:
un lavor**o** semplic**e**,
un paes**e** turistic**o**,
lingu**e** facil**i**

Ho comprato un paio di pantaloni **larghi** e una gonna **lunga.** I pantaloni sono molto **comodi,** la gonna purtroppo è un po' **stretta.**

The adjective agrees in number and gender with the noun it modifies.

La birra e il vino sono **cari.** Ho conosciuto un uomo e una donna **meravigliosi.** Emma e Mario sono molto **vivaci.**

If an adjective modifies a masculine noun and a feminine noun, it is used in the plural and is masculine in gender.

1. Adjectives Ending in -o

	masculine	feminine
singular	un museo modern**o**	una casa modern**a**
plural	i musei modern**i**	le case modern**e**

Adjectives that end in **-o** in the masculine singular have a feminine singular form ending in **-a**.
In the plural, the masculine ending **-o** changes to **–i**, and the feminine ending **-a** becomes **-e**.

2. Adjectives Ending in -e

	masculine	feminine
singular	un uomo gentile	una donna gentile
plural	gli uomini gentili	le donne gentili

Adjectives that end in **-e** in the singular have only one form for both genders: **-e** in the singular and **-i** in the plural.

Special Features of Forming the Plural

Luciana ha i capelli
lunghi, grigi.
①

In Sardegna ci sono
dei posti **fantastici.**
②

Ci sono tante persone
egoiste e non molto
simpatiche.
③

> In forming the plural, the same rules apply for adjectives as for nouns with the corresponding endings.

1. Luciana has long, gray hair. 2. There are some fantastic places in Sardinia.
3. There are many egotistical and not very likable people.

				Adjectives ending in **-co** or **-ca** usually form the plural:
bianco:	i	capelli	bianchi	with **-chi** or **-che** if they are stressed on the second-to-last syllable.
bianca:	le	scarpe	bianche	
pratico:	gli	stivali	pratici	with **-ci** or **-che** if the stress is on the third-from-last syllable.
pratica:	le	borse	pratiche	
lungo:	i	capelli	lunghi	For adjectives ending in **-go** or -ga, the plural ending is **-ghi** or **-ghe**.
lunga:	le	gonne	lunghe	
grigio:	i	capelli	grigi	Adjectives that end in **-io** in the singular have only an **-i** in the plural.
vecchio:	i	vestiti	vecchi	

real**ista**: gli uomini realist**i** real**ista**: le donne realist**e**	Adjectives ending in **-ista** form the plural as follows: the masculine form, by adding -**i**, the feminine form, by adding -**e**.

The Adjectives *bello* and *buono*

When **bello** and **buono** precede a noun, their forms sometimes differ from those used when they follow a noun.

Boston ha un **bel** centro con dei **begli** edifici storici e dei **bei** negozi.

Ho comprato un **buon** vino bianco per il pesce e un **buono** spumante per il dolce.

---

1. Boston has a lovely downtown with pretty historical buildings and beautiful stores.
2. I've bought a good white wine for the fish and a good sparkling wine for the dessert.

1. *Bello* Before Masculine Nouns

Singular

The adjective **bello** behaves like the definite article before masculine nouns. Its form thus depends on the first letter of the following word.

il regalo	un **bel r**egalo	Before a masculine noun in the singular, use: **bel** if it begins with a consonant,
lo stile	un **bello st**ile	**bello** if it begins with **s** + consonant, **z**, **gn**, **ps**, **x**, or **y**,
l'uomo	un **bell'u**omo	**bell'** if the first letter is a vowel.

Plural

i regali	**bei r**egali	In the plural, use the following before masculine nouns: **bei** if they begin with a consonant,
gli specchi **gli z**oo **gli u**omini	**begli sp**ecchi **begli z**oo **begli u**omini	**begli** if they begin with **s** + consonant, **z**, **gn**, **ps**, **x**, **y**, or a vowel.

2. *Bello* Before Feminine Nouns

Singular	Plural
una **bella** mela	**belle** mele
una **bella** storia	**belle** storie
una **bella** opera	**belle** opere
una **bella** idea	**belle** idee

Before feminine nouns, you can treat **bello** as a normal adjective. In the singular use **bella**, and in the plural, **belle**. If the noun begins with **a**, **e**, **i**, **o**, or **u**, you can also use the form of **bella** with the apostrophe in the singular: una **bell'**idea.

3. *Buono* Before Masculine Nouns

Singular

un film	un **buon** film	Before a consonant or a vowel, use **buon**.
un attore	un **buon** attore	
uno sport	un **buono** sport	Before **s** + consonant, **z**, **gn**, **ps**, **x**, or **y**, use **buono**.
uno zio	un **buono** zio	

Before masculine nouns in the singular, the adjective **buono** behaves like the indefinite article.

Plural

buoni film	**buoni** libri	The plural is always **buoni**, regardless of the first letter of the following noun.
buoni attori	**buoni** amici	
buoni gnocchi	**buoni** sport	
buoni zucchini	**buoni** zii	

Before masculine nouns in the plural, **buono** is quite regular.

4. *Buono* Before Feminine Nouns

Singular	Plural
una **buona** famiglia	**buone** famiglie
una **buona** amica	**buone** amiche

Before feminine nouns, you can treat **buono** as a normal adjective and use the form **buona** in the singular and **buone** in the plural. But if the feminine noun begins with a vowel and is singular, you can also use the form of **buona** with the apostrophe: una **buon'**amica.

Invariable Adjectives

Hai visto Marco con i pantaloni **viola** e la camicia **blu**? ①

Sì, ieri portava anche delle scarpe **verde chiaro** e una giacca **rosso fuoco**. ②

1. *Have you seen Marco with the purple pants and the blue shirt?*
2. *Yes, yesterday he also wore light-green shoes and a fire-red jacket.*

Most invariable adjectives denote a color:

gli asciugamani **blu** i pantaloni **beige** il cappotto **lilla** il vestito **rosa** le camicette **turchese** le scarpe **viola**	**blu**, **beige**, **lilla**, **rosa**, **turchese** and **viola**,
una camicetta **giallo chiaro** una gonna **verde scuro**	compound terms for colors consisting of color + adjective, as well as
una macchina **grigio ferro** una borsetta **rosso fuoco**	terms for colors consisting of color + noun.

giallo chiaro –
light yellow
verde scuro –
dark green
grigio ferro –
iron gray

Position of Adjectives

A Stefano piacciono le macchine **veloci**, i mobili **moderni**, l'arte **astratta** il **buon** vino e le **belle** donne.

Stefano likes fast cars, modern furniture, abstract art, good wine, and pretty women.

In Italian, the adjective can precede or follow the noun it modifies. Most adjectives, however, are placed after the noun, in contrast to English.
There are also a few adjectives that usually precede the noun and others that even have different meanings, depending on where they are placed.

1. Adjectives Commonly Placed in Front

First and foremost, these are placed in front:

una **bella**/**brutta** giornata un **piccolo**/**grande** regalo	– **bello** and **brutto**, – **grande** and **piccolo**

The majority of adjectives follow the noun. Therefore you need to pay special attention to those that can also be put in front.

un **buon**/**cattivo** esempio	– **buono** and **cattivo**,
un **vecchio**/**giovane** amico	– **vecchio** and **giovane**,
un **lungo**/**breve** viaggio	– **lungo** and **breve**,
il **primo**/l'**ultimo** giorno	– **primo** and **ultimo**.

▶ Position of Ordinal Numbers with a Noun, p. 228

If these adjectives follow the noun, they are given special weight and thus are strongly contrasted with their antonym:

Ho una macchina **vecchia**.	(= non è nuova)
Ho una casa **piccola**.	(= non è grande)
Ho conosciuto una donna **giovane**.	(= non è vecchia)

2. Change of Meaning of Adjectives, Depending on Position

Adjectives that can change their meaning depending on where they are placed are, for example:

grande:	un **grande** uomo	*a great man*
	un uomo **grande**	*a big man*
caro:	un **caro** amico	*a dear friend*
	un paese **caro**	*an expensive country*
povero:	un **povero** ragazzo	*a poor (pitiable) boy*
	un ragazzo **povero**	*a poor (impoverished) boy*
vecchio:	un **vecchio** amico	*an old (longtime) friend*
	un amico **vecchio**	*an old (elderly) friend*
solo:	una **sola** persona	*only one person*
	una persona **sola**	*a lonely person*

3. Position of the Combination Adverb + Adjective

un film **molto buono** un paese **proprio povero** macchina **troppo vecchia** un viaggio **incredibilmente lungo**	If an adjective is modified by an adverb, such as **molto**, una **abbastanza**, **proprio**, **davvero**, **troppo**, or **incredibilmente**, it always follows the noun and the adverb.

abbastanza – *fairly, quite*
proprio – *really*
davvero – *really, actually*
troppo vecchio – *too old*
incredibilmente – *incredibly*

Comparison of Adjectives

La bicicletta è **più ecologica** della macchina, ma è anche **meno comoda**. ①	Parigi è una **bellissima** città. Per me è **la** città **più bella** del mondo. Secondo mio marito invece Roma è **bella quanto** Parigi. ②

1. The bicycle is more environmentally friendly than the automobile, but it is also less comfortable. 2. Paris is an extremely beautiful city. To me it is the most beautiful city in the world. My husband, however, thinks Rome is just as beautiful as Paris.

1. The Comparative

Carlo è **più gentile** di Sandro.
L'espresso è **più forte** del caffè tedesco.
Rosa è **meno sportiva** di Maria.
Torino è **meno grande** di Roma.

più gentile – *more polite*
più forte – *stronger*
meno sportivo – *less athletic*
meno grande – *smaller*
il motoscafo – *the motorboat*
meno veloce – *slower*

In Italian, an adjective can be positively compared by using **più** and negatively compared by using **meno**. Here the adjectives agree in number and gender with the noun they modify.

Tua sorella è più gentile **di te.**
La gondola è meno veloce **del motoscafo.**

When two persons or things have a common quality and are compared in reference to this quality, Italian expresses the comparison word *than* with **di**. From a grammatical point of view, in this case the comparative is followed by a noun or a pronoun.

In most other cases, *than* is rendered as **che**. For example, when the following types of words follow the comparative:
- an adjective: Questo vino è più caro **che buono.**
- a verb in the infinitive: È più comodo prendere la macchina **che andare** a piedi.
- an adverb: È più bello mangiare fuori **che dentro.**
- a preposition: Da noi ci sono più turisti in estate **che in** inverno.

a piedi – *on foot*

Rendering *just as ... as*

English *just as ... as* has these Italian equivalents:

Oggi fa (**tanto**) caldo **quanto** ieri.	(**tanto**) ... **quanto** (**tanto** can be omitted) or
Il film non era (**così**) divertente **come** pensavo.	(**così**) ... **come** (**così** can be omitted).

2. The Relative Superlative

> I Gotti sono **la** famiglia **più ricca** (**della** città).
> Carlo è **il** collega **meno curioso**.
> Chi è **il** ragazzo **più simpatico** (**della** classe)?
> Questo è l'articolo **meno interessante** (**di** tutti).

ricco – *rich*
curioso – *curious*

With the relative superlative, you state what, within a group of persons or things, possesses a quality in the highest degree.
It is formed with the definite article + **più** or **meno**.
If a comparison is made, it is done by using **di**.

3. The Absolute Superlative

> **Il viaggio** è stato faticosissim**o**.
> Abbiamo passato **una** bellissima **giornata**.
> **Gli spaghetti** sono buonissim**i**.
> **Le pizzette** sono caldissim**e**.

faticoso – *tiring, exhausting*
la pizzetta – *the small pizza*

The absolute superlative is not used to make a comparison. It merely expresses a very high degree of a quality.
These adjectives ending in **-issimo** also agree in gender and number with the noun they modify.

Formation of the Absolute Superlative

car**o**, **-a**: veloc**e**:	ca**rissimo, -a** veloc**issimo, -a**	In place of the final vowel, the ending **-issimo** or **-issima** is attached.
ric**co**, **-a**: bian**co**, **-a**: lun**go**, **-a**:	ric**chissimo, -a** bian**chissimo, -a** lun**ghissimo, -a**	With adjectives ending in **-co** / **-ca** and **-go** / **-ga**, add an **-h-** before the superlative ending.
pra̲ti**co**, **-a**: simpa̲ti**co**, **-a**:	prati**cissimo, -a** simpati**cissimo, -a**	Omit this **-h-**, however, if the adjective is stressed on the third-from-last syllable.

You can also express a very high degree of a quality by using these:
- the adverb **molto**: una macchina **molto veloce**
- adverbs such as **incredibilmente**, **terribilmente**, and **enormemente**: un uomo **incredibilmente attivo**, sono **terribilmente stanco**

terribilmente – *terribly, awfully*
enormemente – *enormously*

4. Adjectives with Two Comparative Forms

Some adjectives have, in addition to the regular forms of comparison, irregular ones, some of which have a figurative meaning.

① La disoccupazione è un **grande** problema, forse il **maggiore** della nostra società.

② Carla è la mia sorella **maggiore**, ma è **più piccola** di me.

---

1. Unemployment is a big problem, perhaps our society's biggest.
2. Carla is my older/oldest sister, but she is shorter than I am.

The Adjectives *buono* and *cattivo*

Positive	Comparative	Relative Superlative	Absolute Superlative
buono	**più buono** **migliore**	**il più buono** **il migliore**	**buonissimo** **ottimo**
cattivo	**più cattivo** **peggiore**	**il più cattivo** **il peggiore**	**cattivissimo** **pessimo**

If the regular forms of comparison of **buono** and **cattivo** are applied to a person, they indicate his or her character.

"Carlo è **il più buono** di tutti" says that he is "the nicest of all." But if you want to refer to the achievement potential of a person, you have to use the irregular forms of comparison. "The best (female) student," then, is "**la migliore** studentessa," and "a very good teacher" is "un **ottimo** insegnante."

The Adjectives *grande* and *piccolo*

Positive	Comparative	Relative Superlative	Absolute Superlative
grande	**più grande** **maggiore**	**il più grande** **il maggiore**	**grandissimo** **massimo**
piccolo	**più piccolo** **minore**	**il più piccolo** **il minore**	**piccolissimo** **minimo**

The irregular forms of comparison of **grande** and **piccolo** generally have a figurative meaning, as here:

un problema **minore**	*a minor problem*
una **minima** differenza	*a very tiny difference*
il fratello **maggiore**	*the older / oldest brother*

1. Fill in the blanks in the questions below with the appropriate adjective endings. *

Lei che cosa preferisce,

a) ... i capelli lung_____ o i capelli cort___?

b) ... la cucina italian___ o quella frances_____?

c) ... le vacanze tranquill___ o le vacanze attiv___?

d) ... il vino bianc___ o quello ross___?

e) ... i mobili modern___ o i mobili antic_____?

f) ... i pantaloni strett___ o quelli larg_____?

g) ... gli stivali ross___ o quelli viol___?

h) ... gli asparagi bianc_____ o gli asparagi verd___?

la cucina – *the kitchen; the cuisine*
gli asparagi – *asparagus*

2. Write the appropriate form of **bello** or **buono** in the blanks. *

bello

a) una _____ donna

b) delle _____ vacanze

c) dei _____ bambini

d) un _____ film

e) un _____ albero

f) un _____ zoo

g) dei _____ stivali

buono

a) un _____ romanzo

b) una _____ cena

c) un _____ scrittore

d) dei _____ sci

e) delle _____ scarpe

f) una _____ amica

g) dei _____ gnocchi

il romanzo – *the novel*
la cena – *the dinner*
le scarpe – *the shoes*

3. Complete the following comparisons with **che** or with the appropriate form of **di**. **

a) Mio padre è più giovane _____ mia madre.

b) Preferisco uscire in gruppo _____ da solo.

c) È più sano finire un pasto con della frutta _____ con un dolce.

d) Luigi è più largo _____ alto.

e) Il fitwalking è più sano _____ jogging.

f) Preferisco andare al cinema _____ vedere un film alla televisione.

preferire – *to prefer*
sano – *healthy*
il pasto – *the meal*
la frutta – *the fruit*
il dolce – *the dessert*

The Adjective

4. Where do the adjectives belong in the following sentences? Pay attention to the endings, and change the articles if necessary. **

a) Ho conosciuto un ragazzo. (simpaticissimo)

   <u>Ho conosciuto un ragazzo simpaticissimo.</u>

b) Ho incontrato alcune persone. (molto interessante)

   _____

ho conosciuto – *I have gotten to know*
ho visto – *I have seen*
ho rotto – *I have broken*
ho passato – *I have spent* (time)
la telefonata – *the telephone call*
l'amico d'infanzia – *the childhood friend*
il bosco – *the woods*
il motorino – *the scooter*

c) Ho visto un film. (ottimo, francese)

   _____

d) Ho rotto il vaso di mia nonna. (bello, antico)

   _____

e) Ho passato una serata con alcuni amici. (molto divertente, vecchio)

   _____

f) Ho fatto una telefonata con un amico d'infanzia. (lungo, caro)

   _____

g) Ho fatto una passeggiata nel bosco. (breve)

   _____

h) Ho comprato un motorino. (blu)

   _____

5. Translate the following. ***

a) Emma is my best friend.

   _____

b) She is younger than I and very pretty.

   _____

c) She is a good translator.

   _____

d) She has three older sisters, Rita, Maria, and Lucia.

   _____

e) But Emma is the biggest of all.

   _____

The Adverb

Anna è **terribilmente** nervosa perché **domani** ha un esame. **Purtroppo** ha dormito **poco** e non riesce a studiare **bene**.

Anna is terribly tired because she has an exam tomorrow. Unfortunately she has slept little and isn't able to study well.

Original and Derived Adverbs

① Sai **già** cosa farai a Pasqua?

② **Forse** vado a Parigi.

1. Do you already know what you'll do at Easter? 2. Maybe I'll go to Paris.

In Italian, there are **original adverbs.** They are not recognizable as such on the basis of their form. The original adverbs include:

adesso, ieri, spesso, tardi, già	adverbs of time,
qui, lì, davanti, fuori, sopra	adverbs of place,
poco, molto, abbastanza, niente	adverbs of quantity,
certo, forse, purtroppo, sì, no	adverbs of probability.

① Carlo è **assolutamente** geniale.

② Sono **perfettamente** d'accordo con te.

1. Carlo is absolutely brilliant. 2. I completely agree with you.

In addition, there are adverbs derived from adjectives and ending in **-mente**, so-called derived adverbs. Most of them are adverbs of manner and are invariable.

As is true of English, not all Italian adverbs resemble the adjectival form. The adverbial form of **buono** is **bene**; compare this with English **good** and **well**.

Luisa parla **bene** il tedesco.	Luisa speaks German **well**.
La pizza è **buona**.	The pizza is **good**.

You can avoid mistakes in the usage of Italian adverbs if you know that adverbs can modify (qualify or limit the meaning of) the following:

Heidrun <u>parla</u> **bene** l'italiano.	a verb,
Questo dolce è **incredibilmente** <u>buono</u>.	an adjective,
Pietro sta **veramente** <u>male</u>.	an adverb,
<u>Non è successo niente</u>, **naturalmente**.	an entire sentence.

Formation of Derived Adverbs

Derived adverbs are formed as follows:

tipico ▶	tipica ▶	tipica**mente**	by attaching the ending **-mente**
lento ▶	lenta ▶	lenta**mente**	to the feminine form of
vero ▶	vera ▶	vera**mente**	adjectives ending in **-o**.
veloce ▶		veloce**mente**	by attaching the ending **-mente**
evidente ▶		evidente**mente**	to the unchanged form of
enorme ▶		enorme**mente**	adjectives ending in **-e**.
regolare ▶		regolar**mente**	by dropping the **-e** of adjectives
familiare ▶		familiar**mente**	ending in **-re** and **-le** and
reale ▶		real**mente**	adding the ending **-mente**.
facile ▶		facil**mente**	

Unfortunately, there are exceptions here too:

leggero	▶	legger	▶	**leggermente**
violento	▶	violente	▶	**violentemente**
folle	▶	folle	▶	**follemente**

Buono and **cattivo** even have irregular adverbs:

buono	▶	**bene**	cattivo	▶	**male**

Position of Adverbs

Adverbs should be placed next to the word or sentence element that they modify.

▶ Word Order, p. 193

Adverbs of manner, adverbs of quantity, and the adverbs of time **adesso**, **presto**, **spesso**, **subito**, and **tardi** are placed:

Fa **incredibilmente** freddo. Dormo **poco.** **Arriviamo** subito.	after the verb.
La Juve ha giocato **meravigliosamente.** Ci siamo divertiti **molto.** Sono tornato **adesso.**	after the past participle in the compound tenses.
Sa spiegare **bene** la grammatica. Dobbiamo alzarci **presto.** Cercate di non bere **troppo.**	after the infinitive with conjugated verb + infinitive.

La Juve – *Juventus of Turin* (soccer club)
divertirsi – *to have fun, enjoy oneself*
spiegare – *to explain*

The adverbs **appena**, **ancora**, **già**, **mai**, and **sempre** are placed:

Siamo **appena** usciti. Ho **ancora** pensato a te. Il concerto è **già** cominciato.	between the auxiliary verb and the past participle, in the compound tenses.
Non vuole **mai** lavare i piatti. Cerca **sempre** di non arrabbiarsi. Volete **già** partire?	for the category of conjugated verb + infinitive, after the conjugated verb.

appena – *just, hardly*
arrabbiarsi – *to get angry*
suonare – *to play* (instrument)
purtroppo – *unfortunately*

Anche tu suoni la chitarra? Suoni **anche la chitarra?**	**Anche** precedes the word that is emphasized.
Purtroppo non ho visto Franco. Non ho visto Franco, **purtroppo.**	Adverbs that refer to an entire sentence are placed at the beginning or at the end of the sentence.

Comparison of Adverbs

1. The Comparative

La domenica mangiamo **più tardi**. ①

Il lavoro avanza **meno rapidamente** del solito. ②

Pia ci telefona **tanto spesso quanto** Paolo. ③

1. On Sundays we eat later. 2. Work is proceeding less rapidly than usual.
3. Pia phones us just as often as Paolo.

vestirsi – *to get dressed*
prontamente – *promptly, with dispatch*
alzarsi – *to get up*

Oggi la posta è arrivata **più tardi** di ieri.	For comparisons of inequality, use **più** to describe "more,"
Mi vesto **meno rapidamente** del solito.	and **meno** to describe "less."
Carlo ha risposto (**così**) **prontamente come** te. Oggi ci siamo alzati (**tanto**) **presto quanto** ieri.	The English *just as … as* is translated as (**così**) **… come** or (**tanto**) **… quanto**, and the first part of both expressions can be omitted.

2. The Relative Superlative

Tu hai reagito **più velocemente di tutti**.

You reacted most quickly of all.

Pia lavora **più rapidamente di tutti** (gli altri / gli impiegati).	The relative superlative is formed with the comparative + **di tutti**. You can also indicate who is meant by **tutti / tutte**.
Pia mangia **più velocemente di tutte** (le altre / le sue colleghe).	

3. The Absolute Superlative

Oggi sono tornato a casa **prestissimo**. ①

Il signor Rosa ci ha accolti **molto calorosamente**. ②

1. Today I came home extremely early. 2. Mr. Rosa received us very warmly.

tardi	▶	**tardissimo**	The absolute superlative of original adverbs is formed by replacing the final vowel with the ending **-issimo**. Like all other adverbs, it is invariable.
presto	▶	**prestissimo**	
spesso	▶	**spessissimo**	

lentamente ▶ **molto lentamente**	Adverbs ending in **-mente** form the absolute superlative with **molto**.
gentilmente ▶ **molto gentilmente**	
rapidamente ▶ **molto rapidamente**	

4. Adverbs with Irregular Forms of Comparison

Rosa balla **bene**. Balla **meglio** di me. Elena però balla **meglio di tutte**.

Carlo ride **molto**, ma suo fratello ride **più** di lui. ②

1. Rosa dances well. She dances better than I. But Elena dances best of all.
2. Carlo laughs a lot, but his brother laughs more than he.

The adverbs **bene**, **male**, **poco**, and **molto** have irregular comparative forms.

	Comparative	Relative Superlative
bene	meglio	meglio di tutti / tutte
male	peggio	peggio di tutti / tutte
poco	meno	meno di tutti / tutte
molto	più	più di tutti / tutte

The formation of the absolute superlative, however, is quite regular:

bene	▶	**benissimo**	poco	▶	**pochissimo**
male	▶	**malissimo**	molto	▶	**moltissimo**

Adjectives as Adverbs

State **zitti**, per favore!
①

Andate **piano**!
②

1. Be quiet, please! 2. Drive slowly!

After some verbs, an adjective is used instead of an adverb. For example, after:

stare fermo – *to be still, keep still*
la giacca – *the jacket*
l'errore – *the error, mistake*
parlar chiaro – *to speak clearly, openly*
parlar forte – *to speak loudly*

Com'è **diventata grande** tua figlia! Dovete **restare calmi**. Le difficoltà **sembrano enormi**. **Stai fermo**, per favore!	**diventare**, **restare**, **sembrare**, **stare**.
La giacca è **costata cara**. I propri errori si **pagano cari**.	**costare**, **pagare**, **comprare**, and **vendere** in connection with the adjective **caro**.
Andate piano, per favore! Con me dovete **parlar chiaro**. Maria, **parla più forte**, non ti sento!	**andare** and **parlare**. They are followed by an adjective, which is invariable, however.

! But Italians say **parlare lentamente** and **andare lentamente**.

Stare is combined both with the adjective **buono** and the adverb **bene** or **male**.

sto bene – *I'm fine.*
il caldo – *the heat*
stare buono – *to be good (kind, nice)*

Ieri la nonna **stava bene**. Oggi con questo caldo **sta male**.	**Bene** and **male** refer to health or to state of mind.
Cercate di **stare buoni** quando noi non ci siamo!	The expression **stare + buono**, however, refers to behavior.

1. What is the adverbial form for the following adjectives? *

a) normale

_____

e) folle

_____

b) raro

_____

f) cattivo

_____

c) leggero

_____

g) violento

_____

d) felice

_____

h) diretto

_____

2. Decide whether the adjective or the adverb is required in each case. With the adjectives, also pay attention to the correct form. **

a) Mario non è una persona (facile) _____ .

b) È uno che si irrita (facile) _____ .

c) Vivere con lui è abbastanza (difficile) _____ .

d) Ha anche delle qualità, (naturale) _____ :

sa cucinare molto (buono) _____ , è un (buono)

_____ padre ed è (puntuale) _____ ;

non è come tante altre persone che agli appuntamenti arrivano

(regolare) _____ in ritardo.

irritarsi – to be irritated
la qualità – the quality, characteristic
cucinare – to cook
puntuale – punctual
in ritardo – late, overdue

3. Where does the adverb belong in each sentence below? **

a) I clienti sono arrivati. (appena)

_____

b) Il film non è cominciato. (ancora)

_____

c) Carlo suona il pianoforte. (anche)

_____

d) Non riesco a finire il lavoro per venerdì. (purtroppo)

_____

il cliente – the client, customer
riuscire a fare qc – to succeed in doing something

The Adverb

e) Sandra è uscita. (tardi)

_____

stancarsi – *to tire,*
get tired

f) Cerca di non stancarti. (tanto)

_____

g) Sono partiti gli ospiti? (già)

_____

h) Dovresti rispondere. (subito)

_____

i) Ines non vuole uscire il sabato sera. (mai)

_____

4. For each item below, complete the first sentence with the comparative and the second with the absolute superlative of the adverb indicated. **

a) Luigi canta male.

Carlo canta _____ di Luigi.

Carlo canta _____.

b) Oggi sto bene.

Oggi sto _____ di ieri.

Oggi sto _____.

c) Emilio beve poco.

Emilio beve _____ di me.

Emilio beve _____.

d) Ieri ci siamo divertiti molto.

Ci siamo divertiti _____ di sabato scorso.

Ci siamo divertiti _____.

e) Stasera torno a casa tardi.

Torno _____ del solito.

Torno a casa _____.

f) Mi preparo rapidamente.

Mi preparo _____ di mio marito.

Mi preparo _____.

The Possessive Pronoun

Posso prendere **la tua** bicicletta? ①

Ma non vedi che **la mia** è rotta? ②

The possessive pronoun is used to indicate possession.

---

1. May I take your bicycle? 2. But don't you see that mine is damaged?

Use

+ Non c'è più **il mio** impermeabile, l'ha preso qualcuno!
~ Si calmi, signora. **Il suo** impermeabile lo troveremo.

Generally the possessive pronoun precedes the noun denoting the thing possessed. This is known as adjectival use.

+ Signora, è questo **il suo** impermeabile?
~ No, **il mio** è più chiaro.

However, it can also stand alone. Then it is considered to be pronominal use.
With possessive pronouns, the same rules apply to both adjectival use and pronominal use.

l'impermeabile –
the raincoat
si calmi – *calm yourself*
trovare – *to find*
chiaro – *light (in color)*

Forms

1. Possession in the Singular

Possession / Possessor	Masculine Singular	Feminine Singular
io	**il mio** amico	**la mia** amica
tu	**il tuo** amico	**la tua** amica
lui / lei	**il suo** amico	**la sua** amica
Lei	**il Suo** amico	**la Sua** amica
noi	**il nostro** amico	**la nostra** amica
voi	**il vostro** amico	**la vostra** amica
Voi	**il Vostro** amico	**la Vostra** amica
loro	**il loro** amico	**la loro** amica

> Watch out! Unlike English, Italian usually uses the definite article along with possessive pronouns.

Except with kinship terms, the possessive pronoun is always accompanied by the definite article.

Both the definite article and the possessive pronoun itself agree in number and gender with the thing possessed. Only **loro** is invariable.

2. Possession in the Plural

Possession / Possessor	Masculine Plural	Feminine Plural
io	**i miei** amici	**le mie** amiche
tu	**i tuoi** amici	**le tue** amiche
lui / lei	**i suoi** amici	**le sue** amiche
Lei	**i Suoi** amici	**le Sue** amiche
noi	**i nostri** amici	**le nostre** amiche
voi	**i vostri** amici	**le vostre** amiche
Voi	**i Vostri** amici	**le Vostre** amiche
loro	**i loro** amici	**le loro** amiche

Even if the thing possessed is in the plural, both the definite article and the possessive pronoun agree in number and gender with the possession. Only **loro** always remains invariable.

3. One of Several Things Possessed

> Il signor Vinti è **un mio** conoscente, la signora Vinti è **una mia** cliente.

Mr. Vinti is one of my acquaintances, Mrs. Vinti is one of my clients.

Carlo è **un nostro** cugino. Cinzia è **una mia** amica. È **una tua** allieva, Simona? Emilio è **un vostro** vicino, vero? Il signor Ruffo è **un Suo** paziente?	If reference is made not to a particular thing possessed but to one of several, then the possessive pronoun is accompanied by the indefinite article.	il cugino – _the cousin_ l'allieva – _the pupil (fem.)_ il paziente – _the patient_

4. Differences Between Italian and English Possessive Pronouns

Emilio ha perso il **suo** libro di **tedesco** e Sandra il **suo libro** d'inglese. ①	Sandra ha venduto **la sua bicicletta.** ②	Rosa e Rocco hanno venduto **la loro casa.** ③

1. Emilio has lost his German book and Sandra her English book. 2. Sandra has sold her bike.
3. Rosa and Rocco have sold their house.

Emilio ha ritrovato **il suo libro.** Anche Sandra ha ritrovato **il suo libro.**	The forms **suo**, **sua**, **suoi**, and **sue** are used for both a male and a female possessor. That is, **il suo libro** can mean either _his book_ or _her book_.	ritrovare – _to recover, retrieve, find again_
Emilio ha perso il **suo** portafoglio con la più bella foto **di lei.** _Emilio has lost **his** wallet with **her** prettiest photo._	Instead of the possessive pronoun, to make the situation clear you can use the preposition **di** along with the appropriate stressed personal pronoun.	
Sandra ha perso il **suo** portafoglio con la più bella foto **di lui.** _Sandra has lost **her** wallet with **his** best-looking photo._		

What English expresses with *her*, *their*, or *your* is rendered in various ways in Italian:

*Pia has sold **her** car.* Pia ha venduto **la sua** macchina.	with the forms of **suo** when you are speaking about a female possessor.
*Rosa and Rocco have sold **their** house.* Rosa e Rocco hanno venduto **la loro** casa.	with **loro** when you refer to several possessors.
*Here is **your** key, Mrs. Grassi.* Ecco **la Sua** chiave, signora Grassi. *Here is **your** key, Mr. Grassi.* Ecco **la Sua** chiave, signor Grassi.	with the forms of **Suo** when you want to refer politely to a male or female possessor.
*How is **your** son?* Come sta **vostro** figlio?	with the forms of **vostro** when you address several persons familiarly.
*Here is **your** room.* Ecco **la Loro** camera.	in a very formal situation, with **Loro**.

The Possessive Pronoun with Kinship Terms

Al mio matrimonio c'erano quasi tutti i miei parenti. Mancavano solo **mio** fratello, **i miei** cugini e **la mia** vecchia zia.

Almost all my relatives were at my wedding. Only my brother, my cousins, and my old aunt were missing.

Mia sorella ha 20 anni. Cosa fa **tuo** padre? **Nostro** figlio è in Inghilterra. I signori Gallo sono venuti con **la loro** figlia.	Generally the definite article is omitted with kinship terms in the singular. Only with **loro** is the definite article required.

Similarly, the definite article must be used when the kinship term:

I miei nonni vivono a Roma.	is in the plural,
Come sta **la tua sorellina?** **La mia mamma** sta bene.	is a diminutive or a term of endearment,
Il nostro vecchio zio è andato a vivere da sua figlia.	is modified by an adjective,
+ Mio figlio quest'anno va in Germania. ~ **Il mio** invece vuole andare in Francia.	or when there is pronominal use of the possessive pronoun.

i nonni –
the grandparents
la sorellina –
the little sister
lo zio – *the uncle*

Special Cases

There are other cases in which the possessive pronoun is used without the definite article:

Vieni **a casa mia** dopo il cinema? Saluta tua madre **da parte mia!** Sandro è sempre **in camera sua.** **È colpa vostra** se arriviamo tardi.	In some expressions with postpositive possessive pronouns.
+ **È tua** questa borsa? ~ No, non **è mia**, è di Chiara.	Often in the combination **essere** + possessive pronoun, which is translated as *to belong to*.

a casa mia – *to my house, at my house*
da parte mia –
on my behalf
la colpa – *the guilt*
la borsa –
the pocketbook

Practice and Application

The Possessive Pronoun

1. Put the possessive pronouns below in the singular or plural, as indicated. *

Singular	Plural
a) il mio disco	_____ dischi
b) _____ foto	le tue foto
c) il suo biglietto	_____ biglietti
d) _____ problema	i nostri problemi
e) la vostra difficoltà	_____ difficoltà
f) il loro cane	_____ cani

2. Massimo is showing old family photos to a friend. Fill in his comments with **suo** and **loro**. **

il fidanzato – *the fiancé*

il partner – *the partner*

il suocero – *the father-in-law*

il cane – *the dog*

a) Questa è mia sorella Luisa con _____ fidanzato.

b) Qui Luisa è con _____ marito e Sara, _____ figlia.

c) Questi sono i miei zii di Imola con _____ figlie Maria e Pia.

d) Questa invece è mia madre al mare con _____ cugine.

e) Qui vedi i miei genitori con Gino e Rosa, _____ migliori amici.

f) E qui vedi i miei nonni con _____ prima macchina. Accanto c'è Socrate, _____ cane.

3. Place the possessive pronouns given below in front of the nouns. Add the definite article if necessary. **

mio

mio padre, _____ famiglia, _____ moglie, _____ vecchia zia

_____ nonni, _____ ragazza, _____ zio

tuo

_____ genitori, _____ fidanzata, _____ amico

_____ sorellina, _____ colleghe, _____ mamma

suo

_____ fratello, _____ cara cugina, _____ nonni

_____ suocero, _____ sorelle, _____ partner

4. Fill in the blanks in the dialogues with the appropriate possessives. **

Two mothers:

a) + _____ figlia quest'anno va in Inghilterra.

~ _____ invece vuole andare in Francia.

b) + _____ figli aiutano molto in casa. Anche _____,

signora?

~ Eh, _____ purtroppo no.

c) + _____ figlio vuole sempre uscire la sera.

~ _____ per fortuna preferisce rimanere a casa.

d) + Quest'anno _____ figlia vuole andare al mare con _____

ragazzo.

~ Ma quanti anni ha _____ figlia?

+ Diciassette.

~ Beh, a diciassette anni anche _____ è andata in vacanza con

_____ ragazzo.

Two girls:

e) + _____ genitori litigano spesso. Anche _____ ?

~ No, _____ no.

f) + _____ fratello ha 18 anni e _____ quanti anni ha?

~ _____ ha già 25 anni.

5. Decide where to place the possessive pronoun. **

a) Chi viene a _____ casa _____ dopo il cinema? (mia)

b) Saluta i nonni da _____ parte _____ e anche da parte

di _____ padre _____. (nostra, mio)

c) Se arriviamo in ritardo è _____ colpa _____. (tua)

d) Roberto è in _____ camera _____ con _____ cugino

_____. (sua, suo)

The Demonstrative Pronoun

Quale vestito preferisci, **questo** o **quello** nero?
①

② **Quello** nero; è più elegante.

The demonstrative pronoun serves to direct the attention of the person addressed to a certain person or thing.

1. Which dress do you prefer, this one or that black one? 2. The black one; it's more elegant.

Use

la marmellata – *the jam*
la camicetta – *the blouse*
maturo – *ripe*
la pera – *the pear*

Questa marmellata è di ciliegie.
Quei pantaloni e **questa** camicetta sono vecchi.

The demonstrative pronoun can appear with the noun it modifies. In this case, we speak of adjectival use.

+ Sono mature le pere? ~ **Queste** sì, **quelle** non ancora.

However, it can also stand alone, and here we speak of pronominal use.

Scusi, è **questo** il treno per Napoli?
Quest'inverno fa proprio freddo.

Use **questo** to refer to a thing or person that is close to you in space or time.

in fondo a – *at the bottom of, in the rear of*
il corridoio – *the corridor, hall*
tanti anni fa – *many years ago*

È carina **quella** ragazza seduta in fondo al corridoio.
Vi ricordate **quella** sera di tanti anni fa quando papà ritornò dal Canada?

Use **quello** to express greater distance in space or time.

Mi piacciono molto **i romanzi** dei giovani scrittori italiani;
quelli di Baricco, per esempio, o **quelli** di De Carlo.
+ Quale **vino** preferisci, **quello** bianco o **quello** rosso? ~ **Quello** rosso.

il romanzo – *the novel*

Without any reference to spatial or temporal distance, **quello** can
replace a previously mentioned noun.

Forms

1. *Questo*

	Singular	Plural
masculine	**questo** vino	**questi** vini
feminine	**questa** borsa	**queste** borse

Questo behaves like
an adjective ending
in **-o** when it is used
pronominally.

The forms **questo** and **questa** are usually written with an apostrophe
before a singular noun beginning with a vowel: **quest'**anno, **quest'**estate,
quest'inverno, **quest'**ora, **quest'**uva.

2. *Quello*

Masculine Forms

The demonstrative
pronoun agrees in
number and gender
with the word it
modifies.

Singular		With masculine singular nouns, use these:
il treno	**quel** treno	**quel** before a consonant,
lo scialle	**quello** scialle	**quello** before **s** + consonant, before
lo zaino	**quello** zaino	**z**, or before **gn**, **ps**, **x**, and **y**,
l' anno	**quell'** anno	**quell'** before a vowel.

Plural		In the plural, use:
i treni	**quei** treni	**quei** before a consonant,
gli scialli	**quegli** scialli	**quegli** before **s** + consonant,
gli zaini	**quegli** zaini	before **z**, or before **gn**, **ps**, **x**,
gli anni	**quegli** anni	and **y**, and before a vowel.

When you use
quello adjectivally,
it behaves like the
definite article.

Feminine Forms

Singular		Before feminine singular nouns, use:
la casa	**quella** casa	**quella** before a consonant,
l' amica	**quell'** amica	**quell'** before a vowel.

Plural		
le case	**quelle** case	In the plural, always use **quelle**.
le amiche	**quelle** amiche	

The Forms of *quello* in Pronominal Use

> When **quello** stands alone, its forms are much simpler.

Preferisci lo yogurt alle fragole o **quello** al limone?
Vi piacciono di più i mobili moderni o **quelli** antichi?

Quale camicia metto, questa o **quella?**
+ Quali scarpe metto per la passeggiata? ~ Metti **quelle** più comode.

As you can tell from the examples, in pronominal use **quello** behaves like an adjective ending in **-o**.

The Demonstrative Pronoun

1. Fill in the blanks with the appropriate forms of **quello**. *

Ti ricordi ...

a) _____ anno in cui siamo andati in Irlanda per la prima volta?

b) _____ famiglia greca che abbiamo conosciuto al mare, anni fa?

c) _____ ragazzi che non avevano i soldi per tornare a casa?

d) _____ estate caldissima in cui dormivamo in terrazza?

e) _____ studente che aveva attraversato l'Italia in bicicletta?

f) _____ giorno in cui ci hanno rubato la macchina?

g) _____ spaghetti che preparammo di notte sulla spiaggia?

2. Decide whether the dialogues need **questo** or **quello**, and which form of the demonstrative pronoun you select is appropriate in each instance. **

a) + Senti, quale gonna metto stasera _____ o _____ blu?

~ Mah, non so, metti _____ più comoda.

b) + Scusi, dov'è il ristorante «Le tre sorelle»?

~ Allora, vede _____ semaforo là in fondo? Ecco, è lì a destra.

c) ı Senti, sai chi sono _____ signori là accanto alla porta?

~ Certo, _____ più piccolo è il professor Minelli, l'altro è l'avvocato Pastrani.

d) + Sai che _____ estate non andiamo in vacanza?

~ Ma come, rimanete in città tutta l'estate?

+ Eh sì, purtroppo è così.

e) + Quali pantaloni preferisci, _____ qui o _____ neri?

~ Mah, secondo me ti stanno meglio _____ rossi.

f) + Scusi, quanto costano _____ stivali, là a destra?

~ Quali, _____ neri?

+ No, _____ beige.

~ _____ costano 150 euro.

comodo – *comfortable*
il semaforo – *the traffic light; semaphore*
là in fondo – *back there*
a destra – *on the right*
accanto a – *beside, next to, by*
rimanere – *to remain, stay*
qui – *here*

The Indefinite Pronouns

> Per il suo matrimonio, mia figlia ha voluto fare una
> grande festa. Ha invitato **tutti i** suoi amici e colleghi
> e persino **qualche** vicino. Non sono venuti **tutti**.
> **Alcuni** purtroppo quel giorno non potevano
> venire, ma c'era lo stesso **tanta** gente.

For her wedding, my daughter wanted to give a big party. She invited all her friends and colleagues and even some neighbors. They didn't all come. Some unfortunately couldn't come that day, but there were a lot of people there all the same.

Use

We distinguish among indefinite pronouns that ...

Ho fatto **tante foto.** Purtroppo **tante** non sono venute bene.
Alla televisione ci sono **tanti film, tanti** purtroppo non sono buoni.

▮ ... can accompany the noun or stand alone. In the former case, we speak of adjectival use, in the latter, of pronominal use.

Ha telefonato **qualcuno?**
È successo **qualcosa?**

▮ ... can be used only pronominally, that is, stand alone.

Ho invitato **qualche** amico.
Ogni mattina faccio ginnastica.

▮ ... can be used only adjectivally; that is, they must accompany a noun.

venire bene –
to turn out well
succedere –
to happen, occur

Indefinite Pronouns with Adjectival and Pronominal Use

> **Tutti** sanno che faccio
> jogging **tutti i** giorni.

Everybody knows that I go jogging every day.

The indefinite pronouns that belong to this category agree in number and gender with the noun they modify:

Ho scritto a **molte** amiche, **poche** mi hanno risposto.	both when used as adjectives and when used as pronouns.

1. *Poco, molto, tanto, troppo*

> **Tutti** sanno chi è la nuova direttrice, ma **pochi** l'hanno vista.

Everyone knows who the new teacher is, but few people have seen her.

> When **poco**, **molto**, **tanto**, and **troppo** are adverbs, however, they are invariable: Ho mangiato **poco** e bevuto **molto**.

Poco, **molto**, **tanto**, and **troppo** generally have the following meanings in English:

C'è **poco** spazio per ballare. Claudia ha **poche** amiche.	**poco, -a:** **pochi, -e:**	*little* *few*
C'è ancora **molto** pane. **Molti** giovani sono disoccupati.	**molto, -a:** **molti, -e:**	*a lot of, much* *many*
C'era **tanta** gente. Ho comprato **tanti** grissini.	**tanto, -a:** **tanti, -e:**	*(so) much* *(so) many*
Nella minestra c'è **troppo** sale. Ci sono **troppe** macchine.	**troppo, -a:** **troppi, -e:**	*too much* *too many*

lo spazio –
the space, room
ballare – *to dance*
disoccupato –
unemployed
la minestra –
the soup

2. *Tutto*

> Oggi ho dormito **tutta la** mattina. Ma di solito mi alzo **tutti i** giorni alle sette.

Today I slept all morning. But normally I get up every day at seven.

> If **tutto** is used with a noun, the noun is always accompanied by the definite article!

	If **tutto** is used with a noun, it means:
Non ho visto **tutto il** film. Ho visto **tutti i** film di Antonioni.	*whole, entire* in the singular and *all* or *every* in the plural.

+ Che cosa vedete? ~ **Tutto**. + Hai mangiato **tutto il** riso? ~ Sì, **tutto**.	If **tutto** stands alone, it usually is equivalent to English *all* or *everything*.
+ Hai salutato **tutti**? ~ Sì, **tutti**.	The plural is rendered as *everybody, everyone, all*.
Ho i vestiti **tutti bagnati**. Claudia è diventata **tutta rossa**. Anna e Sara erano **tutte felici** di andare al concerto di Zucchero. Enzo è **tutto coperto**.	Before an adjective, **tutto** usually is rendered *as all*. It agrees in gender and number with the noun to which it refers, even when it has the function of an adverb.

bagnato – *wet*
felice – *happy*
coperto – *covered*

3. Alcuno

Ho ricevuto **alcuni** fax e **alcune** lettere.

I have received several faxes and some letters.

+ Hanno risposto le tue amiche? ~ **Alcune** sì.	**Alcuno** is quite common in the plural, and it means *some, several, a few*.
Non ho **alcuna** voglia di partire. Sabrina si è arrabbiata **senza alcun** motivo.	In the singular, it is used in sentences that are negated with **non** or **senza**, and it means *none, nobody, no one, not any*, and the like, depending on context.

aver voglia –
to feel like, want to
arrabbiarsi –
to get angry
il motivo – *the reason*

If **alcuno** accompanies the noun and is in the singular, its forms follow the rules for the indefinite article:

lo sbaglio – *the mistake*
l'aiuto – *the help, aid*

Masculine forms:	un	motivo	alcun	motivo
	uno	sbaglio	alcuno	sbaglio
	un	aiuto	alcun	aiuto
Feminine forms:	una	lettera	alcuna	lettera
	un'	idea	alcun'	idea

4. Nessuno

> Oggi non c'è stata **nessuna** telefonata e non ho visto **nessuno**.

_____

Today there was no phone call, and I didn't see anyone.

Nessuno can be used only in the singular.

Non ho **nessun** problema. Non ho fatto **nessuno** sbaglio.	In adjectival use, it means *no*, *not any*.
Qui non conosciamo **nessuno**. Non ha scritto **nessuno**.	Used as a pronoun, **nessuno** means *no one, nobody*.

▶ **Negation**, p. 187

When **nessuno** accompanies a noun and is in the singular, its forms follow the rules for the indefinite article:

Masculine forms:	**un** motivo **uno** sbaglio **un** aiuto	**nessun** motivo **nessuno** sbaglio **nessun** aiuto
Feminine forms:	**una** lettera **un'** idea	**nessuna** lettera **nessun'** idea

Indefinite Pronouns Used as Pronouns

Hai trovato **qualcosa** per Nadia?
Sabato è il suo compleanno.
①

No, non ho trovato
ancora **niente**.
 ②

_____

1. *Have you found something for Nadia? Saturday is her birthday.*
2. *No, I haven't found anything.*

The indefinite pronouns, which you can use only pronominally—that is, alone—include **qualcuno**, **ognuno**, **qualcosa**, **niente**, and **nula**.

1. Qualcuno, ognuno

Qualcuno and **ognuno** can be used only in the singular.

C'è **qualcuno**?	**Qualcuno** means *someone,* *somebody, anybody*.
Conosci **qualcuna** di quelle ragazze?	The feminine form is less common and means *any*.

Ognuno vuole aver ragione.	Ognuno means *each, every (one)* and ognuna is the feminine form.
Ognuna di noi ha dei problemi.	

aver ragione –
to be right
dimmelo –
tell (it to) me
sentire – *to hear*

2. Chiunque, qualcosa

Chiunque and **qualcosa** are invariable.

Chiunque può fare questo lavoro.	Chiunque means *anyone, anybody (whoever)*.
Se sai qualcosa dimmelo.	Qualcosa means *something*.

3. Niente, nulla

▶ Negation, p. 187

Non si vede niente. Non ho sentito niente. Non è successo nulla.	Niente and the somewhat more elevated form nulla are invariable and mean *nothing* in English.

Something and *nothing*, in addition, often appear in expressions such as *something / nothing pretty* or *something / nothing to do*. In Italian, such turns of phrase are expressed by means of the prepositions **di** or **da** as follows:

English	Italian
something / nothing + substantivized adjective: *something / nothing good*	**qualcosa/niente + di +** adjective: **qualcosa/niente di** buono
something / nothing + *to* + verb: *something / nothing to see*	**qualcosa/niente + da +** verb: **qualcosa/niente da** vedere

Indefinite Pronouns Used as Adjectives

Mario è qui da **qualche** giorno. ①	In estate vado **ogni** giorno in piscina. ②

1. Mario has been here for several days. 2. In the summer I go to the swimming pool every morning.

Indefinite pronouns than can be used only adjectivally are, for example, **qualche**, **ogni**, **qualsiasi**, and **qualunque**. They are invariable and occur only in the singular.

1. *Qualche*

Ho invitato **qualche** amica. Ho **qualche** giorno di vacanza.	**Qualche** means *some, a few* and is synonymous with **alcuni, -e**.

Pay attention to the grammatical difference between **qualche** and **alcuni, -e**:

Mario è partito **qualche** giorno fa. **Qualche studente** non ha capito niente.	Mario è partito **alcuni** giorni fa. **Alcuni studenti** non hanno capito niente.

With **qualche**, the following noun is in the singular; with **alcuni, -e**, however, it is plural.

C'è qualche persona **importante.** Qualche cliente non **paga.**	**Ci sono** alcune persone **importanti**. Alcuni clienti non **pagano.**

With **qualche** + noun, the verbs and adjectives that refer to this noun are also singular.

2. *Ogni*

Enzo ed io ci vediamo **ogni** giorno.	**Ogni** means *each, every (one)*.

3. *Qualunque, qualsiasi*

Potete venire a **qualsiasi** ora. Va a sciare con **qualunque** tempo.	**Qualunque** and **qualsiasi** are equivalent to the English *any (whatsoever)*.

The Indefinite Pronouns

1. Which of the indefinite pronouns supplied below fits in each blank? Put it in the right form, if necessary. **

a) **tutto, ogni, ognuno**

_____ anno a Natale, faccio i tortellini.

b) **qualcosa, alcuno, ognuno**

_____ di noi può sbagliare.

c) **tutto, qualche, alcuno**

_____ giorno fa è successo un incidente grave davanti a casa nostra.

d) **qualsiasi, tutto, ognuno**

Per guadagnare un po' durante le vacanze farei _____ lavoro.

e) **qualunque, qualche, tutto**

_____ anni, per il mio compleanno, i miei colleghi mi regalano un enorme mazzo di fiori.

f) **niente, troppo, qualcosa**

Quando vado al mercato compro sempre _____ roba.

g) **qualcuno, nessuno, alcuno**

Marco quando ha mal di testa non vuole vedere_____ .

h) **niente, qualunque, ogni**

Stasera alla televisione non c'è _____ di interessante.

sbagliare – *to make a mistake, err*
un incidente grave – *a serious accident*
guadagnare – *to earn*
il mazzo di fiori – *the bouquet of flowers*
la roba – *the stuff*
il mal di testa – *the headache*

2. Fill in the appropriate form of **nessuno**. *

a) _____ errore

b) _____ film

c) _____ scrittore

d) _____ yogurt

e) _____ macchina

f) _____ foto

g) _____ zoo

h) _____ idea

i) _____ amico

j) _____ amica

k) _____ psicologo

l) _____ città

The Personal Pronouns

> \+ **Noi** rimaniamo a casa; **voi** cosa fate? ①   \+ Quando fai i compiti?
> ~ **Noi** andiamo al cinema.   ~ **Li** faccio subito. ②

> The personal pronouns stand in for people, places, things, and ideas already mentioned.

1. + We're staying at home; what are you doing? ~ We're going to the movies.
2. + When are you doing the homework? ~ I'm doing it right away.

The Subject Pronoun

① Chi lava i piatti, oggi, **tu** o **io**?

② Tu.

1. Who's washing the dishes, you or I? 2. You.

Forms

These are the forms of the subject pronoun in the singular:

Io ho fame, anche	**io** *(I)* for the 1st person,
tu hai fame?	**tu** *(you, familiar)* for the 2nd person,
Lui vuole andare al lago,	**lui** *(he)* for the 3rd person masculine,
lei al mare.	**lei** *(she)* for the 3rd person feminine,
Lei, signor Masu, che cosa prende da bere? **Lei**, signora, prende un'acqua minerale?	**Lei** *(you, polite)* to address a man or woman

> The subject pronoun stands in for the subject. In Italian, all the forms are **stressed**.

The plural forms are:

> **Noi** andiamo al cinema,
>
> **voi** cosa fate?
>
> Anche **voi**, signori, prendete un caffè?
>
> **Loro** sono tedeschi, io sono italiano.

> **noi** *(we)* for the 1st person,
>
> **voi** *(you)* for the 2nd person,
>
> **voi** *(you, familiar)* to address more than one person,
>
> **loro** *(they)* for the 3rd person.

> In very formal situations, to address several people politely, use **Loro**. In letters, **Loro** is usually capitalized.

Use

+ Hai visto i Masu alla festa? ~ **Lei** sì, **lui** no.

The subject pronoun can stand alone, that is, without a verb ...

Io sono italiana, **lui** è svizzero.

... or be used with a verb.

Use the subject pronoun only:

+ Chi va al mare quest'estate? ~ **Noi.**

– to distinguish the person or persons from others,

Noi torniamo a casa in macchina, **loro** preferiscono tornare a piedi.

– to make contrasts,

Lei, signora, che cosa prende?

– commonly, in the polite form of address,

Venite **anche voi** in discoteca?

– after **anche.**

> Unlike English, Italian usually omits the subject pronoun. The verb form indicates which person is meant:
> **Mangio** – *I eat.*
> **Fumi**? – *Do you smoke?*
> **Siamo** stanchi. – *We are tired.*

The forms **lui**, **lei**, and **loro** cannot stand in for objects. With objects, either use the appropriate verb with no subject pronoun, or repeat the corresponding noun, as here:

> I Nardelli hanno comprato <u>una casa</u> . **È** bella e molto spaziosa.
>
> *The Nardellis have bought a house. It is pretty and very spacious.*

> Vi do i compiti . Non **sono** difficili, ma **sono** utili.
>
> *I'm giving you homework assignments. They're not hard, but they are useful.*

The Object Pronouns

① Ti amo.

② Ti ha scritto Lucia?

---

1. I love you. 2. Has Lucia written to you?

Italian has both direct and indirect object pronouns.

+ Hai fatto **la spesa?** ~ Non ancora, **la** faccio più tardi.	The direct object pronouns stand in for a direct object / accusative object.
La sera guardo volentieri **la tivù.** Oggi non ho visto **Carlo.** Dove comperi **la carne**?	The direct object can be identified by the absence of the preposition **a** before the noun in question.
+ Hai scritto **alla nonna?** ~ Certo, **le** ho scritto stamattina.	The indirect object pronouns are used to replace an indirect object / dative object.
Che cosa regali **a tuo marito?** Hai risposto **ai tuoi genitori**? Telefono **al dottor Renzi.**	The indirect object can be identified by the presence of the preposition **a** before the noun in question.

fare la spesa – *to do the shopping*
guardare la tivù – *to watch television*
la carne – *the meat*
rispondere – *to answer*

Perché hai invitato **me** e non **lei?** **A me** la cucina giapponese piace, piace anche **a te**?	There exist **stressed** forms for both the direct and the indirect object pronouns.
Perché **mi** hai invitato? La cucina giapponese **mi piace.** **Ti** piace la cucina francese?	And there exist **unstressed** forms for both types of object pronouns.

invitare – *to invite*
giapponese – *Japanese*

Forms and Use of the Stressed Object Pronouns

The stressed forms of the indirect and the direct object pronouns differ
only by the presence or absence of the preposition **a**, which is used:

A te piace sciare?	with the indirect object pronouns ...
Voglio vedere solo **te**.	... and not with the direct ones.

Indirect Object Pronouns	Direct Object Pronouns
Pia scrive ... *(Pia writes ...)*	**Pia conosce solo ...** *(Pia knows only ...)*
a me. *(me / to me.)*	**me.** *(me.)*
a te. *(you / to you.)*	**te.** *(you.)*
a lui. *(him / to him.)*	**lui.** *(him.)*
a lei. *(her / to her.)*	**lei.** *(her.)*
a Lei. *(you / to you.)*	**Lei.** *(you.)*
a noi. *(us / to us.)*	**noi.** *(us.)*
a voi. *(you / to you.)*	**voi.** *(you.)*
a loro. *(them / to them.)*	**loro.** *(them.)*
a Loro. *(you / to you.)*	**Loro.** *(you.)*
Pia pensa **a sé**. *(Pia thinks about herself.)*	Pia ama solo **sé** stessa. *(Pia loves only herself.)*

A sé and **sé** represent the reflexive pronoun. Before **stesso**, **sé** can
also be written without the accent: **Vede solo se stessa.**

> **A Lei** and **Lei** are
> used as a form of
> polite address for
> one person.

> In formal situations,
> use **a Loro** and **Loro**.

The stressed object pronouns are used:

Flavio guarda solo **te**.
A noi l'aglio piace molto.

when the person or persons are emphasized.

Conosco **lui, lei** no.

in contrasts.

l'aglio – *the garlic*

Io vado al mare, chi viene **con me?**
C'è una lettera **per te.**
Abbiamo parlato **di lui.**
Possiamo venire **da voi** stasera?
Carla è **fuori di sé.**
Secondo me Franca ha ragione.

■ after prepositions, such as **con**, **per**, **di**, **da**, **fuori di**, **sotto di**, **dopo di**, **senza di**, **secondo**.

Mio fratello è più alto **di me.**
Mia sorella è alta **come me.**

■ in comparisons following **di**, **come**, and **quanto**.

Anche a te piace la rucola?

■ after **anche.**

fuori di sé –
beside oneself
secondo me –
in my opinion
aver ragione –
to be right
alto – *tall*

Forms and Use of the Unstressed Object Pronouns

+ Che cosa regali **a Marco?**   + Da quando conosci **Marco?**
~ Forse **gli** regalo un libro.   ~ **Lo** conosco da due anni circa.
① _____   ②

1. + *What are you giving **to Marco**? ~ Maybe I'll give **him** a book.*
2. + *How long have you known **Marco**? ~ I've known him for about two years.*

In the 1st and 2nd persons singular and plural, there is no difference between the unstressed forms of the indirect and the direct object pronouns. With the 3rd person singular and plural, however, pay attention to the difference between the forms of the object pronouns for the masculine and feminine objects!

Indirect Object Pronouns		Direct Object Pronouns	
Pia ...	*(Pia writes ...)*	**Pia ...**	*(Pia greets ...)*
mi scrive.	*(me / to me.)*	**mi** saluta.	*(me.)*
ti scrive.	*(you / to you.)*	**ti** saluta.	*(you.)*
gli scrive.	*(him / to him.)*	**lo** saluta.	*(him.)*
le scrive.	*(her / to her.)*	**la** saluta.	*(her.)*
Le scrive.	*(you / to you.)*	**La** saluta.	*(you.)*

Le and **La** are used as forms of polite address.

<table>
<tr><td>To use the polite form of address for several people, choose Loro or Li / Le.</td></tr>
</table>

ci scrive.	*(us / to us.)*	**ci** saluta.	*(us.)*
vi scrive.	*(you / to you.)*	**vi** saluta.	*(you.)*
gli scrive.	*(them / to them.)*	**li** saluta.	*(them.)* (masculine)
gli scrive.	*(them / to them.)*	**le** saluta.	*(them.)* (feminine)
scrive **Loro**.	*(you / to you.)*	**Li** saluta?	*(you.)* (masculine)
scrive **Loro**.	*(you / to you.)*	**Le** saluta?	*(you.)* (feminine)

▶ **Reflexive Verbs**, p. 161

Perché **si** fa un tè? *(Why is he / she making him / herself tea? / Why are you making yourself tea?)*	Perché **si** scusa? *(Why is he / she excusing him / herself? / Why are you excusing yourself?)*
Perché **si** fanno un tè? *(Why are they making themselves tea?)*	Perché **si** scusano? *(Why are they excusing themselves?)*

Except in the 3rd person singular and plural, the reflexive pronouns have the same form as the direct and indirect object pronouns.

The unstressed object pronouns cannot stand alone. They are always used together with a verb.

+ **Mi** telefoni? ~ Certo, appena arrivo **ti** telefono.
  Vi prego di ascoltar**mi**.
+ Quando fai i compiti? ~ **Li** faccio subito.

appena – *as soon as*
pregare – *to ask, request*
subito – *immediately*

Regarding **lo**, **la**, **li**, and **le**, note the following:

+ Hai già letto l'ultimo libro di Baricco? ~ No, non **l'h**o ancora letto.
+ Potresti aiutare **Carla?** ~ Certo, **l'a**iuto subito.

Before **h** and often before a vowel as well, **lo** and **la** are used in their contracted forms, with an apostrophe.

+ Conoscete **i film di Visconti**? ~ Certo, **li** abbiamo visti tutti.
+ Hai preso **la medicina?** ~ **L'**ho presa stamattina.

When **lo**, **la**, **li**, or **le** occur before a past participle that is conjugated with **avere** in a compound tense, the participle agrees in gender and number with the preceding direct object pronoun.

Li and **le** are never written with apostrophes!

+ Chi ha telefonato? ~ Non **lo** so.

The form **lo** can also refer to a fact or circumstance and mean *it*.

Position of the Unstressed Object Pronouns

+ **Vi** disturba se fumo? ~ No, non **ci** disturba affatto.	Generally the unstressed object pronouns precede the conjugated verb.
Perché non sei venuto? **Ti** abbiamo aspettato tutta la sera.	In the compound tenses, they precede the auxiliary verb.
Signori, posso offrire **Loro** un aperitivo?	Only the very formal **Loro**, which is a polite form of address for several people, follows the verb.

disturbare – *to disturb*
fumare – *to smoke*
offrire – *to offer*

In certain instances, however, the unstressed pronouns are attached, as here:

Ho cercato di telefonar**ti**. Siamo felici di veder**vi**.	to the infinitive, which loses the final vowel in the process.
Vedendo**mi** è diventato tutto rosso.	to the present participle.
Guarda**mi**! Che bella frutta, prendiamo**la**! Riposate**vi**, se siete stanchi!	to the imperative.
Signora, questo prosciutto è ottimo, **lo** prenda!	not, however, to the polite imperative.
+ Ma dove siete? ~ Ecco**ci**. + Mi dai le chiavi? ~ Ecco**le**.	to **ecco**.

▶ **The Imperative**, p. 138

eccoci – *here we are*
eccole – *here they are (feminine)*
eccoli – *here they are (masc or masc & fem)*

There are also instances in which you can place the unstressed object pronoun before the conjugated verb or attach it to the verb. This is true:

Vi devo parlare./Devo parlar**vi**. **Li** ho potuti vedere./Ho potuto veder**li**.	when a verb in the infinitive follows **dovere**, **potere**, **volere**, or **sapere**.
Ti vengo a prendere. Vengo a prender**ti**.	when **andare** or **venire** are followed by a verb in the infinitive.

venire a prendere – *to pick up*

<table>
<tr>
<td>▶ The Imperative,
p. 138</td>
<td>Non far**lo**!/Non **lo** fare!
Non fate**lo**!/Non **lo** fate!

Signora, non **lo** faccia!</td>
<td>with the negative imperative,

but not with the polite imperative. Here it can be placed only before the verb.</td>
</tr>
</table>

Italian Verbs That Require an Object in a Certain Case

There are some Italian verbs that require a direct object, including these:

<table>
<tr><td>

Tip! To avoid mistakes, it is always best to memorize a verb along with its object!

</td><td>

aiutare qu	*to help someone*
ascoltare qu	*to belong to someone*
aspettare qu	*to wait for someone*
ringraziare qu	*to thank someone*
seguire qu	*to follow someone*

</td></tr>
</table>

Others, however, always require an indirect object:

domandare a qu	*to ask someone a question*
chiedere a qu	*to ask someone to do something*
pensare a qu	*to think about someone*
telefonare a qu	*to telephone someone*

The Pronominal Adverbs *ci* and *ne*

Vai spesso al ristorante?
①

Ci vado abbastanza spesso, sì.
②

Signora, prende dello zucchero?
③

Ne ho già preso, grazie.
④

---

1. *Do you often go to the restaurant?* 2. *Yes, I go there fairly often.*
3. *Ma'am, do you take sugar?* 4. *I've already taken some, thank you.*

The pronominal adverbs **ci** and **ne** perform several functions.

1. *ci*

+ Andate spesso **a Monaco?** ~ **Ci** andiamo ogni anno in autunno. + Quando vai **dal parrucchiere?** ~ **Ci** vado sabato.	The pronominal adverb **ci** stands for places and means *there* in English.
+ Credi **a quello che scrivono i giornali?** ~ No, non **ci** credo. + Pensi ancora **all'esame?** ~ No, adesso non **ci** penso più.	**Ci** also stands for objects with **a** that refer to things or circumstances. It is rendered *as it* or *of it / them*.

l'autunno – *autumn, fall*
il parrucchiere – *the hairdresser*
il giornale – *the newspaper*
l'esame – *the exam*

2. *ne*

+ Ho comprato **troppe ciliegie, ne** vuoi un po'? ~ Grazie, ma **ne** ho comprate anch'io. + Hai **dei colleghi stranieri**? ~ Sì, **ne** ho due.	**Ne** can refer to previously named persons or things and designate a subset of them. In such cases **ne** may be rendered as *some* or may remain untranslated in English.
+ Hai fatto **delle foto?** ~ Sì, **ne** ho fatte tante. + **Quanti biglietti** hai preso? ~ **Ne** ho presi quattro. + Vuoi **una birra**? ~ Grazie, ma **ne** ho bevuta già abbastanza.	If **ne** denotes a subset and occurs in a compound tense before a past participle linked with **avere**, the participle agrees in number and gender with the term **ne** is replacing.
+ Sei convinto **di quello che** dici? ~ **Ne** sono convinto, sì. + Hai voglia **di uscire** stasera? ~ No, stasera non **ne** ho tanta voglia. + Hai bisogno **del dizionario?** ~ No, adesso non **ne** ho bisogno.	**Ne** can also stand for objects with **di**. It often is rendered as *of it, of them*. In some cases it may remain untranslated.
Il gatto è salito sul tetto, ma non **ne** è più sceso. **(ne = dal tetto)** Ho visto il tuo quadro. **Ne** sono affascinato. **(ne = dal quadro)**	**Ne** can also replace objects with **da** and means *from there* or *about it*, for example, depending on the context.

▶ **The Position of the Unstressed Object Pronouns**, p. 71

ottimo – *very good*
la metà – *the half*

3. The Position of *ci* and *ne*

+ Quando vai al corso di italiano? ~ **Ci** vado il martedì sera. + Hai tanti compiti? ~ **Ne** ho sempre tanti.	Like the unstressed object pronouns, **ci** and **ne** generally are placed before the conjugated verb.
+ È vero che hai abitato a Parigi? ~ Certo, **ci** ho abitato per tre anni. + Carla ha fatto un ottimo tiramisù. ~ Sì, **ne** ho mangiato la metà.	With the compound tenses, **ci** and **ne** precede the auxiliary verb.

The Double Pronouns

+ Mi dai il giornale, per favore? ~ Aspetta, finisco di leggere un articolo e **te lo** do. ①	+ Ci sono ancora delle uova? ~ No, non **ce ne** sono più. ②

---

1. + Will you give me the newspaper, please? ~ Wait, I'll finish reading an article and give it to you.
2. + Are there still some eggs? ~ No, there aren't any more.

Often an unstressed indirect object pronoun occurs beside an unstressed direct object pronoun.

Ci date **il vostro indirizzo?** ▶ **Ce lo** date? Pia **si** fa **un caffè.** ▶ Pia **se lo** fa. **Ti** do **la mia giacca.** ▶ **Te la** do.	In the combination thus created, the indirect object pronoun always precedes the direct one, with the **-i** of the indirect object pronoun changing to **-e.**
Darò **i libri a Gianni.** ▶ **Glieli** darò. Presto **la macchina a Rosa.** ▶ **Gliela** presto. Signora, **Le** do **il mio libro.** ▶ **Glielo** do.	The unstressed dative pronouns **gli**, **le**, and **Le** in combination with a direct object pronoun become **glie** and join with that pronoun to form a single word.
Potresti dar**mi il tuo dizionario?** ▶ Potresti dar**melo?** Dam**mi la lettera!** ▶ Dam**mela!**	The other combinations form a single word only when they are attached to the verb.

Possible Combinations

+	lo	la	li	le	ne
mi *(to me)*	me lo	me la	me li	me le	me ne
ti *(to you)*	te lo	te la	te li	te le	te ne
gli *(to him)* **le** *(to her)* **Le** *(to you)*	glielo	gliela	glieli	gliele	gliene
ci *(to us)*	ce lo	ce la	ce li	ce le	ce ne
vi *(to you)*	ve lo	ve la	ve li	ve le	ve ne
gli *(to them)*	glielo	gliela	glieli	gliele	gliene
si *(reflexive, 3rd pers. sing. and pl.)*	se lo	se la	se li	se le	se ne
ci *(there)*	ce lo	ce la	ce li	ce le	ce ne

The double pronouns follow the same rules as the unstressed pronouns.
Therefore, pay attention to their position relative to the verb:

Che bello scialle! **Me lo** dai? **Me lo** devi dare. Devi dar**melo.**	They precede the conjugated verb or are attached to the infinitive.
Che buono questo dolce! **Dam**mene un pezzo! **Me ne** dia un pezzo!	They are attached to the imperative, with the exception of the polite form of the imperative.

In addition, note the following:

+ I vicini sanno già che mi sposo. ~ Ah sì, e chi **gliel'h**a detto?	**lo** and **la** are written as contractions before **h** and often before a vowel.
Che **bei fiori!** Chi **te li** ha portati? Ho conosciuto **la fidanzata** di Marco. **Me l'**ha presentata ieri.	the agreement in number and gender of the past participle with **avere** in the compound tenses, with **lo**, **la**, **li**, **le**, or **ne**, when they precede the past participle.

il pezzo – *the piece*
il vicino – *the neighbor*
sposarsi – *to marry*
il fiore – *the flower*
la fidanzata –
the fiancée
presentare qu –
to introduce someone

The Personal Pronouns

1. Read the dialogue, and fill in the appropriate subject pronouns and stressed object pronouns, as well as the pronominal adverb **ci**. **

+ Ragazzi, _____ quest'estate vado in Germania, _____

che cosa fate?

~ Mah, _____ vado prima in montagna con i miei genitori, sto

due settimane con _____ e poi vado in Inghilterra. _____

vado con Sandro. _____ siamo già stati l'anno scorso, e ci siamo

divertiti moltissimo. Poi non so, forse andrò al mare.

+ E _____ Elena, vai a Savignano Mare come ogni anno?

~ Sì, ma non _____ sto tutta l'estate. Quest'anno _____

sarà anche mia cugina Graziella e siccome _____ e _____

non andiamo molto d'accordo, preferisco non starci troppo a lungo.

prima – *first*
poi – *then*
siccome – *since, as*
andare d'accordo –
to get on well with
someone

2. The sentences in the left-hand column are addressed to a person for whom the familiar pronoun is used. In the right-hand column, the same sentences are addressed to someone for whom the polite pronoun is used. Fill in the blanks with the appropriate pronouns. **

TU	LEI
a) Ti piace la musica classica?	a) Signora Rota, _____ piace la musica classica?
b) Ti ringrazio per il bel regalo.	b) Signora, _____ ringrazio per il bel regalo.
c) Ti dovrei chiedere qualcosa, posso?	c) Signor Valli, _____ dovrei chiedere qualcosa, posso?
d) Cosa ti posso offrire?	d) Professore, cosa _____ posso offrire?
e) Ti vorrei invitare a cena.	e) Signorina, _____ vorrei invitare a cena.
f) A che ora ti posso telefonare?	f) Ingegnere, a che ora _____ posso telefonare?

3. Match the sentences in the left-hand column with the appropriate item in the right-hand column. The pronouns in the column on the right will help you get the correct match. *

a) Ottimo questo pesce!

b) Che buoni questi cioccolatini!

c) Abbiamo sentito che cambiate casa.

d) Sai che ho un nuovo computer?

e) Avete visto la mia nuova bicicletta?

f) Buongiorno, sono Carla Franchi, c'è il professor Carli?

g) Che bella borsetta!

h) Non trovo i miei occhiali.

1) Te l'ha regalata Mario?

2) No, faccela vedere!

3) Ce n'è ancora un po'?

4) Chi ve l'ha detto?

5) Me ne dai ancora uno?

6) Me li hai presi tu, forse?

7) Glielo passo subito.

8) Ah sì, e te lo sei comprato tu?

il pesce – *the fish*

il cioccolatino – *the (piece of) chocolate candy*

cambiar casa – *to move (change residence)*

la borsetta – *the handbag*

passare qu a qu – *to connect someone with someone else*

a)   b)   c)   d)   e)   f)   g)   h)

4. Mark the appropriate pronoun in the pairs below. *

a) + Siete già stati a Los Angeles? ~ Sì, ci / ne siamo stati due anni fa.

b) + Anche tu porti gli occhiali? ~ Eh sì, per leggere gli / li devo mettere.

c) + Guardate spesso la televisione? ~ Ne / La guardiamo spesso, sì.

d) + Che cosa hai portato a Gino? ~ Gli / Le ho portato del vino.

e) + È ottima la tua carne! ~ La / Ne vuoi ancora una fetta?

f) + Hai scritto alla nonna? ~ Senti, le / la scriverò.

g) + Incontri le tue amiche, oggi? ~ No, gli / le incontro domani.

h) + È pratico questo vestito, vero? ~ Sì, lo / ne metto spesso.

i) + Vuoi un po' d'uva? ~ Ci / Ne ho già presa, grazie.

j) + Cosa mangiano i bambini? ~ Se vuoi li / gli puoi preparare della pasta.

k) + Hai trovato qualcosa per Anna? ~ Sì, gli / le ho comprato un foulard.

l) + Andiamo al cinema stasera? ~ No, guarda, non ci / ne ho voglia.

la carne – *the meat*

la fetta – *the slice*

il foulard – *the scarf, neckerchief*

vero? – *isn't that so?*

The Personal Pronouns

5. For each item, provide an alternative to the underlined portion. *

assaggiare –
to sample, taste
trasferirsi –
to transfer, move
spiegare – *to explain*
presentare –
to introduce

a) Quando <u>ci vieni a prendere</u>?   <u>Quando vieni a prenderci?</u>

b) <u>Le posso telefonare</u> stasera?   _____

c) _____   <u>Posso assaggiarne</u> un po'?

d) <u>Ci dobbiamo vedere</u> stasera.   _____

e) _____   Carlo <u>deve trasferirsi</u> a Roma.

f) <u>Mi vorrei scusare</u> per ieri sera.   _____

g) Al cinema non <u>ci voglio andare</u>.   _____

h) _____   <u>Vorrei presentarvi</u> un mio collega.

i) _____   Purtroppo non <u>so spiegarti</u> niente.

6. Translate the following. ***

a) I excuse myself / apologize.

_____

b) Can I help you, Mrs. Nuti?

_____

c) I'll call him tomorrow.

_____

d) I'll send you an e-mail.

_____

e) I thank you, Mr. Carli.

_____

f) I'm waiting for you, Mrs. Lanzi.

_____

7. Complete the dialogues with the appropriate double pronouns. *

a) + Hai detto a Mario che partiamo tra una settimana?

~ No, _____ dirò stasera.

b) + Ho comprato dei bellissimi stivali.

~ Ah sì? _____ fai vedere?

c) + Mamma, non ci prepari mai il tiramisù, quando _____ prepari ? ~ Se volete _____ faccio sabato.

d) + Signora, sono arrivati dei bellissimi vestiti estivi; _____ faccio vedere? ~ Sì, volentieri.

The Present Tense

Tu che cosa **fai** stasera? **Guardi** la partita di calcio?

①

No, **vado** a teatro; **ho** un biglietto per lo spettacolo di Dario Fo.

②

---

1. *What are you doing this evening? Are you watching the soccer game?*
2. *No, I'm going to the theater; I have a ticket for the play by Dario Fo.*

On the basis of the ending of their infinitive, Italian verbs can be divided into three conjugations:

> Most verbs ending in **-are** and **-ire** are regular.

Infinitive	
guard**are**	1st conjugation, or verbs ending in **-are**,
prend**ere**	2nd conjugation, or verbs ending in **-ere**,
dorm**ire**	3rd conjugation, or verbs ending in **-ire**.

A distinction is made between regular and irregular verbs.

Infinitive	(io)	
guardare	**guard**o	In the process of conjugation, the verb stem (for example, **guard-, prend-, dorm-**) of regular verbs remains unchanged.
prendere	**prend**o	
dormire	**dorm**o	
andare	**vad**o	With irregular verbs, however, the stem changes.
uscire	**esc**o	

guardare – *to look*
prendere – *to take*
dormire – *to sleep*
andare – *to go, move*
uscire – *to go out, leave, exit*

The Present Tense of Regular Verbs

La domenica **guardo** la televisione,
leggo un po' e **pulisco** la casa.

On Sundays I watch television, read a little, and clean the house.

Tip! The stress
of the 3rd person plu-
ral forms is not easy!
Practice by first
pronouncing the
1st person singular,
and immediately
thereafter the 3rd
person plural.
guardo ▶ guardano
prendo ▶ prendono
dormo ▶ dormono

1. Verbs Ending in -are, -ere and -ire

Verbs Ending in -are

	guardare	The present tense of regular
		verbs ending in **-are** is formed
(io)	guardo	by adding the endings for the
(tu)	guardi	individual persons: **-o, -i, -a,**
(lui/lei/Lei)	guarda	**-iamo, -ate,** and **-ano.** They are
(noi)	guardiamo	attached to the verb stem, for
(voi)	guardate	example, **guard-.**
(loro)	guardano	

Verbs Ending in -ere

	prendere	For regular verbs ending in
		-ere, the personal endings are
(io)	prendo	**-o, -i, -e, -iamo, -ete,** and
(tu)	prendi	**-ono.** They are attached to the
(lui/lei/Lei)	prende	verb stem, for example, **prend-.**
(noi)	prendiamo	
(voi)	prendete	
(loro)	prendono	

Have you noticed that
the verb forms of the
three conjugations
differ from one
another only in the
2nd and 3rd person
plural?

Verbs Ending in -ire Without an Expanded Stem

	dormire	Regular verbs ending in **-ire**
		are conjugated by adding the
(io)	dormo	personal endings **-o, -i, -e,**
(tu)	dormi	**-iamo, -ite,** and **-ono** to the
(lui/lei/Lei)	dorme	appropriate verb stem, for
(noi)	dormiamo	example, **dorm-.**
(voi)	dormite	
(loro)	dormono	

Verbs Ending in *-ire* with an Expanded Stem

	capire	
(io)	capisco	For almost 500 verbs ending in **-ire**, the endings of the present tense are attached to the expanded verb stem **-isc-**: for example, **cap-** + **-isc-** ▸ **capisc-**. Only the 1st and 2nd person plural, that is, **noi** and **voi**, are an exception.
(tu)	capisci	
(lui/lei/Lei)	capisce	
(noi)	capiamo	
(voi)	capite	
(loro)	capiscono	

Tip! You have to memorize which verbs belong to which group. Thus, in addition to the infinitive, always learn the 1st person singular (**io**) as well!

The most important verbs ending in **-ire** with an expanded stem are:

abolire	*(to abolish)*	impedire	*(to hinder)*
abortire	*(to abort)*	preferire	*(to prefer)*
agire	*(to act)*	proibire	*(to prohibit)*
capire	*(to understand)*	pulire	*(to clean up, polish)*
chiarire	*(to clarify)*	punire	*(to punish)*
colpire	*(to strike)*	reagire	*(to react)*
contribuire	*(to contribute)*	restituire	*(to return, give back)*
costruire	*(to construct, build)*	riferire	*(to report)*
definire	*(to define)*	smentire	*(to deny)*
digerire	*(to digest)*	sostituire	*(to substitute)*
distribuire	*(to distribute)*	sparire	*(to disappear)*
fallire	*(to fail, go wrong)*	spedire	*(to send)*
favorire	*(to favor, encourage)*	subire	*(to undergo)*
ferire	*(to injure)*	suggerire	*(to suggest)*
finire	*(to finish)*	tossire	*(to cough)*
fornire	*(to supply, provide)*	tradire	*(to betray)*
gestire	*(to manage, lead)*	ubbidire	*(to obey)*
guarire	*(to heal)*	unire	*(to unite, join)*

2. Special Features

Verbs Ending in *-care* and *-gare*

	giocare	pagare	
(io)	gioco	pago	To preserve the pronunciation of **-c-** or **-g-** throughout all the persons ([k] or [g]), verbs ending in **-care** or **-gare** insert an **-h-** before the 2nd person singular (**tu**) and before the 1st person plural (**noi**).
(tu)	giochi	paghi	
(lui/lei/Lei)	gioca	paga	
(noi)	giochiamo	paghiamo	
(voi)	giocate	pagate	
(loro)	giocano	pagano	

giocare – *to play*
pagare – *to pay*

Verbs Ending in -*iare*

	studiare	Verbs ending in **-iare** generally have only an **-i** in the 2nd person singular (**tu**) and in the 1st person plural (**noi**).
(io)	studio	
(tu)	stu**di**	
(lui/lei/Lei)	studia	
(noi)	stud**i**amo	
(voi)	studiate	
(loro)	studiano	

studiare – *to study*
sciare – *to ski*

	sciare	Only a few verbs ending in **-iare**, such as **sciare**, have **-ii** in the 2nd person singular. They retain the stressed **-i-** of the verb stem.
(io)	scio	
(tu)	sc**ii**	
(lui/lei/Lei)	scia	
(noi)	sciamo	
(voi)	sciate	
(loro)	sciano	

The following verbs are conjugated like **sciare**:
avviare (*to launch, start*), **deviare** (*to deviate, deflect*),
espiare (*to expiate*), **inviare** (*to send*), **rinviare** (*to send back*),
and **spiare** (*to spy*).

Verbs Ending in -*(s)cere* and -*gere*

	conoscere	leggere
(io)	conosco [k]	leggo [g]
(tu)	conosci	leggi
(lui/lei/Lei)	conosce	legge
(noi)	conosciamo	leggiamo
(voi)	conoscete	leggete
(loro)	conoscono [k]	leggono [g]

conoscere – *to know*
leggere – *to read*
vincere – *to win*

With verbs ending in **-(s)cere**, such as **conoscere** or **vincere**, and in **-gere**, such as **leggere**, the pronunciation of **-c-** and **-g-** is determined by the following vowel. Therefore it changes in the 1st person singular (**io**) and in the 3rd person plural (**loro**) and sounds like [k] or [g].

The Present Tense of Irregular Verbs

> Io **vado** al cinema,
> tu cosa **fai?**
> ①

> Io **rimango** a casa, non
> **ho** voglia di uscire.
> ②

---

1. I'm going to the movies, what are you doing? 2. I'm staying home; I don't want to go out.

There are quite a number of irregular verbs. Many of them are part of the basic vocabulary and can be placed into groups.

1. Very Frequently Used Verbs

Some irregular verbs are used with great frequency. They include:

	essere	avere
(io)	sono	ho
(tu)	sei	hai
(lui/lei/Lei)	è	ha
(noi)	siamo	abbiamo
(voi)	siete	avete
(loro)	sono	hanno

> Don't confuse these:
> **è** (with accent) and
> **e** (without accent).
> **è** = *he / she / it is*
> **e** = *and*

Essere is irregular in all persons.
With **avere**, only the verb form **avete** is regular.

	dovere	potere	volere	sapere
(io)	devo	posso	voglio	so
(tu)	devi	puoi	vuoi	sai
(lui/lei/Lei)	deve	può	vuole	sa
(noi)	dobbiamo	possiamo	vogliamo	sappiamo
(voi)	dovete	potete	volete	sapete
(loro)	devono	possono	vogliono	sanno

dovere – *to have to*
potere – *to be able to, can*
volere – *to want, wish*
sapere – *to know, be able to*

The 2nd person plural is regular for all four verbs.

	andare	dare	fare	stare
(io)	vado	do	faccio	sto
(tu)	vai	dai	fai	stai
(lui/lei/Lei)	va	dà	fa	sta
(noi)	andiamo	diamo	facciamo	stiamo
(voi)	andate	date	fate	state
(loro)	vanno	danno	fanno	stanno

> Don't confuse the verb form **dà** (with a written accent) with the preposition **da** (without an accent).

Andare, dare, fare, and **stare** are the only irregular verbs ending in **-are**.

	dire	uscire	venire
(io)	dico	esco	vengo
(tu)	dici	esci	vieni
(lui/lei/Lei)	dice	esce	viene
(noi)	diciamo	usciamo	veniamo
(voi)	dite	uscite	venite
(loro)	dicono	escono	vengono

Dire, **uscire**, and **venire** are among the few verbs ending in **-ire** that are irregular in their conjugation. Quite a number of verbs related to them follow the same conjugational pattern.

contraddire –
to contradict
disdire – *to cancel*
ridire – *to say again*
riuscire – *to succeed*
avvenire – *to happen*
convenire – *to agree*
prevenire – *to prevent; to inform*
svenire – *to faint*
trarre – *to derive*

dire ▶ **contraddire, disdire,** and **ridire**
uscire ▶ **riuscire**
venire ▶ **avvenire, convenire, intervenire, prevenire,** and **svenire**

2. Verbs Ending in *-arre*, *-urre*, and *-orre*

	trarre
(io)	traggo
(tu)	trai
(lui/lei/Lei)	trae
(noi)	traiamo
(voi)	traete
(loro)	traggono

These are conjugated the same way as **trarre**:

attrarre *(to attract, charm)*, **contrarre** *(to contract, narrow)*, **distrarre** *(to distract)*, **protrarre** *(to protract, prolong)*.

	produrre	Treat these the same way as **produrre**:
(io)	produco	
(tu)	produci	**condurre** (to lead, conduct),
(lui/lei/Lei)	produce	**introdurre** (to introduce),
(noi)	produciamo	**sedurre** (to seduce) and
(voi)	producete	**tradurre** (to translate).
(loro)	producono	

produrre – *to produce*

	porre	These follow the conjugational pattern of **porre**:
(io)	pongo	
(tu)	poni	**esporre** (to expose, show),
(lui/lei/Lei)	pone	**imporre** (to impose), **opporre**
(noi)	poniamo	(to oppose) and **proporre** (to
(voi)	ponete	propose, suggest).
(loro)	pongono	

porre – *to put, position*

3. Verbs Ending in *-gliere*

	scegliere	These verbs display two irregularities: In the 1st person singular (**io**) and in the 3rd person plural (**loro**), the stem ends in **-lg-**. In the 2nd person singular (**tu**) and in the 1st person plural (**noi**), the **-i-** of the stem is omitted.
(io)	scelgo	
(tu)	scegli	
(lui/lei/Lei)	sceglie	
(noi)	scegliamo	
(voi)	scegliete	
(loro)	scelgono	

scegliere – *to choose, select*

This group includes, among others: **accogliere** (to welcome, receive), **cogliere** (to pluck; to overhear), **raccogliere** (to pick up, gather; to collect), **sciogliere** (to melt; to let loose), and **togliere** (to remove, take off).

4. Verbs with Doubling of -c-

	piacere	The same irregularity is exhibited by:
(io)	piaccio	
(tu)	piaci	**compiacere** (to play up to),
(lui/lei/Lei)	piace	**dispiacere** (to displease),
(noi)	piacciamo	and **tacere** (to be silent,
(voi)	piacete	to hush).
(loro)	piacciono	

piacere – *to please*

5. Verbs with Irregularities in the 1st Person Singular and the 3rd Person Plural

Verbs Ending in -ere

rimanere – *to stay, remain*
spegnere – *to put out, turn off*
valere – *to be worth*

	rimanere	spegnere	valere
(io)	rimango	spengo	valgo
(tu)	rimani	spegni	vali
(lui/lei/Lei)	rimane	spegne	vale
(noi)	rimaniamo	spegniamo	valiamo
(voi)	rimanete	spegnete	valete
(loro)	rimangono	spengono	valgono

These are conjugated:
- like **rimanere: permanere** *(to linger on)*.
- like **valere: equivalere** *(to be equivalent)*, **prevalere** *(to prevail)*.

Verbs Ending in -ire

apparire – *to appear*
salire – *to rise, go up*

	apparire	salire
(io)	appaio	salgo
(tu)	appari	sali
(lui/lei/Lei)	appare	sale
(noi)	appariamo	saliamo
(voi)	apparite	salite
(loro)	appaiono	salgono

These are conjugated:
- like **apparire: comparire** *(to appear)*, **disparire** *(to disappear)*, **scomparire** *(to vanish)*, **trasparire** *(to shine through, transpire)*.
- like **salire: assalire** *(to attack, assault)*, **risalire** *(to rise, go up again)*.

6. Other Irregular Verbs

	bere	morire	sedere	tenere
(io)	bevo	muoio	siedo	tengo
(tu)	bevi	muori	siedi	tieni
(lui/lei/Lei)	beve	muore	siede	tiene
(noi)	beviamo	moriamo	sediamo	teniamo
(voi)	bevete	morite	sedete	tenete
(loro)	bevono	muoiono	siedono	tengono

Possedere (*to possess*) is conjugated like **sedere**, and the following follow the pattern of **tenere**: **appartenere** (*to belong, to appertain*), **contenere** (*to contain*), **intrattenere** (*to entertain*), **mantenere** (*to maintain*), **ottenere** (*to obtain*), **trattenere** (*to restrain*).

Use

Oggi **fa** molto caldo. Chi non **deve** uscire **rimane** chiuso in casa.

- As in English, the present tense is used to express actions and circumstances in the present time, at the moment of speaking.

A mezzogiorno **non torno mai** a casa.
Il lunedì **esco** sempre con le mie amiche.

- The present tense is also used to express habitual action, ...

L'Africa **è** un continente.

- facts that are not dependent on time, ...

Domani devo alzarmi presto.
Fra due giorni iniziano le vacanze.
La settimana prossima è il compleanno di mio padre.

- and events that lie in the near future, when the future time is made clear with a time expression.

fa caldo – *it is hot*
il lunedì – *on Mondays*
fra due giorni –
in two days
la settimana prossima –
next week

The Present Tense

1. Which present tense forms occur in the sentences below? Match them with the correct personal pronouns. *

a) Che cosa cercate?

b) Tutti dicono che Elio è un bravo ragazzo.

c) Perché non leggi mai il giornale?

d) A tavola bevo volentieri un po' di vino.

e) Mi tieni un momento la borsetta, per favore?

f) Chi vuole ancora una fetta di dolce?

g) A che ora parte il treno?

h) La sera non mangiamo mai prima delle otto.

io	_____	noi	_____
tu	_____	voi	_____
lui/lei/Lei	_____	loro	_____

2. What are the other forms of the following verbs?*

	avere	dare	essere	sapere
(io)	ho	_____	_____	_____
(tu)	_____	dai	_____	_____
(lui/lei/Lei)	_____	_____	è	_____
(noi)	_____	_____	_____	sappiamo
(voi)	_____	date	_____	_____
(loro)	_____	_____	sono	_____

3. Complete the text with the verbs supplied, each in the appropriate form. *

~ Noi questo fine settimana _____(andare) tutti via.

Io _____ (andare) a Bologna, Carlo _____ (andare) a

Torino e i bambini _____ (andare) in montagna con degli

amici. E voi cosa _____ (fare)?_____ (andare)

via anche voi?

+ No, noi _____ (rimanere) qui.

4. By putting the letters in the correct order, you will obtain the
verb form of one of the verbs supplied. Write down the infinitive
as well. **

a) o a i g m n r   _____   rimanere

b) n n p g s o e o   _____   _____

c) o o a s l g n   _____   _____

d) i e e n t   _____   _____

e) t n n g o o e   _____   _____

f) o i o a i c p c n   _____   _____

g) i o o o l g v n   _____   _____

h) o o e g l c n s   _____   _____

i) e u o c p d r   _____   _____

rimanere

produrre

spegnere

tenere

scegliere

salire

piacere

volere

5. Complete the text with the appropriate verb forms. *

a) Io in estate _____ (andare) sempre dai miei nonni.

b) _____ (loro – stare) in una vecchia casa vicino al mare.

c) La mattina _____ (io – dormire) fino a tardi, _____
(io – fare) colazione e poi _____ (io – andare) in spiaggia.

d) Lì _____ (io – incontrare) i miei amici.

e) Qualche volta _____ (noi – rimanere) in spiaggia e
_____ (noi – giocare) a pallavolo, _____
(noi – chiacchierare), _____ (noi – andare) a fare il
bagno o non _____ (noi – fare) assolutamente niente.

f) Certe volte invece _____ (noi – decidere) di andare a
giocare a calcetto nel bar del paese.

g) Quando _____ (io – essere) stanco _____
(io – preferire) stare a casa: _____ (io – leggere) un po',
o _____ (io – guardare) la televisione.

h) La sera _____ (io – uscire) sempre. Purtroppo a mezzanotte
_____ (io – dovere) essere di nuovo a casa.

la pallavolo –
the volleyball

chiacchierare –
to chatter, gossip

il calcetto –
table soccer

The Present Perfect

Allora, com'è **andata** ieri sera? ①

Bene. È **stata** una bella serata. Prima **siamo andati** al cinema e poi in pizzeria. **Abbiamo parlato** molto; **sono tornata** a casa tardi ... ②

The **passato prossimo** is used where English uses the present perfect or, often, the simple past.

---

1. So, how did it go yesterday evening? 2. Fine. It was a lovely evening. First we went to the movies and then to a pizzeria. We talked a lot; I came home late ...

Formation of the Present Perfect

The present perfect, or **passato prossimo** (literally, "recent past"), is a past tense. It is formed with the present tense of **avere** or **essere** and the past participle of the main verb in question.

1. The Present Perfect with *avere*

	lavorare		
(io)	**ho**	lavora**to**	When the past perfect is formed
(tu)	**hai**	lavora**to**	with **avere**, the participle
(lui/lei/Lei)	**ha**	lavora**to**	remains unchanged. It always
(noi)	**abbiamo**	lavora**to**	ends in **-o**.
(voi)	**avete**	lavora**to**	
(loro)	**hanno**	lavora**to**	

+ Hai incontrato **Gianni**, vero? ~ Sì, **l'**ho incontrat**o** ieri. + Hai fatto **i compiti**? ~ No, non **li** ho fatt**i**. + Avete mangiato **la pizza**? ~ Sì, **l'**abbiamo mangiat**a**. + Hai visto **le tue amiche**? ~ No, non **le** ho vist**e**. + Avete fatto **delle foto**? ~ Sì, **ne** abbiamo fatt**e** molte.	The present perfect formed with **avere** changes, however, when a direct object in the form of the direct object pronouns **lo**, **la**, **li**, **le**, or **ne** precedes the auxiliary verb. Then the past participle agrees in number and gender with the direct object (pronoun).

+ **Anna**, ma perché Gianni non **ti** ha salutato/salutata? ~ **Perché** mi ha già visto/vista mezz'ora fa.	With the direct object pronouns **mi**, **ti**, **ci**, and **vi**, agreement is optional.

mezz'ora fa – *half an hour ago*

2. The Present Perfect with *essere*

	arrivare		
(io)	**sono**	arrivat**o**, **-a**	When the present perfect is conjugated with **essere**, the past participle agrees in gender and number with the subject.
(tu)	**sei**	arrivat**o**, **-a**	
(lui/lei/Lei)	**è**	arrivat**o**, **-a**	
(noi)	**siamo**	arrivat**i**, **-e**	
(voi)	**siete**	arrivat**i**, **-e**	
(loro)	**sono**	arrivat**i**, **-e**	

Il fax è arrivat**o**.	The past participle ends: in **-o** in the masculine singular,
Rita è arrivat**a**.	in **-a** in the feminine singular,
I clienti sono arrivat**i**.	in **-i** in the masculine plural,
Le cartoline sono arrivat**e**.	in **-e** in the feminine plural.
Fabio è andat**o** a Berlino. **Rita** è andat**a** a Berlino. **Fabio e Rita** sono andat**i** a Berlino.	When the subject consists of several persons or things of different genders, the participle ends in **-i**.

la cartolina – *the picture postcard*

Formation of the Past Participle

1. The Regular Past Participle

The regular past participle is formed by replacing the infinitive ending with the following endings:

and**are**	▶ and**ato**	**-ato** with verbs ending in **-are**,
av**ere**	▶ av**uto**	**-uto** with verbs ending in **-ere**,
dorm**ire**	▶ dorm**ito**	**-ito** with verbs ending in **-ire**.
cap**ire**	▶ cap**ito**	

conos**cere** cres**cere** pia**cere**	▶ conosc**iuto** ▶ cresc**iuto** ▶ piac**iuto**	Verbs ending in **-(s)cere** that have a regular participle form it with **-iuto**.
att**rarre**	▶ att**ratto**	Verbs ending in **-arre** form the past participle with **-atto**.
prod**urre**	▶ prod**otto**	For verbs ending in **-urre**, the ending of the past participle is **-otto**.
prop**orre**	▶ prop**osto**	For verbs ending in **-orre**, the past participle ends in **-osto**.

2. The Most Important Irregular Participles

accendere	▶ **acceso**	nascere	▶ **nato**
accorgersi	▶ **accorto**	offrire	▶ **offerto**
apparire	▶ **apparso**	perdere	▶ **perso**
aprire	▶ **aperto**	prendere	▶ **preso**
bere	▶ **bevuto**	ridere	▶ **riso**
chiedere	▶ **chiesto**	rimanere	▶ **rimasto**
chiudere	▶ **chiuso**	risolvere	▶ **risolto**
cogliere	▶ **colto**	rispondere	▶ **risposto**
concedere	▶ **concesso**	rompere	▶ **rotto**
correre	▶ **corso**	scegliere	▶ **scelto**
decidere	▶ **deciso**	scendere	▶ **sceso**
dire	▶ **detto**	scrivere	▶ **scritto**
dirigere	▶ **diretto**	spegnere	▶ **spento**
discutere	▶ **discusso**	spendere	▶ **speso**
escludere	▶ **escluso**	succedere	▶ **successo**
essere	▶ **stato**	togliere	▶ **tolto**
fare	▶ **fatto**	valere	▶ **valso**
insistere	▶ **insistito**	vedere	▶ **visto**
leggere	▶ **letto**	venire	▶ **venuto**
mettere	▶ **messo**	vincere	▶ **vinto**
morire	▶ **morto**	vivere	▶ **vissuto**
muovere	▶ **mosso**		

It is important to know that verbs made up of a prefix, such as **ac-**, and a basic verb, such as **cogliere**, resulting in **accogliere**, form the past participle the same way as the basic verb: **cogliere** ▶ **colto**, **accogliere** ▶ **accolto**.

Some additional examples are:

dire	▶ **detto**	contraddire ▶ **contraddetto**	
		disdire ▶ **disdetto**	
mettere	▶ **messo**	promettere ▶ **promesso**	
		trasmettere ▶ **trasmesso**	
venire	▶ **venuto**	convenire ▶ **convenuto**	
		intervenire ▶ **intervenuto**	

Use of *avere* or *essere* to Form the Present Perfect

> Ieri **ho invitato** alcuni amici a cena. **Sono venuti** verso le otto.
> **Abbiamo preso** un aperitivo e poi **siamo andati** a tavola.

*Usually **avere** is used with transitive verbs, and **essere** with intransitive verbs.*

Yesterday I invited some friends to dinner. They came around eight o'clock. We drank an aperitif and then we went to the table.

1. When Is the Present Perfect Formed with *essere*?

Verbs that do not take a direct object—intransitive verbs—generally form the present perfect with **essere**. These include:

Siamo stati in montagna.	**essere, diventare, dormire,**
Pia e Rosa **sono diventate** amiche.	**ridere, sembrare, rimanere,**
La risposta di Carlo mi **è** sembrata strana.	and most verbs of motion.
I vicini **sono partiti** per gli Stati Uniti.	
Siamo usciti senza ombrello.	

In the following cases as well, the present perfect must be formed with **essere**:

Ci siamo divertiti moltissimo.	with reflexive verbs.
I panini **sono bastati**.	with the verbs **bastare,**
Quant'**è costata** la cena di ieri?	**costare, dispiacere, durare,**
Ci **è dispiaciuto** molto.	**esistere, mancare, parere**
È durato a lungo lo spettacolo?	**piacere, sembrare, servire**
Il tuo consiglio non mi **è servito**.	

diventare – *to become*
sembrare – *to seem*
strano – *strange*
l'ombrello – *the umbrella*
bastare – *to be enough, suffice*
dispiacere – *to be sorry, regret*
durare – *to last, endure*
mancare – *to lack; to be missed*
parere – *to seem*
servire – *to be useful, serve*

In colloquial speech, however, the auxiliary verb **avere** is often used:
Ho dovuto rimanere. Non ho potuto partire. Ha voluto venire.

Siamo dovuti rimanere a casa. (siamo rimasti) Non **siamo potuti partire.** (siamo partiti) **È voluta venire** da sola. (è venuta) **Ho voluto invitare** i colleghi. (ho invitato)	with **dovere**, **potere**, and **volere**, when they are followed by an infinitive of a verb that forms the present perfect with **essere**. Otherwise, use **avere** to form the present perfect.
È bastato lasciare un messaggio.	with impersonal verbs.

With verbs that describe atmospheric phenomena, you can form the present perfect with either **essere** or **avere**, as here:

> ▸ **Impersonal Verbs and Expressions,** p. 166

È piovuto.	**Ha piovuto.**	*It (has) rained.*
È nevicato.	**Ha nevicato.**	*It (has) snowed.*

Use **avere**, however, with atmospheric phenomena that are expressed with fare, as in these examples:

Ha fatto molto **caldo.**	*It was very hot.*
Stanotte **ha fatto** molto **freddo.**	*Last night it was very cold.*
Ha fatto bel tempo.	*The weather was nice.*

2. When Is the Present Perfect Formed with *avere*?

All verbs that take a direct object—transitive verbs—form the present perfect with **avere**.

> **Abbiamo noleggiato** una macchina.
> **Abbiamo visitato** Ferrara e Mantova.

noleggiare – *to rent out*
camminare – *to walk*
nuotare – *to swim*
passeggiare – *to go for a walk*
sciare – *to ski*
viaggiare – *to travel*
marciare – *to march*

With verbs indicating a type of movement, **avere** is used to form the present perfect. Such verbs include:

Abbiamo camminato per due ore almeno. **Ho nuotato** nel lago. Dopo cena **ho passeggiato** lungo il fiume. **Ho sciato** tutto il pomeriggio. Mio nonno **ha viaggiato** molto.	**camminare, marciare, nuotare, passeggiare, sciare** and **viaggiare.**
Ho corso sotto la pioggia. Non **ho** ancora mai **volato.**	The verbs **correre** and **volare** use **avere** as the auxiliary verb when neither the starting point nor the goal of the movement is stated.

Sono corsa a casa al più presto. Siamo volati ad Amburgo.	Otherwise, form the present perfect with **essere**.

correre – *to run, race*
volare – *to fly*

Some verbs form the present perfect with **avere** when they are followed by a direct object or by the preposition **a** or **di** + infinitive. Otherwise, they form it with **essere**. The meaning of the verb may change in this case:

Ho cambiato dei soldi. Carla è cambiata.	*to change, exchange* *to undergo change, change oneself*
Abbiamo cominciato una nuova lezione. Ho cominciato a dipingere. Il film è già cominciato.	*to begin* *to begin to* *to start, begin*
Ho finito la traduzione. Ho finito di scrivere È finito lo spettacolo?	*to finish* *to get done* *to be at an end, be over*

Use

Sabato scorso **siamo andati** a giocare a golf.

The present perfect is used to give information about non-recurring actions and events in the past, ...

sabato scorso – *last Saturday*
andare a prendere qu – *to go get, go pick up someone*

Dopo il lavoro **ho fatto** prima la spesa, poi **sono andata** a prendere la bambina e l'**ho portata** dal parrucchiere.

... to depict several consecutive and completed actions and events in the past, ...

Ho fatto la patente tanti anni fa.
Mio padre **è andato** in pensione nel 1978.
Ho conosciuto mia moglie nell'estate del 1969.

... to tell about actions and events whose meaning continues in the present time or has effects on the present.

In addition to the present perfect, Italian has another important past tense, the imperfect, or **imperfetto**. Some things in the past can be told correctly only by means of the present perfect and the imperfect.

▶ **The Imperfect**, p. 98

Practice and Application

The Present Perfect

1. Fill in the missing forms of the present perfect. *

lavorare	partire	capire	sapere
ho lavorato	_____	_____	_____
_____	sei partito, -a	_____	_____
_____	_____	_____	ha saputo
_____	_____	_____	_____
_____	_____	_____	_____
_____	_____	hanno capito	_____

2. Which participle goes with which infinitive? Fill in the blanks. *

dovuto   messo   vissuto   risposto   venuto   visto
rimasto   ~~proposto~~   rotto   promesso   deciso   mosso

a)   proporre   rispondere   muovere   vedere

      proposto   _____   _____   _____

b)   rompere   dovere   decidere   mettere

    _____   _____   _____   _____

c)   venire   promettere   vivere   rimanere

    _____   _____   _____   _____

3. Complete each past participle with the appropriate ending: **-o, -a, -i,** or **-e.** *

il regalo – the gift
da tempo – for a long time
la traduzione – the translation
l'errore – the error, mistake

a)   + Hai già comprat_____ i regali di Natale?

    ~ Certo, li ho già comprat_____ da tempo.

b)   + Bravo, hai fatt_____ un' ottima traduzione!

    ~ L'ho fatt_____ bene veramente?

    + Come no, ho trovat_____ solo due o tre errori.

c)   + Che buone queste paste! Da chi le hai pres_____?

    ~ Le ho comprat_____ da Rossi.

4. What is the 1st person singular of the present perfect for these verbs? **

a) dire   conoscere   aprire   disdire

   ho detto   _____   _____   _____

b) essere   produrre   bere   chiedere

_____   _____   _____   _____

c) discutere   offrire   leggere   nascere

_____   _____   _____   _____

5. Put these sentences in the present perfect. **

      Oggi   Ieri

a) Pia va in città.   Pia è andata in città.

b) Pia compra un paio di scarpe.   _____

c) Le scarpe costano molto.   _____

d) I soldi non bastano.   _____

e) Deve pagare con la carta di   _____

   credito.   _____

f) Paola e Maria escono alle 8.   _____

g) Rosa e Enzo vanno al bar.   _____

h) Gino e Elena mangiano in ufficio. _____

i) Orazio va al cinema.   _____

j) Il film comincia alle 7.30 e   _____

   finisce alle 8.   _____

k) Il film gli piace.   _____

l) Dopo il film Orazio deve tornare   _____

   subito a casa.   _____

m) Fa molto caldo.   _____

n) Chiara non vuole uscire.   _____

un paio di scarpe –
a pair of shoes

The Imperfect

The imperfect, or **imperfetto**, is also a past tense.

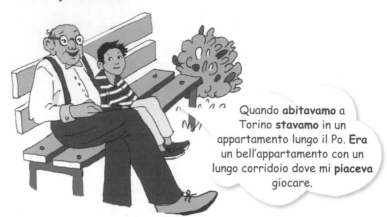

Quando **abitavamo** a Torino **stavamo** in un appartamento lungo il Po. **Era** un bell'appartamento con un lungo corridoio dove mi **piaceva** giocare.

When we lived in Turin, we lived in an apartment on the Po. It was a pretty apartment with a long corridor where I liked to play.

Formation

1. Regular Verbs

Most verbs are regular in the imperfect. They are easy to learn.

Verbs Ending in -*are*

	abit**are**
(io)	abit**avo**
(tu)	abit**avi**
(lui/lei/Lei)	abit**ava**
(noi)	abit**avamo**
(voi)	abit**avate**
(loro)	abit**avano**

The imperfect of verbs ending in **-are** is formed by adding the personal endings for the imperfect, **-avo**, **-avi**, **-ava**, **-avamo**, **-avate**, and **-avano** to the verb stem.

Tip! You can practice the stress of the 3rd person plural by first saying the 1st person singular, and immediately thereafter the 3rd person plural. The stress stays on the same syllable:

abit<u>a</u>vo ▶ abit<u>a</u>vano
av<u>e</u>vo ▶ av<u>e</u>vano
dorm<u>i</u>vo ▶ dorm<u>i</u>vano

Verbs Ending in -*ere*

	av**ere**
(io)	av**evo**
(tu)	av**evi**
(lui/lei/Lei)	av**eva**
(noi)	av**evamo**
(voi)	av**evate**
(loro)	av**evano**

With verbs ending in **-ere**, the personal endings for the imperfect are **-evo**, **-evi**, **-eva**, **-evamo**, **-evate**, and **-evano**. They too are attached to the verb stem.

Verbs Ending in *-ire*

	dormire
(io)	dorm**ivo**
(tu)	dorm**ivi**
(lui/lei/Lei)	dorm**iva**
(noi)	dorm**ivamo**
(voi)	dorm**ivate**
(loro)	dorm**ivano**

Verbs ending in **-ire** add the imperfect endings **-ivo**, **-ivi**, **-iva**, **-ivamo**, **-ivate**, and **-ivano** to the verb stem.

2. Irregular Verbs

	essere
(io)	**ero**
(tu)	**eri**
(lui/lei/Lei)	**era**
(noi)	**eravamo**
(voi)	**eravate**
(loro)	**erano**

The verb **essere** is a special case among the irregular verbs, since it is completely irregular.

	dire	fare	bere
(io)	**dic**evo	**fac**evo	**bev**evo
(tu)	**dic**evi	**fac**evi	**bev**evi
(lui/lei/Lei)	**dic**eva	**fac**eva	**bev**eva
(noi)	**dic**evamo	**fac**evamo	**bev**evamo
(voi)	**dic**evate	**fac**evate	**bev**evate
(loro)	**dic**evano	**fac**evano	**bev**evano

The remaining verbs with an irregular imperfect are easy to memorize: Take the imperfect endings of verbs ending in **-ere**, that is, **-evo**, **-evi**, **-eva**, **-evamo**, **-evate**, and **-evano**, and attach them to the expanded verb stem.

Trarre, **porre**, and **produrre** serve as models for the other verbs ending in **-arre**, **-orre**, and **-urre**.

	trarre	porre	produrre
(io)	**tra**evo	**pon**evo	**produc**evo
(tu)	**tra**evi	**pon**evi	**produc**evi
(lui/lei/Lei)	**tra**eva	**pon**eva	**produc**eva
(noi)	**tra**evamo	**pon**evamo	**produc**evamo
(voi)	**tra**evate	**pon**evate	**produc**evate
(loro)	**tra**evano	**pon**evano	**produc**evano

For verbs ending in **-arre**, attach the endings of the imperfect directly to the **-a-** of the verb stem. For **porre** and **produrre**, the imperfect endings are attached to a changed stem.

Use

Quando ancora non **esisteva** il telefonino, raggiungere una persona **poteva** essere difficile, e chi non **era** a casa, se **voleva** telefonare, **doveva** cercare un bar o una cabina telefonica.
Una volta **c'erano** meno divorzi.

The imperfect is used to describe previous conditions and situations, ...

Ezio **era** un bell'uomo. **Era** alto e snello e **aveva** dei bellissimi capelli neri. **Era** anche molto gentile e simpatico.

... persons and things as they once were, ...

Quando **andavo** a scuola **mi alzavo** sempre tardi, **mi** lavavo e **mi vestivo** in fretta e **correvo** a scuola.

... former habits and regularly repeated actions in the past, ...

Ieri sera, mentre io **studiavo,** gli altri **guardavano** la televisione.

... and two simultaneously occurring actions in the past.

Scusi, **volevo** solo un'informazione.

You can also use the imperfect to make requests ...

+ Andiamo al cinema, stasera? ~ Mah, **pensavo** di rimanere a casa.

... and to politely express objections.

il telefonino –
the cell phone
raggiungere – *to reach*
il divorzio – *the divorce*
snello – *slender, slim*
in fretta – *in a rush*

Present Perfect or Imperfect?

Erano le tre di notte, **dormivamo** tutti tranquillamente, quando un tuono fortissimo ci **ha svegliati.**

It was three o'clock at night, we were all sleeping peacefully, when a loud thunderclap woke us.

The imperfect and the present perfect have different uses.

Erano le tre di notte, **dormivamo** tutti tranquillamente,	The **imperfect** answers the question "What were things like when something happened?" It describes the accompanying conditions of an event in the past.
quando un tuono fortissimo ci **ha svegliati.**	The **present perfect**, however, expresses the event itself and answers the question "What happened?" It is the main narrative tense of the past.

There are cases in which both the imperfect and the present perfect can be used. Admittedly, they have different meanings then:

Quando mi **vedeva** mi **salutava.**	The imperfect tells us that the event was habitual: **quando** = *whenever.*
Quando mi **ha visto** mi **ha salutato.**	The past perfect, however, says that there were two unique actions: **quando** = *when.*
	The imperfect indicates a condition existing in the past:
Ieri **avevo** mal di testa.	*The headache may have lasted the entire day.*
Nel 1998 **abitavo** a Forlì.	*I lived all that year in Forlì and maybe also spent the preceding and subsequent years there.*

	The **present perfect** delimits the past event:
Ieri **ho avuto** mal di testa.	*The headache came and went.*
Nel 1998 **ho abitato** a Forlì.	*I lived in Forlì for only a part of the year or the whole year, but not before or after that.*
Ieri **ho avuto** mal di testa **tutto il giorno.** **Dal** 1992 **al** 1999 **ho abitato** a Forlì. **Ho camminato per tre ore.**	Once the beginning and / or end of the occurrence is precisely defined by an expression of time, such as **tutto il giorno**, **da ... a ...**, **per ... ore**, the present perfect is required.

per tre ore –
for three hours

After **mentre** (*while*), the imperfect is used. For the subsequent actions, both the imperfect and the present perfect can be used. Here there are differences in meaning with regard to the duration of the actions:

Mentre tu **dormivi**, Giulio **telefonava.** Mentre la madre **preparava** la cena, il padre **leggeva** e i bambini **giocavano.** Mentre **aspettavo** il tuo ritorno, **fumavo** una sigaretta dopo l'altra.	If the other actions are in the imperfect, then they all occurred simultaneously. The duration of the various actions is uncertain.
Mentre tu **dormivi**, Giulio **ha** telefonato. Mentre **aspettavo** il tuo ritorno, **ho acceso** una sigaretta.	If the other actions are in the present perfect, then they ended before the first action began.

Some verbs and expressions have a different meaning, depending on whether they are in the imperfect or in the present perfect:

sapere:

Non **sapevo** niente.	*I knew nothing.*
Ho saputo che ti sei sposato.	*I learned that you got married.*

conoscere:

Non **conoscevo** nessuno.	*I knew no one.*
Ho conosciuto tanta gente.	*I got to know a lot of people.*

aver paura:

Avevo paura.	*I was afraid.*
Quando l'ho visto **ho avuto paura**.	*When I saw him, I was afraid.*

The Imperfect

1. What is the imperfect of the following verbs? *

	stare	sapere	partire	capire
(io)	stavo	_____	_____	_____
(tu)	_____	_____	_____	_____
(lui/lei/Lei)	_____	_____	_____	_____
(noi)	_____	_____	_____	_____
(voi)	_____	_____	_____	_____
(loro)	_____	_____	_____	_____

2. Ottavio is telling about his youth. Fill in the text with the appropriate forms of the imperfect. *

a) Quando _____ (io – avere) quindici anni, mi _____ (piacere) molto i Beatles. b) _____ (comprare) tutti i loro dischi e quando _____ (tornare) da scuola, invece di studiare _____ (ascoltare) un disco dopo l'altro.

c) I miei genitori naturalmente _____ (essere) molto preoccupati, perché non _____ (studiare) abbastanza e infatti non _____ (essere) certamente il migliore della classe.

il disco –
the (phonograph) record
preoccupato – *worried*

3. Silvia is telling about her school days. Complete the text with the appropriate form of the present perfect or the imperfect. **

a) Io a scuola non _____ (essere) brava. b). Studiare proprio non mi _____ (piacere). c) La materia che _____ (detestare) di più _____ (essere) matematica. d) In 2ª liceo _____ (arrivare) un nuovo professore di matematica, il professor Malvasi. e) _____ (essere) abbastanza severo, ma a me _____ (piacere) molto e così _____ (cominciare) a studiare e in poco tempo, in matematica, _____ (diventare) una delle migliori.

la materia –
the (school) subject
detestare – *to detest*
severo – *strict*

The Preterit

> Manzoni **nacque** a Milano nel 1785. Nel 1805 **si trasferì** a Parigi, dove **rimase** fino al 1810. **Morì** nel 1873.

Manzoni was born in Milan in 1785. In 1805 he moved to Paris, where he remained until 1810. He died in 1873.

The preterit, or simple past, the **passato remoto**, is a past tense that is common in literary texts, historical accounts, and biographies. For you the main thing is to recognize the forms of the preterit.

Formation

1. Regular Verbs

Verbs Ending in -*are*

	andare
(io)	and**ai**
(tu)	and**asti**
(lui/lei/Lei)	and**ò**
(noi)	and**ammo**
(voi)	and**aste**
(loro)	and**arono**

Most verbs ending in **-are** have a regular preterit. To form it, attach the personal endings **-ai**, **-asti**, **-ò**, **-ammo**, **-aste**, and **-arono** to the verb stem.

Verbs Ending in -*ere*

	credere
(io)	cred**ei/etti**
(tu)	cred**esti**
(lui/lei/Lei)	cred**é/ette**
(noi)	cred**emmo**
(voi)	cred**este**
(loro)	cred**erono/ettero**

For regular formation, attach the personal endings **-ei**, **-esti**, **-è**, **-emmo**, **-este**, and **-erono** to the verb stem. The 1st and 3rd persons singular have, besides the short form, a long form: **-etti**, **-ette**, and **-ettero**.

Only a few verbs ending in **-ere** are regular in the preterit!

Verbs Ending in -*ire*

	finire
(io)	fin**ii**
(tu)	fin**isti**
(lui/lei/Lei)	fin**ì**
(noi)	fin**immo**
(voi)	fin**iste**
(loro)	fin**irono**

Most verbs ending in **-ire** are regular in the preterit. The personal endings **-ii**, **-isti**, **-ì**, **-immo**, **-iste**, and **-irono** are attached to the verb stem.

2. Irregular Verbs

Verbs with Three Irregular Forms

	avere	venire
(io)	**ebbi**	**venni**
(tu)	avesti	venisti
(lui/lei/Lei)	**ebbe**	**venne**
(noi)	avemmo	venimmo
(voi)	aveste	veniste
(loro)	**ebbero**	**vennero**

The following holds true for almost all verbs with an irregular preterit: Only the 1st and 3rd persons singular and the 3rd person plural are irregular. For these persons, only the stem, as in **ebb-** or **venn-**, is irregular. Then the 2nd person singular always ends in **-i**, the 3rd person singular in **-e**, and the 3rd person plural in **-ero**.

The Most Important Verbs with Three Irregular Forms

Infinitive	lui/lei/Lei	Infinitive	lui/lei/Lei
accendere	**accese**	piovere	**piovve**
accorgersi	**si accorse**	prendere	**prese**
bere	**bevve**	ridere	**rise**
cadere	**cadde**	rimanere	**rimase**
chiedere	**chiese**	risolvere	**risolse**
chiudere	**chiuse**	rispondere	**rispose**
cogliere	**colse**	rompere	**ruppe**
concedere	**concesse**	sapere	**seppe**
conoscere	**conobbe**	scegliere	**scelse**
correre	**corse**	scendere	**scese**
crescere	**crebbe**	scrivere	**scrisse**
decidere	**decise**	spegnere	**spense**
dirigere	**diresse**	spendere	**spese**
discutere	**discusse**	succedere	**successe**
escludere	**escluse**	tacere	**tacque**
leggere	**lesse**	tenere	**tenne**
mettere	**mise**	togliere	**tolse**
muovere	**mosse**	vedere	**vide**
nascere	**nacque**	vincere	**vinse**
perdere	**perse**	vivere	**visse**
piacere	**piacque**	volere	**volle**

Verbs with a Completely Irregular Preterit

Among the verbs with a completely irregular preterit are the very commonly used verbs **dare**, **fare**, **stare**, **essere**, and **dire**.

	dare	fare	stare
(io)	diedi/detti	feci	stetti
(tu)	desti	facesti	stesti
(lui/lei/Lei)	diede/dette	fece	stette
(noi)	demmo	facemmo	stemmo
(voi)	deste	faceste	steste
(loro)	diedero/dettero	fecero	stettero

Related verbs are conjugated in the same way, so **rifare** forms the preterit like **fare**, **mantenere** like **tenere**, and **accogliere** like **cogliere**.

	essere	dire
(io)	fui	dissi
(tu)	fosti	dicesti
(lui/lei/Lei)	fu	disse
(noi)	fummo	dicemmo
(voi)	foste	diceste
(loro)	furono	dissero

In addition, **trarre**, **porre**, and **produrre** are completely irregular.

	trarre	porre	produrre
(io)	trassi	posi	produssi
(tu)	traesti	ponesti	producesti
(lui/lei/Lei)	trasse	pose	produsse
(noi)	traemmo	ponemmo	producemmo
(voi)	traeste	poneste	produceste
(loro)	trassero	posero	produssero

Trarre, porre, and **produrre** serve as patterns for the other verbs ending in **-arre, -orre,** and **-urre.**

Use

The preterit is used predominantly in written Italian. In spoken Italian, it can be heard chiefly in southern and central Italy. In northern Italy in particular, the present perfect is used instead of the preterit.

Alessandro Manzoni **si sposò** nel 1808.

▌The preterit describes a single completed event in the past ...

Giacomo Puccini **nacque** a Lucca nel 1858. Nel 1880 **si trasferì** a Milano dove **frequentò** il conservatorio. Il primo successo di Puccini **fu** «Manon Lescaut» (1893). **Seguirono** poi le opere «La Bohème», «Tosca» e «Madame Butterfly».

▌... as well as several consecutive events, each of them completed in the past.

In interaction with the imperfect, the preterit has the same function as the present perfect:

Toni faceva il panettiere in una panetteria vicino a Milano. Nella stessa panetteria **lavorava** anche una bella ragazza. Toni **era** innamorato di lei e, per conquistarla, ogni giorno **sperimentava** nuove ricette che poi **dava** alla ragazza. Un giorno **mise** del burro nella solita pagnotta che **diventò** più morbida e gustosa.

▌The imperfect describes, for example, situations, states, and attendant circumstances, as well as habits, in the past.
The preterit relates the individual incidents that, taken together, constituted the events. It serves as the narrative tense of the past.

However, the preterit can also occur alongside the present perfect in newspaper articles or in the spoken language:

Quando il film «Ladri di biciclette» **uscì** nel 1948, non **piacque** al pubblico e **restò** pochissimo nelle sale di prima visione.

▌Actions and processes that lie in the distant past and no longer have any connection with the present are rendered by using the preterit.

sposarsi – *to marry, get married*
il successo – *the success*
il panettiere – *the baker*
la panetteria – *the bakery*
conquistare – *to conquer*
sperimentare – *to test, verify*
la ricetta – *the recipe*
solito – *usual, common*
la pagnotta – *the loaf of bread*
morbido – *soft*
gustoso – *tasty*
la prima visione – *the premiere, first release*

Nel frattempo «Ladri di biciclette» **è diventato** uno dei film più importanti nella storia del cinema italiano.

If an event in the past does have a relationship to the present or has meaning for the present, you need to use the present perfect.

1. Complete the three conjugations with the appropriate verb forms. *

dormisti – dovette – doveste – pagarono – dormii – dormì – pagasti
dovemmo – pagò – pagaste – dormiste – pagammo – dovettero
dormimmo – dovetti

	pagare	dovere	dormire
(io)	pagai	_____	_____
(tu)	_____	dovesti	_____
(lui/lei/Lei)	_____	_____	_____
(noi)	_____	_____	_____
(voi)	_____	_____	_____
(loro)	_____	_____	dormirono

2. Write down the forms of the preterit, and supply the infinitive of the corresponding verb. **

la casa editrice –
the publishing house
lo scrittore –
the writer
condannare –
to condemn, sentence
il confino –
the exile, banishment
il diario – *the diary*

Cesare Pavese nacque nel 1908 a Santo Stefano Belbo, un paese delle Langhe. Studiò e si laureò a Torino. Dopo gli studi cominciò a lavorare per la casa editrice Einaudi e tradusse scrittori inglesi e americani. Nel 1935 venne condannato al confino in Calabria a causa delle sue attività antifasciste; lì scrisse «Il mestiere di vivere», una specie di diario che fu pubblicato nel 1952, due anni dopo la sua morte. Dopo il suo ritorno a Torino pubblicò altri libri, ma il successo definitivo arrivò con «La luna e i falò», nel 1950. Nell'agosto dello stesso anno, in un albergo di Torino, Pavese si tolse la vita.

nacque	_____	_____
nascere	_____	_____
_____	_____	_____
_____	_____	_____
_____	_____	_____
_____	_____	_____
_____	_____	_____

3. Match the following preterit forms with their infinitives. *

presero – crebbi – discusse – lessi – scese – successero – furono
piovve – si accorsero – venne – ebbe – vollero – corse – chiusero
vinsi – videro – persi – conobbe – chiese – misero

a) chiedere _____   discutere _____

b) chiudere _____   conoscere _____

c) crescere _____   avere _____

d) correre _____   essere _____

e) perdere _____   succedere _____

f) prendere _____   accorgersi _____

g) mettere _____   scendere _____

h) piovere _____   vedere _____

i) leggere _____   vincere _____

k) volere _____   venire _____

4. Krizia is a famous Italian designer. The following passage tells about her professional development as a designer. When is the preterit required, and when is the imperfect needed? Mark the correct verb form in each pair below. ***

Da bambina fece / faceva i vestiti alle bambole. Disegnò / disegnava modellini e poi li realizzò / realizzava. A 18 anni prese / prendeva il diploma d'insegnante e cominciò / cominciava a lavorare.

Tutti i giorni quando tornò / tornava a casa da scuola riempì / riempiva una valigia con le gonne e i golfini che aveva inventato e li andò / andava a vendere nei negozi della sua città. Nel 1953 si trasferì / si trasferiva a Milano e iniziò / iniziava un giro d'affari. Poi comprò / comprava l'appartamento di un amico e aprì / apriva il suo primo laboratorio. Investì / investiva tutti i soldi che ebbe / aveva per comprare due macchine da cucire, un tavolone e delle stoffe e si mise / si metteva a produrre. «Krizia» nacque / nasceva così.

> **Tip!** Remember that in interaction with the imperfect, the preterit has the same functions as the present perfect.

la bambola – *the doll*
riempire – *to fill*
inventare – *to invent*
il giro d'affari – *the turnover, volume of sales*
la macchina da cucire – *the sewing machine*
il tavolone – *the large table*
la stoffa – *the fabric, material*

The Past Perfect

The past perfect, or pluperfect, is known in Italian as the **trapassato proximo**.

① Hai potuto parlare con Elio?

② No, quando sono arrivato, lui **era** già **partito**.

---

1. Were you able to talk to Elio? 2. No, when I came, he had already left.

Formation

The past perfect is formed with the imperfect of **essere** or **avere** and the past participle of the main verb in question.

	prendere		
(io)	**avevo**	pres**o**	If the past perfect is formed with **avere**, the past participle remains unchanged. In this case it always ends in **-o**.
(tu)	**avevi**	pres**o**	
(lui/lei/Lei)	**aveva**	pres**o**	
(noi)	**avevamo**	pres**o**	
(voi)	**avevate**	pres**o**	
(loro)	**avevano**	pres**o**	

	uscire		
(io)	**ero**	uscit**o, -a**	If it is formed with **essere**, however, then the past participle agrees in number and gender with the subject.
(tu)	**eri**	uscit**o, -a**	
(lui/lei/Lei)	**era**	uscit**o, -a**	
(noi)	**eravamo**	uscit**i, -e**	
(voi)	**eravate**	uscit**i, -e**	
(loro)	**erano**	uscit**i, -e**	

	The past participle ends in:
Elio era uscit**o**.	**-o** in the masculine singular,
Laura era uscit**a**.	**-a** in the feminine singular,
I figli erano uscit**i**.	**-i** in the masculine plural,
Laura e sua sorella erano uscit**e**.	**-e** in the feminine plural.

If you have mastered the formation of the present perfect, then you already know when the past perfect is formed with **avere** and when it is formed with **essere**. The rules are identical.

▶ **The Present Perfect**, p. 93

Use

Avevo dimenticato di chiudere il finestrino e quando sono tornato, la macchina era vuota.

Eravamo stanchi morti perché **avevamo camminato** tutto il giorno.

▌ The Italian past perfect, like the English past perfect, is used to express that an event in the past took place before another occurrence or state in the past.

Ti ricordi quel ragazzo americano che ti **avevo presentato** tempo fa?

▌ The past perfect can also be used in conjunction with the present tense. In this case, you are saying that the events are far in the past.

vuoto – *empty*
stanco morto – *dead tired, tired out*
presentare qu –
to introduce someone

Practice and Application

The Past Perfect

1. Complete the sentences with the appropriate forms of the past perfect. *

erano tornati

erano tornate

era tornato

era tornata

a) Simona era stanca perché _____ a casa tardi.

b) I miei genitori erano stanchi perché _____ a casa tardi.

c) Giancarlo era stanco perché _____ a casa tardi.

d) Silvia e Luisa erano stanche _____ a casa tardi.

2. Mrs. Brezzo was away for a few days. You can read below how things looked at home upon her return. Fill in the blanks with the verbs supplied, using the appropriate form of the past perfect. *

a) Anna aveva la tosse perché _____ (uscire) senza giacca e

_____ (prendere) freddo.

litigare – to quarrel, dispute

cadere – to fall

rompere – to break

il braccio fasciato – the bandaged arm

b) Andrea e Simona piangevano perché _____ (litigare)

c) La nonna aveva il braccio fasciato perché _____

(cadere) e _____ (farsi) male.

d) Il marito era stanco morto perché _____ (lavorare) fino a tardi tutti i giorni.

e) In cucina c'era una montagna di piatti sporchi perché nessuno li _____

_____ (lavare) e nell'entrata mancava il bel vaso

cinese perché qualcuno lo _____ (rompere).

f) Socrate, il cane, invece era tutto contento perché sul tavolo della

cucina _____ (trovare) un bell'arrosto di vitello.

3. Which past tenses occur in the text below? Write them in the appropriate columns. **

scappare – to escape, run away

Fufù è un gatto che era scappato da casa otto anni fa. Ma ieri ha ritrovato il posto dove aveva vissuto per sei mesi e così è ritornato

dalla sua padrona, la signora Maria. Questa ha riconosciuto subito il suo gatto perché aveva un taglio alla coda e gli mancavano due denti.

La signora Maria racconta che Fufù sparì perché non sopportava un cane che stava nella stessa casa e che a gennaio scorso, però è morto.

Passato prossimo	Imperfetto	Trapassato prossimo	Passato remoto
_____	_____	_____	_____
_____	_____	_____	_____
_____	_____	_____	_____
_____	_____	_____	_____

4. Enter the appropriate verb form in each blank. Use the present perfect, the imperfect, or the past perfect. ***

a) La settimana scorsa _____(essere) terribile per Claudia. b) Lunedì mattina _____ (perdere) il portafoglio con tutti i documenti. c) Probabilmente _____ (succedere) mentre _____ (correre) per prendere la metropolitana. d) Martedì _____ (arrivare) in ufficio in ritardo, perché non _____ (sentire) la sveglia. e) Giovedì sera _____ (andare) in palestra e lì, mentre _____ (fare) la doccia, qualcuno le _____ (rubare) la sua giacca di pelle. f) Venerdì, mentre _____ (andare) da un cliente che abita fuori città, _____ (rimanere) ferma in piena campagna, perché _____ (dimenticare) di fare benzina. g) Sabato mattina, mentre _____ (tornare) a casa dalla spesa non _____ (vedere) un gradino ed _____ (cadere). h) Naturalmente la bottiglia d'olio che _____ (comprare) al mercato _____ (rompersi).

la sveglia –
the alarm clock
rubare – *to steal*

il gradino – *the step*

> The future (simple future) tense is easy to learn. The endings are always -ò, -ai, -à, -emo, -ete, and -anno.

The Future

Allora, cosa **succederà**? ①

I primi giorni di maggio non **saranno** facili, ma verso la metà del mese tutto **cambierà** e **troverà** una soluzione ai Suoi problemi. ②

---

1. So, what will happen? 2. The first days of May will not be easy, but toward mid-month everything will change and you will find a solution for your problems.

Formation

1. Verbs with a Regular Future Tense

Verbs Ending in -*are*, -*ere*, and -*ire*

	trov**are**	mett**ere**	cap**ire**
(io)	trov**erò**	mett**erò**	cap**irò**
(tu)	trov**erai**	mett**erai**	cap**irai**
(lui/lei/Lei)	trov**erà**	mett**erà**	cap**irà**
(noi)	trov**eremo**	mett**eremo**	cap**iremo**
(voi)	trov**erete**	mett**erete**	cap**irete**
(loro)	trov**eranno**	mett**eranno**	cap**iranno**

For verbs with a regular future tense, replace the infinitive ending **-e** with the future endings. For verbs ending in **-are**, the **-a-** of the ending **-are** changes to **-e-**.

dare, *fare*, and *stare*

dare ▶ darò	Unlike the other verbs that end in **-are**, **dare**, **fare**, and **stare** retain the **-a-**.
fare ▶ farò	
stare ▶ starò	

Verbs Ending in -*care* and -*gare*

	cer**care**	pa**gare**
(io)	cer**che**rò	pa**ghe**rò
(tu)	cer**che**rai	pa**ghe**rai
(lui/lei/Lei)	cer**che**rà	pa**ghe**rà
(noi)	cer**che**remo	pa**ghe**remo
(voi)	cer**che**rete	pa**ghe**rete
(loro)	cer**che**ranno	pa**ghe**ranno

To retain the pronunciation of the **-c-** and **-g-** of the infinitive in all the persons, verbs ending in **-care** and **-gare** insert an **-h-**.

Verbs Ending in -*sciare*, -*ciare*, and -*giare*

	la**sciare**	ba**ciare**	man**giare**
(io)	la**sce**rò	ba**ce**rò	man**ge**rò
(tu)	la**sce**rai	ba**ce**rai	man**ge**rai
(lui/lei/Lei)	la**sce**rà	ba**ce**rà	man**ge**rà
(noi)	la**sce**remo	ba**ce**remo	man**ge**remo
(voi)	la**sce**rete	ba**ce**rete	man**ge**rete
(loro)	la**sce**ranno	ba**ce**ranno	man**ge**ranno

baciare – *to kiss*
sciare – *to ski*

As you see, with verbs that end in **-sciare**, **-ciare**, and **-giare**, the **-i-** of the verb stem is omitted.
Sciare, however, retains the **-i-**: **scierò**, **scierai**, etc.

2. Verbs with an Irregular Future

	essere
(io)	**sar**ò
(tu)	**sar**ai
(lui/lei/Lei)	**sar**à
(noi)	**sar**emo
(voi)	**sar**ete
(loro)	**sar**anno

For **essere**, attach the standard future endings to the irregular stem **sar-**.

Verbs with a Shortened Verb Stem

A number of verbs—usually, frequently used verbs ending in **-ere**—have a shortened stem. The future endings, which always remain the same, are attached to this shortened stem. Thus, for example, the future of **andare**: **andrò**, **andrai**, **andrà**, **andremo**, **andrete**, **andranno**.

Infinitive	Shortened Verb Stem	Endings
andare	**andr**	
avere	**avr**	
bere	**berr**	
cadere	**cadr**	
dovere	**dovr**	
godere	**godr**	-ò
potere	**potr**	-ai
rimanere	**rimarr**	-à
sapere	**sapr**	-emo
tenere	**terr**	-ete
valere	**varr**	-anno
vedere	**vedr**	
venire	**verr**	
vivere	**vivr**	
volere	**vorr**	

mantenere – *to maintain, support*
contenere – *to contain*
ottenere – *to obtain, achieve*
accadere – *to happen, occur*
convenire – *to agree*
avvenire – *to happen, occur*

la pensione – *the retirement*

Remember that verbs which contain another verb are conjugated in the same way as that verb. For example, **mantenere**, **contenere**, and **ottenere** form the future like **tenere**, while **accadere** follows the pattern of **cadere**, and **convenire** and **avvenire** behave like **venire**.

Use

Domani **pioverà**.
Fra due anni **andrò** in pensione.
Un giorno mi **sposerò**.

The future, or simple future, is used to discuss events and conditions that lie in the future.

Domani rimango a casa tutto il giorno.
Tomorrow I will stay / I'm staying / I'm going to stay home all day.

In colloquial speech, the present is often used instead of the future to refer to events and conditions that are in the near future. Compare this with the English options.

+ Che ora è? ~ **Saranno** le quattro.

The future also can be used to express speculation or supposition, ...

Avrai fame, penso.
Sarà vero quello che dice Pia?

... uncertainty and doubts, ...

Non **partirete** senza il nostro permesso.

... prohibitions and commands, ...

Ammetterai che ho ragione.

... or even weakened declarations.

When an action is about to happen, you can express this with **stare per** + infinitive. Then **stare** is in the present tense:

Il treno **sta per partire**.
The train is about to leave.

Stanno per arrivare gli ospiti.
The guests are about to arrive.

Sta per finire il vino.
The wine is about gone.

> Don't confuse **stare per** + infinitive with **stare** + present participle.

Practice and Application

The Future

1. Write down the forms of the future tense for the following verbs. *

a) io – vedere

_____

f) io – ottenere

_____

k) io – lasciare

_____

b) tu – avere

_____

g) tu – bere

_____

l) tu – sapere

_____

c) lui – volere

_____

h) lui – cercare

_____

m) lui – mangiare

_____

d) noi – rimanere

_____

i) noi – dovere

_____

n) noi – fare

_____

e) loro – vivere

_____

j) voi – stare

_____

o) loro – pagare

_____

2. Fill in the blanks in the dialogue by placing the verbs supplied in the appropriate person of the future tense. **

a) + Tu quando _____ (andare) in vacanza quest'estate?

~ Purtroppo non _____ (potere) partire prima di settembre.

b) + Che progetti avete per le prossime vacanze?

~ Probabilmente _____ (andare) in Sardegna come

ogni anno e in settembre _____ (fare) forse un

viaggetto in Spagna.

c) + Carlo e Luca _____ (passare) il Natale con voi,

immagino.

~ Luca sì, lui _____ (venire) da noi. Carlo invece lo

_____ (passare) con i suoi futuri suoceri. Lui e la sua

fidanzata _____ (essere) però con noi a Capodanno.

d) + Il prossimo fine settimana Mariella ed io _____ (essere)

a Zurigo.

~ Ah, allora _____ (potere) vedere la mostra su Leonardo da

Vinci.

il progetto – *the plan, project*
il viaggetto – *the little trip*
la fidanzata – *the fiancée*

The Future Perfect

1. As soon as I've finished high school, I'll go to the United States. 2. You'll write me, I hope.
3. But of course, I'll send you an e-mail as soon as I've arrived.

Formation

The future perfect is formed with the future tense of **essere** or **avere** and
the past participle of the main verb in question.

	fare		
(io)	**avrò**	fat**to**	If the future perfect is formed with **avere**, the past participle remains unchanged. In this case, it always ends in **-o**.
(tu)	**avrai**	fat**to**	
(lui/lei/Lei)	**avrà**	fat**to**	
(noi)	**avremo**	fat**to**	
(voi)	**avrete**	fat**to**	
(loro)	**avranno**	fat**to**	

	uscire		
(io)	**sarò**	uscit**o, -a**	If it is formed with **essere**, however, the past participle, like an adjective, agrees in number and gender with the subject.
(tu)	**sarai**	uscit**o, -a**	
(lui/lei/Lei)	**sarà**	uscit**o, -a**	
(noi)	**saremo**	uscit**i, -e**	
(voi)	**sarete**	uscit**i, -e**	
(loro)	**saranno**	uscit**i, -e**	

	The past participle ends in:
Elio sarà uscit**o**. **Laura** sarà uscit**a**. **I figli** saranno uscit**i**. **Le ragazze** saranno uscit**e**.	**-o** in the masculine singular, **-a** in the feminine singular, **-i** in the masculine plural, **-e** in the feminine plural.

▶ The Present
Perfect, p. 90

Since the formation of the future perfect is analogous to that of the present perfect, the rules on the variability of the past participle as well as the use of **essere** and **avere** are the same as those for the present perfect.

Use

appena – *as soon as*

Quando arriverai, **saremo** già **partiti.**
Appena mi **sarò trasferito** a Londra, studierò l'inglese.

The future perfect tells us that one future action will occur before another future action.

Appena **mi trasferirò** a Londra, studierò l'inglese.
Quando **smetterà** di piovere, faremo una passeggiata.

The same time relationship, however, can also be expressed by the simple future tense in many cases.

scappare – *to escape,*
run away

A quest'ora Viola **sarà** già **arrivata** a casa e **avrà** anche già **mangiato,** penso.
Chissà dov'è il gatto; non **sarà scappato**, spero.

The future perfect can also be used to express a supposition, an uncertainty, or a doubt with regard to an event that occurred earlier ...

Fra un'ora **avrai scritto** la lettera, chiaro?!

... or to give an order.

1. Complete the sentences, using the future perfect. **

a) Mi farò viva appena _____ (arrivare) a casa.

b) Partiremo quando _____(smettere) di nevicare.

c) Quando _____ (fare) i compiti potrai andare a giocare.

d) Nina terrà il suo discorsetto appena _____
(arrivare) tutti gli ospiti.

e) Quando _____ (io – rimettersi) farò una grande festa.

farsi vivo – *to get in touch*

smettere – *to stop*

il discorsetto – *the little talk*

rimettersi – *to recuperate*

2. Simple future or future perfect? Mark the correct verb form in each pair below. **

a) Quando avrò finito / finirò gli studi sarò partita / partirò per il Messico.

b) Quando sarai tornato / tornerai a casa avremo mangiato / mangeremo già da un pezzo.

da un pezzo – *for quite some time*

c) Dopo che sarai stato /sarai in Inghilterra parlerai /avrai parlato meglio l'inglese.

d) Ti avrò prestato/presterò il libro appena lo avrò letto / leggerò.

e) I miei genitori saranno rientrati / rientreranno in Italia appena mio padre sarà andato / andrà in pensione.

3. Why don't the ladies feel well? Formulate a suitable speculation in each case by putting the verbs supplied in the future perfect. *

a) Luisa ha mal di testa. _____ (dormire) troppo poco.

b) La signora Monelli ha il raffreddore. _____ (uscire)
senza cappotto e _____ (prendere) freddo.

c) Luca ha mal di stomaco. _____ (mangiare) troppo.

d) A Chiara bruciano gli occhi. _____ (lavorare) a
lungo al computer.

bruciare – *to burn*

e) Gloria ha male a un ginocchio. _____ (fare)
troppa aerobica.

> Most verbs form the conditional in a regular manner.

The Conditional

> **Sarebbe** bello essere al mare, adesso.

It would be nice to be at the ocean now.

Formation

> Please keep in mind that the 1st person plural has only one **-m-** in the future tense, but two in the conditional: trover**emo** (future) trover**emmo** (conditional)

In the conditional, the endings for all verbs are the same: **-ei**, **-esti**, **-ebbe**, **-emmo**, **-este**, and **-ebbero**.

1. Verbs with a Regular Conditional

Verbs Ending in *-are*, *-ere*, and *-ire*

	trov**are**	mett**ere**	cap**ire**
(io)	trov**erei**	mett**erei**	cap**irei**
(tu)	trov**eresti**	mett**eresti**	cap**iresti**
(lui/lei/Lei)	trov**erebbe**	mett**erebbe**	cap**irebbe**
(noi)	trov**eremmo**	mett**eremmo**	cap**iremmo**
(voi)	trov**ereste**	mett**ereste**	cap**ireste**
(loro)	trov**erebbero**	mett**erebbero**	cap**irebbero**

For verbs that are regular in the conditional, replace the infinitive ending **-e-** with the conditional endings. For verbs that end in **-are**, the **-a-** of the ending becomes **-e-**.

dare, *fare*, and *stare*

dare	▶	darei
fare	▶	farei
stare	▶	starei

Unlike the other verbs ending in **-are**, **dare**, **fare**, and **stare** retain the **-a-**.

Verbs Ending in *-care* and *-gare*

	cercare	pagare
(io)	cercherei	pagherei
(tu)	cercheresti	pagheresti
(lui/lei/Lei)	cercherebbe	pagherebbe
(noi)	cercheremmo	pagheremmo
(voi)	cerchereste	paghereste
(loro)	cercherebbero	pagherebbero

To retain the pronunciation of **-c-** and **-g-** in all the persons, verbs that end in **-care** and **-gare** insert an **-h-**.

Verbs Ending in *-sciare*, *-ciare*, and *-giare*

	lasciare	baciare	mangiare
(io)	lascerei	bacerei	mangerei
(tu)	lasceresti	baceresti	mangeresti
(lui/lei/Lei)	lascerebbe	bacerebbe	mangerebbe
(noi)	lasceremmo	baceremmo	mangeremmo
(voi)	lascereste	bacereste	mangereste
(loro)	lascerebbero	bacerebbero	mangerebbero

In verbs that end in **-sciare**, **-ciare**, and **-giare**, the **i** of the verb stem is omitted.

Sciare, however, retains the **-i-**: **scie**rei, **scie**resti.

2. Verbs with an Irregular Conditional

	essere	
(io)	sarei	For **essere**, attach the conditional endings to the irregular stem **sar-**.
(tu)	saresti	
(lui/lei/Lei)	sarebbe	
(noi)	saremmo	
(voi)	sareste	
(loro)	sarebbero	

Verbs with a Shortened Verb Stem

A number of verbs, most of them frequently used verbs ending in **-ere**, have a shortened stem. The conditional endings, which always remain the same, are attached to this shortened stem. Thus, for example, the conditional of **andare** is as follows: **andrei**, **andresti**, **andrebbe**, **andremmo**, **andreste**, **andrebbero**.

Infinitive	Shortened Verb Stem	Endings
andare	**andr**	
avere	**avr**	
bere	**berr**	
cadere	**cadr**	
dovere	**dovr**	
godere	**godr**	-ei
potere	**potr**	-esti
rimanere	**rimarr**	-ebbe
sapere	**sapr**	-emmo
tenere	**terr**	-este
valere	**varr**	-ebbero
vedere	**vedr**	
venire	**verr**	
vivere	**vivr**	
volere	**vorr**	

The endings of the conditional are attached to the same shortened verb stem as the endings of the future tense.

Use

Vi **farebbe** bene uscire un po'.
In montagna **staresti** meglio.

The conditional is used to express what might be or what could happen.

Andrei al cinema se avessi tempo.

It is used in conditional sentences, and ...

▶ The Conditional Sentence, p. 208

Vorrei una camera tranquilla.
Ci **piacerebbe** andare al mare.
Che ne **diresti** di invitare Rosa?
Potresti chiudere la finestra?
Lei **dovrebbe** lavorare di meno.
Dovresti andare dal dentista.

... to formulate statements in a weakened form. Wishes, suggestions, requests, advice, and challenges sound more polite in the conditional than in the present or in the imperative.

Il quadro di Picasso **costerebbe** più di un milione di dollari.
Il ministro **sarebbe** disposto ad un colloquio con il sindacalista C.
Molti parlamentari **sarebbero** contrari alla nuova legge.

In the media in particular, the conditional is used to deliver news in a cautious way.

sarebbe disposto –
is said to be willing
il parlamentare –
the representative,
member of parliament
sarebbero contrari –
are said to be opposed

The Conditional

1. Reading from right to left and from top to bottom, you will find 12 verbs in the conditional hidden in the rows of letters below. Write them down and fill in the appropriate infinitive. *

a s a r e b b e f m v e r r e s t e

n d a r e i s t i b e r r e m m o a

d o v r e b b e r o f t e r r e i v

r s a p r e s t i v m v i v r e i r

e o b b o v e d r e s t i n p e o e

i r i m a r r e b b e r o r o b b i

Conditional: Infinitive:

Conditional:	Infinitive:
_____	_____
_____	_____
_____	_____
_____	_____
_____	_____
_____	_____
_____	_____
_____	_____
_____	_____
_____	_____
_____	_____
_____	_____

2. Four people are telling what they would do with ten thousand euros. Complete their statements with the conditional forms of the verbs supplied. *

a) Con 10.000 euro io _____ (realizzare) finalmente un

il sogno – *the dream*   sogno: _____ (prendere) un anno di vacanza e

_____ (partire) per l'India.

b) Franco ed io ci sposiamo l'anno prossimo e i soldi ci _____

_____ (servire) per il matrimonio. Io _____ (potere)

comprarmi un bel vestito da sposa e poi _____ (noi –

potere) fare un viaggio di nozze un po' speciale.

c) Noi abbiamo comprato una casa un anno fa e 10.000 euro ci _____
_____ (fare) molto comodo.

d) Io penso che non li _____ (spendere), li _____
(mettere) in banca e più tardi li _____ (dare) a mia figlia.

3. Express the following concerns in a more polite way, by replacing the
present tense with the conditional. *

a) Accompagni tu il bambino all'asilo?

_____

b) Mi fa vedere la borsetta verde là in vetrina?

_____

c) Mi può fare uno sconto per queste scarpe?

_____

d) Ci fate vedere le foto delle vostre vacanze?

_____

e) Posso provare questo vestito?

_____

f) Ci porta ancora un po' di pane, per favore?

_____

g) Ci aiutate a fare il trasloco?

_____

h) Può dirmi che ore sono?

_____

i) Mi passi il pane, per favore?

_____

j) Letizia, fai un caffè, per piacere?

_____

k) Signora, Le dispiace chiudere la finestra? Fa freddo.

_____

The Conditional Perfect

*Io non **sarei** mai **partita** con questo tempo!* ①

*E io non **avrei** mai **dovuto sposarti!*** ②

1. I would never have left home in such weather! 2. And I should never have married you!

Formation

The conditional perfect is formed with the conditional of **essere** or **avere** and the past participle of the main verb in question.

	parlare		
(io)	avrei	parlato	If the conditional perfect is formed with **avere**, the past participle remains unchanged. In this case it always ends in **-o**.
(tu)	avresti	parlato	
(lui/lei/Lei)	avrebbe	parlato	
(noi)	avremmo	parlato	
(voi)	avreste	parlato	
(loro)	avrebbero	parlato	

	partire		
(io)	sarei	partito, -a	If it is formed with **essere**, however, then the past participle, like an adjective, agrees in number and gender with the subject.
(tu)	saresti	partito, -a	
(lui/lei/Lei)	sarebbe	partito, -a	
(noi)	saremmo	partiti, -e	
(voi)	sareste	partiti, -e	
(loro)	sarebbero	partiti, -e	

	The past participle ends in:
Elio sarebbe partit**o**.	**-o** in the masculine singular,
Laura sarebbe partit**a**.	**-a** in the feminine singular,
I figli sarebbero partit**i**.	**-i** in the masculine plural,
Le ragazze sarebbero partit**e**.	**-e** in the feminine plural.

The formation of the conditional perfect is analogous to that of the present perfect. For the variability of the past participle and the use of **essere** and **avere**, the same rules apply as for the present perfect.

Use

Ti **avrei telefonato,** ma non avevo il tuo numero.
Io **avrei detto** la verità.

▮ The conditional perfect is used to say what could have been or happened in the past.

Mi **sarebbe piaciuto** fare il dentista.

▮ It is also used to express wishes that went unfulfilled, ...

Sarei andato al cinema se avessi avuto tempo.

▮ ... in conditional sentences, ...

Avresti dovuto andare dal dentista.

▮ ... in demands and requests that have not been carried out, ...

Lei **avrebbe dovuto** lavorare di meno.

▮ ... and with advice that was not followed.

La villa **sarebbe costata** quasi due milioni di euro.
A distanza di quattro anni e 2300 chilometri, un gatto **avrebbe ritrovato** i suoi padroni.

▮ The media uses the conditional perfect to formulate news about a past event without a guarantee of truth.

sarebbe costata – *is said to have cost*
avrebbe ritrovato – *is said to have found again*

▶ For more on the use of the conditional perfect, see:
Indirect Discourse, p. 212
The Sequence of Tenses with the Subjunctive, p. 154

The Conditional Perfect

1. By putting the verbs in the conditional perfect, you will find out what these people would have liked to do. *

a) _____ (io – venire) volentieri con te al cinema, ma purtroppo dovevo lavorare.

b) Ci dispiace molto per domenica scorsa, ci _____ (fare) molto piacere fare pic-nic, ma dovevamo andare dai miei genitori.

c) Carla ed io _____ (volere) partire per le vacanze sabato scorso. Poi però mia suocera si è ammalata e adesso siamo ancora qui.

d) Riccardo _____ (preferire) passare le vacanze in Sicilia. Ma io non sopporto il caldo e così siamo andati nelle Dolomiti.

e) Ma perché non ci hai detto niente? Ti _____ (noi – aiutare) volentieri a fare il trasloco.

f) _____ (tu – dovere) dirmi che il pesce non ti piace. Ti _____ (io – preparare) un'altra cosa.

2. Try your hand as a journalist, and formulate the following reports with caution by replacing the present perfect with the conditional perfect. *

a) Un cane pastore ha salvato la vita a due bambini caduti nel fiume.

_____

b) Una delle opere più famose di Picasso è sparita dal «Kunstmuseum» di Basilea.

_____

c) I due uomini di stato sono giunti a un accordo.

_____

d) Molti parlamentari si sono opposti alla nuova legge.

_____

The Imperative

Mettiti la giacca!
①

Non dirmi sempre quello che devo fare!
②

---

1. Put the jacket on! 2. Don't always tell me what I should do!

In Italian, there is a type of imperative for things that one ought to do: the so-called "affirmative imperative." The type of imperative for things that one ought not to do, accordingly, is called the "negative imperative."

The Affirmative Imperative

1. The 2nd Person Singular (*tu*) Imperative

+ Scusa, posso entrare?   ~ Ma certo, **entra** pure!
①   ②

---

1. Excuse me, may I come in? 2. But of course, come right in!

When you give a command to a person whom you address with the familiar pronoun, you use the **tu** form of the imperative.

Verbs with a Regular Imperative

Verb Ending in:	Infinitive	Imperative (tu)	The familiar form of the imperative is as follows:
-are	guard**are**	guard**a**!	with verbs ending in **-are**, the 3rd person singular of the present tense.
	scus**are**	scus**a**!	
-ere	prend**ere**	prend**i**!	with verbs ending in **-ere** and **-ire**, the 2nd person singular of the present tense.
	legg**ere**	legg**i**!	
-ire	sent**ire**	sent**i**!	
	fin**ire**	fin**isci**!	

The 2nd person singular of the present tense is also used as the familiar imperative for most verbs that are irregular in the present tense. For example:

Infinitive	Present Tense **(tu)**	Imperative **(tu)**
tenere	tieni *(you hold)*	**tieni!** *(hold!)*
uscire	esci *(you go out)*	**esci!** *(go out!)*
venire	vieni *(you come)*	**vieni!** *(come!)*
tradurre	traduci *(you translate)*	**traduci!** *(translate!)*

Verbs with Short Forms

andare:	**va'!/vai!**	**Andare, dare, fare,** and **stare** have two imperative forms: a long form and a short form. The short form is very frequently used.
dare:	**da'!/dai!**	
fare:	**fa'!/fai!**	
stare:	**sta'!/stai!**	
dire:	**di'!**	**Dire,** however, has only the short form **di'.**

Verbs with an Irregular Imperative

avere:	**abbi!**	Only **avere, essere,** and **sapere** have an irregular imperative in the familiar form.
essere:	**sii!**	
sapere:	**sappi!**	

2. The 3rd Person Singular (*Lei*) Imperative

Scusi, posso entrare?
①

Ma certo, **entri** pure!
②

1. Excuse me, may I come in? 2. But of course, come right in!

When you give a command to someone whom you address with the polite pronoun, you use the **Lei** form of the imperative.

Verbs with a Regular Imperative

Verb Ending in:	Infinitive	Imperative (Lei)	
-are	guardare	guardi!	The **Lei** form of the imperative is formed:
	scusare	scusi!	by adding an **-i** to the verb stem of verbs ending in **-are**.
-ere	prendere	prenda!	by adding an **-a** to the verb stem or expanded stem (**-isc-**) of verbs ending in **-ere** and **-ire**.
	leggere	legga!	
-ire	sentire	senta!	
	finire	finisca!	

All verbs that are regular in the present tense also have a regular imperative.

Otherwise, verbs ending in **-are** exhibit the same characteristics in the **Lei** imperative as in the present tense:

Infinitive	Imperative (Lei)	
cercare	cerchi!	Verbs ending in **-care** and **-gare** have an **-h-** before the imperative ending **-i**.
pagare	paghi!	
mangiare	mangi!	Verbs ending in **-iare** have only an **-i**.
lasciare	lasci!	

Verbs with an Irregular Imperative

Derivable Imperatives

Infinitive	Present Tense (io)	Imperative (Lei)
andare	vado	**vada!**
dire	dico	**dica!**
fare	faccio	**faccia!**
proporre	propongo	**proponga!**
tenere	tengo	**tenga!**
tradurre	traduco	**traduca!**
uscire	esco	**esca!**
venire	vengo	**venga!**

Generally, the derivable imperatives are forms of verbs that are irregular in the present tense, and the imperative of the **Lei** form can be derived from the 1st person singular of the present tense. All you have to do is replace the present tense ending **-o** with the ending **-a**.

Completely Irregular Forms

avere:	**abbia!**	**Avere, dare, essere, sapere,**
dare:	**dia!**	and **stare** have a completely
essere:	**sia!**	irregular imperative in the **Lei**
sapere:	**sappia!**	form.
stare:	**stia!**	

3. The 1st Person Plural Imperative (*noi*)

① Allora, cosa facciamo, entriamo?

② Ma certo, su, **entriamo!**

1. So, what are we doing, are we going in? 2. But of course, come on, let's go in!

When you give a command to several people, including yourself, you use the **noi** form of the present tense for all verbs.

	Infinitive	Imperative **(noi)**
verbs ending in **-are**	guard**are**	guard**iamo!**
	and**are**	and**iamo!**
verbs ending in **-ere**	prend**ere**	prend**iamo!**
	legg**ere**	legg**iamo!**
verbs ending in **-ire**	sent**ire**	sent**iamo!**
	fin**ire**	fin**iamo!**

4. The 2nd Person Plural Imperative (*voi*)

① Possiamo entrare?

② Ma certo, **entrate** pure!

1. Can we come in? 2. But of course, come on in!

When you give a command to several people whom you address with the familiar or the polite pronoun, you simply use the **voi** form of the present tense.

Verbs with a Regular Imperative

	Infinitive	Imperative **(voi)**
verbs ending in -**are**	scus**are**	scus**ate**!
	lasci**are**	lasci**ate**!
verbs ending in -**ere**	prend**ere**	prend**ete**!
	legg**ere**	legg**ete**!
verbs ending in -**ire**	sent**ire**	sent**ite**!
	fin**ire**	fin**ite**!

Verbs with an Irregular Imperative

avere:	**abbiate!**	**Avere**, **essere**, and **sapere**
essere:	**siate!**	have an irregular imperative
sapere:	**sappiate!**	in the **voi** form.

The Negative Imperative

Senta, **non dimentichi** di telefonare al dottor Ronchi! E tu, Carla, **non dimenticare** di confermare la camera!

Listen, don't forget to telephone Dr. Ronchi! And you, Carla, don't forget to confirm the room.

(tu)	**non aspettare!** **non venire!** **non bere!** **non parlare!**	The negative imperative of the **tu** form is made up of **non** + the infinitive of the main verb in question.
(Lei)	**non aspetti!** **non beva!**	Otherwise, place **non** before the forms of the affirmative imperative.
(noi)	**non aspettiamo!** **non parliamo!**	
(voi)	**non aspettate!** **non venite!**	

Once you know the affirmative imperative, the only new thing you have to learn for the negative imperative is the **tu** form!

137

Personal Pronouns with the Imperative

Mi dia due etti
di parmigiano,
per favore.

①

Dimmi la verità!
Di**mmela** subito!

②

1. Give me 200 grams of Parmesan, please. 2. Tell me the truth! Tell it to me right now!

1. Personal Pronouns with the Affirmative Imperative

(tu)	aspetta**mi**! compra**ne** un chilo! scrivi**melo**!	The personal pronouns, the pronominal adverbs **ci** and **ne**, and the combined personal pronouns (double pronouns)
(noi)	aspettiamo**lo**! andiamo**ci** subito! scriviamo**glielo**!	are appended to the imperative of **tu**, **noi**, and **voi**. If two pronouns are attached to the imperative, then the direct object pronouns (**lo**, **la**, **li**, **le**)
(voi)	aspettate**ci**! comprate**ne** poco! scrivete**celo**!	and **ne** always come second; that is, they follow the unstressed dative pronouns and **ce**.
(Lei)	**ci** aspetti, per favore! **ne** prenda un po'! **ce lo** scriva!	With the imperative of the **Lei** form, however, the pronouns precede the verb.

Personal Pronouns with Verbs Having a Short Form

andare:	Va**cci** tu!	*You go!*
	Va**gli** incontro!	*Go toward him!*
dare:	Da**nne** un po' anche a me!	*Give me a little of it too!*
dire:	Di**lle** tutto!	*Tell her everything!*
	Di**gli** tutto!	*Tell him everything!*
fare:	Fa**llo** per noi!	*Do it for us!*
stare:	Sta**mmi** bene!	*Stay healthy!*

With the 2nd person singular (**tu**) imperative of **andare**, **dare**, **dire**, **fare**, and **stare**, the personal pronouns, as well as **ci** and **ne**, are attached to the short form. In the process, the consonant of the pronoun is doubled, except with **gli**.

2. Personal Pronouns with the Negative Imperative

(tu)	non **ci** aspettare!	non aspettar**ci**!
	non **me lo** dire!	non dir**melo**!
(noi)	non **lo** aspettiamo!	non aspettiamo**lo**!
	non **glielo** diciamo!	non diciamo**glielo**!
(voi)	non **ci** aspettate!	non aspettate**ci**!
	non **ce lo** dite!	non dite**celo**!

With the negative imperative of **tu**, **noi**, and **voi**, the pronouns are placed before the imperative or appended to the imperative. With the infinitive in the **tu** form, the final **-e** is omitted.

(Lei)	non **ci** aspetti!	With the **Lei** form, the pronouns
	non **ce lo** dica!	must precede the imperative.

Use

Non bere tanto!
Aspettate!

▐ The imperative is used to give commands ...

Entri pure!
Accomodati!
Lasciatemi lavorare, per favore!

▐ ... and express challenges, invitations, and requests.

Senta, scusi!	*Excuse me, may I ask you something?*
Dica!	*Yes, I'm listening!*
Non si preoccupi!	*Don't worry!*
Faccia pure!	*But of course! Go right ahead!*
Si figuri! S'immagini!	*Naturally! Please do!*
Abbi pazienza!	*Be patient!*
Ma **fammi** il favore!	*Now listen here!*

▐ The imperative is also used to formulate many phrases of civility and turns of speech.

The Imperative

1. Separate the **tu** imperatives from the **Lei** imperatives. Enter the appropriate letters in the corresponding boxes. **

a) Scusami!

b) Entri pure!

c) Si serva!

d) Stia attenta!

e) Fa' attenzione!

f) Lascia fare a me!

g) Dica pure!

h) Abbi pazienza!

i) Senti!

j) Si calmi!

Tu: ☐ ☐ ☐ ☐ ☐   Lei: ☐ ☐ ☐ ☐ ☐

2. How do the following requests sound when you address them to a person for whom you use the polite pronoun? **

a) Aiutami, per favore!   _____

b) Sta' tranquilla!   _____

c) Guarda un po'!   _____

d) Per favore, ascoltami!   _____

e) Aspettaci!   _____

f) Non preoccuparti!   _____

g) Vieni prima delle otto.   _____

h) Rispondi tu, per favore!   _____

i) Sii gentile e fammi questo favore!   _____

preoccuparsi – *to worry*
fare un favore – *to do a favor*

3. Change the following affirmative imperatives to negative imperatives. **

a) Guarda!   _____

b) Ci aspetti!   _____

c) Prendete il treno!   _____

d) Telefonami in ufficio!   _____

e) Si fermi!   _____

f) Venga prima delle nove!   _____

g) Usciamo prima di cena!   _____

h) Vattene!   _____

i)   Lasciatemi solo!   _____

j)   Passi dal centro!   _____

k)   Prendi l'autostrada!   _____

4. Complete the dialogues by adding the appropriate verbs from the group in the right margin.**

a)   + _____, posso entrare?

~ Ma certo, _____ ! In che cosa Le posso essere

utile?

+ Ecco, avrei bisogno di un consiglio.

~ Sì, mi _____ !

b)   + _____, La disturba se apro un po' il finestrino?

~ Ma no, per niente, _____!

faccia pure

dica

scusi

senta

entri pure

5. These sentences may come in handy. Translate them with the **Lei** form. ***

a)   Please telephone me!

_____

b)   Please leave a message!

_____

c)   Wait a moment, please!

_____

d)   Sit down, please!

_____

e)   Excuse the delay!

_____

f)   Take the first street on the right!

_____

to leave – lasciare
the message –
il messaggio
to sit down –
accomodarsi
the delay –
il ritardo

The Subjunctive

Peccato che Nicola non **voglia** venire! Credevo che gli **facesse** piacere rivedere i vecchi amici.

Too bad Nicola wasn't able to come! I thought he would enjoy seeing his old friends again.

The Present Subjunctive

① Sandro vuole partecipare alla gara benché **abbia** la febbre.

② Cerco qualcuno che mi **aiuti** nei lavori di casa.

1. Sandro wants to participate in the race even though he has a fever.
2. I'm looking for someone to help me with the housework.

Formation

The forms of the present subjunctive are easy to learn, since the forms of **io**, **tu**, **lui**, **lei**, **Lei** all have the same ending, and the 1st person plural of the present subjunctive is identical to the equivalent person of the present indicative.

Tip! Do you already know the 3rd person singular imperative? Then you don't need to learn any new forms for the 1st, 2nd, and 3rd persons singular of the present subjunctive. They are identical to the imperative of the **Lei** form.

1. Verbs with a Regular Subjunctive

Verbs Ending in *-are*

	parl**are**	
io	parl**i**	You form the present subjunctive of verbs ending in **-are** by adding the endings **-i**, **-iamo**, **-iate**, and **-ino** to the verb stem.
tu	parl**i**	
lui/lei/Lei	parl**i**	
(noi)	parl**iamo**	
(voi)	parl**iate**	To distinguish between the persons **io**, **tu**, **lui**, **lei**, **Lei**, the personal pronoun frequently is added.
(loro)	parl**ino**	

Verbs that are regular in the present tense are also regular in the subjunctive. Moreover, they retain the same special features as in the present tense. Thus verbs ending in **-care** and **-gare** have an **-h-** before the **-i-**:

	io, tu, lui/lei/Lei	(noi)	(voi)	(loro)
cer**care**:	cer**chi**	cer**chiamo**	cer**chiate**	cer**chino**
pa**gare**:	pa**ghi**	pa**ghiamo**	pa**ghiate**	pa**ghino**

And verbs ending in **-iare** have only one **-i-**:

	io, tu, lui/lei/Lei	(noi)	(voi)	(loro)
stud**iare**:	stud**i**	stud**iamo**	stud**iate**	stud**ino**
mang**iare**:	mang**i**	mang**iamo**	mang**iate**	mang**ino**

Verbs Ending in *-ere* and *-ire*

For verbs ending in **-ere** and **-ire**, add the endings **-a**, **-iamo**, **-iate**, and **-ano** to the verb stem or to the expanded stem **-isc-**.

	scriv**ere**	part**ire**	cap**ire**
io	scriv**a**	part**a**	capisc**a**
tu	scriv**a**	part**a**	capisc**a**
lui/lei/Lei	scriv**a**	part**a**	capisc**a**
(noi)	scriv**iamo**	part**iamo**	cap**iamo**
(voi)	scriv**iate**	part**iate**	cap**iate**
(loro)	scriv**ano**	part**ano**	capisc**ano**

2. Verbs with an Irregular Subjunctive

Verbs that are irregular in the present tense have the endings **-a**, **-iamo**, **-iate**, and **-ano** in the present subjunctive.

Infinitive	Present Indicative	Subjunctive			
	(io)	io, tu, lui lei, Lei	(noi)	(voi)	(loro)
andare	vado	vada	and**iamo**	and**iate**	vad**ano**
bere	bevo	beva	bev**iamo**	bev**iate**	bev**ano**
dire	dico	dica	dic**iamo**	dic**iate**	dic**ano**
fare	faccio	faccia	facc**iamo**	facc**iate**	facc**iano**
potere	posso	possa	poss**iamo**	poss**iate**	poss**ano**
tenere	tengo	tenga	ten**iamo**	ten**iate**	teng**ano**
uscire	esco	esca	usc**iamo**	usc**iate**	esc**ano**
venire	vengo	venga	ven**iamo**	ven**iate**	veng**ano**
volere	voglio	voglia	vogl**iamo**	vogl**iate**	vogl**iano**

143

Formation of the Irregular Present Subjunctive

Infinitive	Present Indicative	Subjunctive	
	1st person singular	1st, 2nd, 3rd person singular	3rd person plural
andare	vad**o** ▶	vad**a** ▶	vad**ano**
tenere	teng**o** ▶	teng**a** ▶	teng**ano**
uscire	esc**o** ▶	esc**a** ▶	esc**ano**

The present subjunctive of the singular and the 3rd person plural are derived from the 1st person singular of the present indicative. The endings of the present subjunctive replace the endings of the present indicative.

Infinitive	Present Indicative	Subjunctive
	1st person plural	1st person plural
andare	and**iamo**	and**iamo**
tenere	ten**iamo**	ten**iamo**
uscire	usc**iamo**	usc**iamo**

The 1st person plural of the present subjunctive and that of the present indicative are identical.

Infinitive	Subjunctive	Subjunctive
	1st person plural	2nd person plural
andare	and**iamo**	and**iate**
tenere	ten**iamo**	ten**iate**
uscire	usc**iamo**	usc**iate**

The 2nd person plural of the present subjunctive is derived from the 1st person plural of the present subjunctive.

3. Completely Irregular Forms

Infinitive	io, tu, lui lei, Lei	(noi)	(voi)	(loro)
avere	**abbia**	abbiamo	**abbiate**	**abbiano**
dare	**dia**	diamo	**diate**	**diano**
dovere	**debba**	dobbiamo	**dobbiate**	**debbano**
essere	**sia**	siamo	**siate**	**siano**
sapere	**sappia**	sappiamo	**sappiate**	**sappiano**
stare	**stia**	stiamo	**stiate**	**stiano**

The present subjunctive of **avere**, **dare**, **dovere**, **essere**, **sapere**, and **stare** is not derived from any other verb form.

Use

The present subjunctive is used in main clauses that begin with **che**:

Qualcuno ha suonato alla porta. **Che sia** di nuovo la vicina?

che sia...? – *might it be ...?*

Main clauses with the present subjunctive express a doubting question, ...

Che faccia attenzione! *He ought to pay attention!*

... a request, command, or suggestion, ...

Che Dio vi **benedica!** *God bless you!*

... or a wish.

The present subjunctive is used primarily in subordinate clauses:

Ti aiuto **benché abbia** poco tempo.
Vi presto la macchina **a condizione che torniate** prima di mezzanotte.
Diglielo **prima che** sia troppo tardi.
Cerca di entrare **di modo che** nessuno ti **senta.**

benché – *although, even though*
a condizione che – *provided that, providing*
prima che – *before*
di modo che – *so that*

The present subjunctive follows certain conjunctions, including **benché**, **affinché**, **purché**, **a condizione che**, **a meno che**, **prima che**, **sebbene**, **senza che**, **di modo che**.

▶ **Conjunctions,**
p. 233

Parla lentamente, **di modo che** tutti **possano** capirti.
Speak slowly, so that everyone can understand you.

After the conjunction **di modo che**, the subjunctive is required if the dependent clause contains something that is wished for.

Ho dimenticato la carta di credito **di modo che** non **posso** pagare il conto.
I forgot the credit card, so (that) I can't pay the bill.

Otherwise, **di modo che** is followed by the indicative mood.

augurarsi –
to wish, hope
non vedere l'ora –
to look forward to

Mio padre **non vuole che esca** tutte le sere.
Mi auguro che tutto **vada** bene.
Aspettiamo che arrivi il dott. Rota.
Spero che non **succeda** niente.
Preferiamo che tu non **parta** da solo.

The subjunctive follows the conjunction **che** with verbs and phrases expressing that something is wanted, wished, demanded, expected, or hoped for. These include, for example:
aspettare, augurarsi, desiderare, permettere, preferire, sperare, non vedere l'ora, volere.

In colloquial speech, the indicative often is used after **penso che** and **trovo che**:
Penso/trovo che hai ragione.

Penso che sia meglio partire subito.
Mi sembra che Stefano non **stia** bene.
Trovo che i tuoi genitori **abbiano** ragione.
Immagino che l'opera non vi **piaccia** tanto.
Credo che Anna **sia** in vacanza.

The subjunctive also is used after the conjunction **che** with verbs and expressions of opinion, thinking, and believing, such as these:
avere l'impressione, capire, credere, essere dell'opinione/del parere, immaginare, pensare, sembra/pare a qu, supporre, ritenere, trovare.

immaginare –
to imagine, think
supporre –
to suppose, presume
ritenere – *to deem, consider*
dubitare che –
to doubt that

Dubito che Enzo **sappia** bene il tedesco.
Non so se mio marito **possa** venire.
Non sono sicuro che il film **piaccia** a tutti.

The subjunctive is used after the conjunction **che** or **se** (*if, whether*) with verbs and expressions of doubt and uncertainty.
These include:
dubitare, non essere sicuro, non sapere, non pensare, non credere.

So che **hai** ragione tu.
Sono sicuro che Michele non **è** in casa.

The indicative, not the subjunctive, is used after verbs and
expressions indicating certainty. For example, it is used after
sapere, **essere sicuro/certo/convinto** …

Dico che **siete** tutti matti.
Affermo che **è** la verità.
Il direttore **conferma** che non **ci sono** più camere libere.

… as well as after verbs and expressions of saying, assuring, and
confirming, such as **dire**, **affermare**, **confermare.**

The subjunctive is not
used after **dire che**.

▶ **Indirect Discourse**,
p. 210

Ho paura che mia madre **venga** a sapere tutto.
Sono contento che tu non **abbia** la febbre.
Non m'importa che Rita non **venga.**
Ci dispiace che non **possiate** rimanere.
Non sopporto che nel soggiorno **ci sia** disordine.
Temo che arrivino in ritardo.

The subjunctive also is used after the conjunction **che** with verbs
and expressions that render a feeling, such as fear, joy, indifference,
sadness, regret, anger, amazement.
Among these are:
aver paura, **dispiacere a qu**, **essere contento/felice/sorpreso/
triste**, **non importare a qu**, **far piacere a qu**, **non sopportare**,
temere.

ho paura che – *I fear
that, I'm afraid that*
non m'importa che – *it
doesn't matter to me, it's
not important to me*
ci dispiace che – *we're
sorry that*
non sopportare – *to not
bear / tolerate / put
up with*
temere che – *to fear
that*

È assurdo che **faccia** tu i compiti di tuo fratello.
Bisogna che **faccia** più caldo.
Basta che mi **telefoniate** stasera.
È meglio che il cane **rimanga** a casa.
Peccato che non **abbiate** tempo di venire a trovarci.
Può darsi che non **riesca** a finire la traduzione entro lunedì.
Sembra che Sandra **voglia** divorziare.

The subjunctive also follows impersonal verbs and expressions
introducing a dependent clause with **che**, such as:
**è assurdo che, bisogna che, basta che, è bene/meglio che, è
bello che, è incredibile che, è (in)giusto che, è (im)possibile
che, è necessario che, pare che, (è un) peccato che, può darsi
che, sembra che, è strano che, è una vergogna che.**

è evidente che –
it's obvious that
si sa che – *it's well
known that*

È certo che qui non **accettano** carte di credito.
È chiaro che hai ragione tu.
È evidente che non **dici** la verità.

È sicuro che domani **è** festa.
Si sa che l'olio d'oliva **è** sano.
È vero che ci **sono** troppe macchine.

However, if the impersonal verbs and phrases express something certain or obvious, then the **indicative** follows, as after:
è certo che, **è chiaro che**, **è evidente che**, **è sicuro che**, **si sa che**, **è vero che**.

Cerchiamo **un albergo che accetti** i cani.
Mi può consigliare **un libro che piaccia** agli adulti e ai bambini?

The subjunctive also occurs in relative clauses that reflect a wish, a demand, or an expectation ...

l'unico – *the only one*

Il dott. Bruni è **la persona più gentile che** io **conosca**.
Carla è **l'unica che sappia** veramente bene il tedesco.
Non c'è **nessun film che** gli **piaccia**.

... or contain an expression that has the nature of exclusivity, such as **l'unico**, **l'ultimo**, **il solo**, **niente**, **nessuno**.

Non aprire, **chiunque sia**.
Qualunque cosa ti **offra**, tu non comprarla.
Non cambierò idea, **qualsiasi** cosa tu mi **dica**.
Dovunque tu **vada**, io ti seguirò.
Comunque vadano le cose, io ti scriverò.

Similarly, use the subjunctive after generalizing expressions such as **chiunque** *(whoever)*, **qualunque/qualsiasi** *(whichever)*, **dovunque** *(wherever)*, **comunque** *(however)*.

When the main clause and the dependent clause have the same subject, use an infinitive construction instead of a dependent clause with the subjunctive:

Sono contento **di essere** a casa.	*I'm glad to be home.*
But:	
Sono contento **che tu sia** a casa.	*I'm glad that **you**'re home.*
Non voglio **rimanere** qui.	*I don't want to stay here.*
But:	
Non voglio **che tu rimanga** qui.	*I don't want **you** to stay here.*

The Present Perfect Subjunctive

① È bene che **abbiate raccontato** tutto.

② Carlo non risponde. Che **sia** già **partito?**

---

1. It's good that you told everything. 2. Carlo doesn't answer. Could it be that he has already left?

Formation

The present perfect subjunctive is formed with the present subjunctive of **essere** or **avere** and the past participle of the verb in question.

	prendere	
io	**abbia**	preso
tu	**abbia**	preso
lui/lei/Lei	**abbia**	preso
(noi)	**abbiamo**	preso
(voi)	**abbiate**	preso
(loro)	**abbiano**	preso

If the present perfect subjunctive is formed with **avere**, the past participle remains unchanged. In this case, it always ends in **-o**.

▶ For more about the formation and variability of the past participle and the use of **essere** and **avere**, see this chapter: **The Present Perfect**, p. 91

	partire	
io	**sia**	partito, -a
tu	**sia**	partito, -a
lui/lei/Lei	**sia**	partito, -a
(noi)	**siamo**	partiti, -e
(voi)	**siate**	partiti, -e
(loro)	**siano**	partiti, -e

If it is conjugated with **essere**, however, then the past participle agrees in number and gender with the subject:

Penso che Rosa sia già partita.

Use

Ho paura che sia successo qualcosa a Michele.
Può darsi che abbia perso il treno.
Pia non è ancora arrivata. **Che sia successo** qualcosa?
Barbara è **l'unica donna che** mi **abbia** veramente **amato.**

The present perfect subjunctive follows the same rules as the present subjunctive in a main clause or a dependent clause. Here the present perfect subjunctive indicates events that have already taken place.

▶ For more about the use of the present perfect subjunctive, see this section: **Sequence of Tenses with the Subjunctive**, p. 153

The Imperfect Subjunctive

Fossi già a Parigi!	E se **mandassimo** un fax?	Parla come se **fosse** ubriaco.
①	②	③

1. If only I were already in Paris! 2. And what if we sent a fax?
3. He speaks as if he were drunk.

1. Verbs with a Regular Imperfect Subjunctive

Verbs Ending in -*are*, -*ere*, and -*ire*

Tip! The 1st and 2nd persons singular are always identical in the imperfect subjunctive.

	and**are**	av**ere**	cap**ire**
(io)	and**assi**	av**essi**	cap**issi**
(tu)	and**assi**	av**essi**	cap**issi**
(lui/lei/Lei)	and**asse**	av**esse**	cap**isse**
(noi)	and**assimo**	av**essimo**	cap**issimo**
(voi)	and**aste**	av**este**	cap**iste**
(loro)	and**assero**	av**essero**	cap**issero**

The regular forms of the imperfect subjunctive are formed by adding the personal endings to the verb stem in question, such as **and-**, **av-**, **cap-**.

2. Verbs with an Irregular Imperfect Subjunctive

Infinitive	Irregular stem	Ending of the **imperfect subjunctive**
bere	**bev**	
dare	**d**	-essi
dire	**dic**	-essi
fare	**fac**	-esse
trarre	**tra**	-essimo
porre	**pon**	-este
produrre	**produc**	-essero
stare	**st**	

Verbs with an irregular imperfect subjunctive use these personal endings: **-essi, -essi, -esse, -essimo, -este, -essero.** These endings are attached to the stem of the imperfect tense, as in these examples: **dessi, dessi, desse, dessimo, deste, dessero.**

You can use **trarre**, **porre**, and **produrre** as patterns for verbs ending in **-arre**, **-orre**, and **-urre**:

dist**rarre:**	(io) distraessi, (tu) distraessi, (lui/lei/Lei) distraesse, (noi) distraessimo, (voi) distraeste, (loro) distraessero
prop**orre:**	(io) proponessi, (tu) proponessi, (lui/lei/Lei) proponesse, (noi) proponessimo, (voi) proponeste, (loro) proponessero
cond**urre:**	(io) conducessi, (tu) conducessi, (lui/lei/Lei) conducesse, (noi) conducessimo, (voi) conduceste, (loro) conducessero

	essere	
(io)	**fossi**	The verb **essere** is a special case.
(tu)	**fossi**	
(lui/lei/Lei)	**fosse**	
(noi)	**fossimo**	
(voi)	**foste**	
(loro)	**fossero**	

Use

Venisse almeno da solo!
Potessi partire con voi!
Sapessi le lingue come le sai tu!

The imperfect subjunctive occurs in wishes that are unfulfillable or whose fulfillment is unlikely, ...

E se andassimo al cinema?

... in cautiously formulated suggestions, ...

Si comporta **come se fosse** lui il direttore.

... and after the conjunction **come se**, to express something that is not real at the present time.

Above all, the imperfect subjunctive is used in conditional sentences and, in accordance with the sequences of tenses, with verbs and expressions that require the subjunctive, as well as in indirect questions.

E se andassimo ...? –
What if we were to go ...?

▶ **The Conditional Sentence**, p. 208

▶ **Sequence of Tenses with the Subjunctive**, p. 155

▶ **Indirect Questions**, p. 214

The Past Perfect Subjunctive

Non l'**avessi** mai
conosciuto!
①

E se **fossero**
già **arrivati?**
②

Mi guarda come se non
mi **avesse** mai **visto!**
③

1. If only I had never met him! 2. And what if they had already arrived?
3. He looks at me as if he had never seen me.

Formation

The past perfect subjunctive is formed with the imperfect subjunctive of
avere or **essere** and the past participle of the verb in question.

<table>
<tr><td colspan="3">prendere</td><td></td></tr>
<tr><td>(io)</td><td>avessi</td><td>preso</td><td rowspan="6">If the past perfect subjunctive is formed with avere, the past participle ends in -o.</td></tr>
<tr><td>(tu)</td><td>avessi</td><td>preso</td></tr>
<tr><td>(lui/lei/Lei)</td><td>avesse</td><td>preso</td></tr>
<tr><td>(noi)</td><td>avessimo</td><td>preso</td></tr>
<tr><td>(voi)</td><td>aveste</td><td>preso</td></tr>
<tr><td>(loro)</td><td>avessero</td><td>preso</td></tr>
</table>

▶ For more about
the formation and
variability of the
past participle as
well as the use of
essere or **avere**,
see this chapter:
The Present Perfect,
p. 91

<table>
<tr><td colspan="3">partire</td><td></td></tr>
<tr><td>(io)</td><td>fossi</td><td>partito, -a</td><td rowspan="6">However, if it is formed with essere, the past participle agrees in number and gender with the subject:
E se Rosa fosse già partita?</td></tr>
<tr><td>(tu)</td><td>fossi</td><td>partito, -a</td></tr>
<tr><td>(lui/lei/Lei)</td><td>fosse</td><td>partito, -a</td></tr>
<tr><td>(noi)</td><td>fossimo</td><td>partiti, -e</td></tr>
<tr><td>(voi)</td><td>foste</td><td>partiti, -e</td></tr>
<tr><td>(loro)</td><td>fossero</td><td>partiti, -e</td></tr>
</table>

Use

Fosse almeno **venuto** da solo!

The past perfect subjunctive occurs in wishes that cannot be
fulfilled, ...

E se **fossimo andati** al cinema?

... in reflections about things that could have happened, ...

Si comporta **come se avesse** vinto al lotto.

▶ The Conditional
Sentence, p. 208

■ ... and after the conjunction **come se**, to express something that
was not real in the past.

The past perfect subjunctive also occurs in conditional sentences and, in
accordance with the sequence of tenses, with verbs and expressions
that require the subjunctive, as well as in indirect questions.

▶ Sequence of
Tenses with the
Subjunctive,
p. 155

▶ Indirect
Questions, p. 214

Sequence of Tenses with the Subjunctive

Pensi che Silvia si
sia arrabbiata?
①

Credevo che fosse successo
qualcosa di grave.
②

1. Do you think that Silvia was angry? 2. I thought that something serious had happened.

In order to use the correct tense in a dependent clause with the
subjunctive, you first have to know whether the action of the dependent
clause took place before that of the main clause (prior), at the same
time (simultaneous), of after it (subsequent).

Second, the tense that must be selected depends on the tense of the
verb in the main clause: present, future, one of the past tenses, or
conditional.

1. The Verb in the Main Clause Is in the Present,
   Future, or Imperative

Credo che Carlo
sia arrivato.
①

Penso che
stia bene.
②

Spero che non **parta/
partirà** già domani!
③

1. I believe that Carlo has arrived. 2. I think he's doing fine.
3. I hope he's not already leaving tomorrow.

Main Clause:		Dependent Clause (prior):	**Past Perfect Subjunctive**
Present	Penso		
Future	Penserà	che **sia arrivata.**	
Imperative	Non pensare		

Main Clause:		Dependent Clause (simultaneous):	**Present Subjunctive**
Present	Penso		
Future	Penserà	che **arrivi** adesso.	
Imperative	Non pensare		

Main Clause:		Dependent Clause (subsequent):	**Present / Future Subjunctive**
Present	Penso		
Future	Penserà	che **arrivi/arriverà** più tardi.	
Imperative	Non pensare		

Additional Possibilities for Combination

Present tense – Conditional:

Penso che Luca **si sposerebbe** volentieri.
I think that Luca would like to get married.

If the verb in the main clause is in the present tense, then the conditional can be used in the dependent clause, if this clause expresses what could be or might happen now or later.

Present tense – Conditional perfect:

Penso che Pia **si sarebbe sposata** volentieri.
I think that Pia would have liked to get married.

However, the conditional perfect is required in the dependent clause if you want to say what could have been or might have happened.

2. The Verb in the Main Clause Is in One of the Past Tenses

Credevo che Carlo **fosse già arrivato.**	**Pensavo** che **stesse** bene.	**Speravo** che non **sarebbe ripartito/ ripartisse** troppo presto.
①	②	③

1. I thought that Carlo had already arrived. 2. I thought he was doing fine.
3. I hoped that he wouldn't leave again too soon.

Main Clause:		Dependent Clause (prior):	**Past Perfect Subjunctive**
Imperfect	Pensavo		
Present perfect	Ho pensato		
Preterit	Pensai	che **fosse arrivata**.	
Past perfect	Avevo pensato		

Main Clause:		Dependent Clause (simultaneous):	**Imperfect Subjunctive**
Imperfect	Pensavo		
Present perfect	Ho pensato		
Preterit	Pensai	che **arrivasse** subito.	
Past perfect	Avevo pensato		

Main Clause:		Dependent Clause (subsequent):	**Conditional Perfect /Imperfect Subjunctive**
Imperfect	Pensavo		
Present perfect	Ho pensato		
Preterit	Pensai	che **sarebbe arrivata/arrivasse** più tardi.	
Past perfect	Avevo pensato		

Additional Possibilities for Combination

Present tense – Imperfect subjunctive:

Mi sembra che **fosse** l'una quando è successo.
It seems to me that it was one o'clock when it happened.
Sembra che da bambina **andasse** ogni estate in Sardegna.
It appears that as a child she went to Sardinia every year.

If the verb in the main clause is in the present tense, then the imperfect subjunctive can be used in the dependent clause, if a past condition or a past habit is being described.

Present tense – Past perfect subjunctive:

Non so se nel 1945 Luisa **si fosse** già **trasferita** a Roma.
I don't know whether Luisa had already moved to Rome in 1945.

If the verb in the main clause is in the present tense, then the prior action or state in the dependent clause is expressed by using the past perfect subjunctive, if the event in question is far in the past.

3. The Verb in the Main Clause Is in the Conditional

Mi dispiacerebbe se
non **venisse** più.
①

Mi sarebbe dispiaciuto
se non **fosse venuto**.
②

---

1. I would be sorry if he didn't come any more. 2. I would have been sorry if he had not come.

When verbs and expressions that express a wish, such as **desiderare**, **preferire**, **volere**, **è bene**, **è meglio**, **è necessario**, are in the conditional, then the imperfect subjunctive or the past perfect subjunctive is used in the dependent clause.

Main Clause:		Dependent Clause (prior):	**Past Perfect Subjunctive**
Conditional	Vorrei	che **fosse arrivata**.	
Conditional perfect	Avrei voluto		

Main Clause:		Dependent Clause (simultaneous):	**Imperfect Subjunctive**
Conditional	Vorrei	che **arrivasse** subito.	
Conditional perfect	Avrei voluto		

Main Clause:		Dependent Clause (subsequent):	**Imperfect Subjunctive**
Conditional	Vorrei	che **arrivasse** più tardi.	
Conditional perfect	Avrei voluto		

1. Mark the verbs that are in some form of the subjunctive. *

a) + Senti, pensi che faccia freddo in Germania?

~ Beh, in settembre non si sa mai. Può far freddo, ma può anche far caldo.

b) + Vi dispiace se non vengo al cinema con voi? Sono troppo stanco.

~ Ma no, per niente! Se sei stanco è bene che tu vada a letto presto.

c) + Senti, dove abita adesso il professor Sangiorgi?

~ Mah, di preciso non lo so, ma credo che abbia cambiato casa e che ora stia in piazza Carlo Felice.

d) + Sai che c'è anche Teresa?

~ No, davvero?! Pensavo che dovesse rimanere a casa a studiare.

e) + Ma perché non hai detto ai tuoi che a Natale non andremo da loro?   i tuoi – *your parents*

~ Mah, mi sembrava che non fosse il momento per dirglielo.

> **Tip!** Would you like to express an opinion without using the subjunctive? Instead of **penso / credo che**, simply use the expression **secondo me** (*in my opinion*):
> **Secondo me è** troppo tardi per il cinema.

2. Write out the present subjunctive and imperfect subjunctive of the following verbs. *

		Present Subjunctive	Imperfect Subjunctive
a)	io – parlare	_____	_____
b)	tu – cercare	_____	_____
c)	lui – crescere	_____	_____
d)	noi – vivere	_____	_____
e)	voi – partire	_____	_____
f)	loro – finire	_____	_____
g)	io – sapere	_____	_____
h)	tu – potere	_____	_____
i)	lui – dovere	_____	_____
j)	noi – volere	_____	_____
k)	loro – andare	_____	_____
l)	io – essere	_____	_____
m)	tu – avere	_____	_____

The Subjunctive

3. When is the indicative required, and when must the subjunctive be used? Mark the form that is appropriate in each of the pairs below. **

a) È necessario che la gente è / sia informata.

b) So che Sergio ha / abbia ragione.

c) Non c'è nessun libro che io ho letto / abbia letto con maggior interesse.

d) Non venire, qualsiasi cosa succede / succeda.

e) Il dottore ha detto che fra due giorni puoi / possa alzarti.

f) È evidente che Maurizio sa / sappia bene l'inglese.

i miei – *my parents*   g) Non è ancora sicuro che i miei possono /possano venire a Pasqua.

4. Rewrite the sentences in the left column in the past, putting the verbs in **bold** in the imperfect subjunctive, the past perfect subjunctive, or the conditional perfect. ***

a) Crede che tu **stia** male.   Credeva che tu _____ male.

b) Penso che Ezio **sia uscito**.   Pensavo che Ezio _____ .

c) Credo che i miei genitori   Credevo che i miei genitori _____
   ritorneranno in Italia.   _____ in Italia.

d) Non so se il telefonino **sia**   Non sapevo se il telefonino _____
   veramente indispensabile.   _____ veramente indispensabile.

e) Temo che Carla **abbia fatto**   Temevo che Carla _____
   tanti debiti.   _____ tanti debiti.

f) Non vogliamo che **paghiate**   Non volevamo che _____
   voi il conto.   _____ voi il conto.

g) Non è sicuro che l'anno prossimo   Non era sicuro che l'anno dopo io
   io **possa** passare un mese al mare. _____
                                         passare un mese al mare.

h) Vuoi che si **vada** al cinema?   Volevi che si _____
                                         al cinema?

5. Complete the sentences below, using the verbs supplied, either in the present subjunctive or in the present perfect subjunctive. **

a) Non penso che Luca (volere) _____ partecipare alla regata.

b) Sembra che Franco e Silvia (sposarsi) _____

l'anno prossimo.

c) Temo che Sandro (annoiarsi) _____ ieri sera.

d) Pare che Lucia e Andrea (divorziare) _____

già da tempo.

*divorziare – to get
a divorce*

e) Siamo contenti che voi due (andare) _____ d'accordo.

f) Credo che ieri mia figlia non mi (dire) _____ la

verità.

g) È un peccato che sabato prossimo tu e Gianna non (potere) _____

_____ venire alla festa.

h) Bisogna che a scuola tu (fare) _____ più

attenzione.

i) Mi dispiace che il film di ieri sera non ti (piacere) _____ .

j) Se non potete venire, basta che mi (telefonare) _____ .

6. Present subjunctive or imperfect subjunctive? Mark the appropriate verb form in each pair below. ***

a) Secondo me sarebbe bene che tu faccia/facessi ordine nella tua
stanza. Non è necessario che tu lo faccia/facessi subito, ma fallo.

b) Non vogliamo che tu esca/uscissi tutte le sere. Preferiremmo che tu
rimanga/rimanessi a casa almeno il fine settimana.

c) Non è bene che tu prenda/prendessi la macchina per andare in centro.
Sarebbe meglio che ci vada/andassi con i mezzi pubblici.

d) Alla nonna piacerebbe che per il suo compleanno si riunisca/si
riunisse tutta la famiglia. E poi vorrebbe che Carletto suoni/suonasse
qualcosa alla chitarra.

e) Sarebbe bene che qualcuno resti/restasse a casa con il nonno. Non è
bene che stia/stesse solo tutto il fine settimana.

The Reflexive Verbs

Franca **si alza** alle sette. **Si lava, si veste,** prende un caffè ed esce.

Franca gets up at seven. She washes, gets dressed, drinks coffee and goes out.

Italian has verbs that can be reflexive or not reflexive, such as **lavare** (*to wash*) and **lavarsi** (*to wash* [*oneself*]). Some even change their meaning, as these do:

alzare	*to raise*	alzarsi	*to arise, get up*
cambiare	*to change*	cambiarsi	*to change clothes*
chiamare	*to call*	chiamarsi	*to be called, named*
sedere	*to sit*	sedersi	*to sit down*
trovare	*to find*	trovarsi	*to be located*
tenere	*to hold*	tenersi	*to hold on (tight)*

In colloquial speech, nonreflexive verbs are often used as reflexives. In this way the speaker lends an especially personal note to his statement, as here:

Adesso **mi bevo** una bella birra.	*Now I'm going to drink (myself) a nice beer.*
Ci siamo mangiati un panino.	*We ate (ourselves) a sandwich.*

Some important verbs are reflexive in Italian:

accorgersi di qc	to notice something	chiamarsi	to be called, named
addormentarsi	to go to sleep	fermarsi	to stop, come to a halt
alzarsi	to get up	ammalarsi	to fall ill
mettersi qc	to put something on	andarsene	to go away, leave
svegliarsi	to wake up		

Many verbs having to do with personal grooming are reflexive; the action of the verb affects the speaker.

truccarsi	to put on makeup
pettinarsi	to comb one's hair
lavarsi i denti	to brush one's teeth
farsi la barba	to shave

The Reflexive Verbs in the Present Tense

① Non **ti senti** bene?

② No, non tanto. Forse **mi siedo** un po' all'ombra.

Where the reflexive pronouns are concerned, only the forms for the 3rd person singular and plural are new to you. The other forms correspond to those for the direct and indirect object pronouns.

---

1. Don't you feel well? 2. No, not so well. Maybe I'll sit down in the shade for a little.

1. Regular Forms

	alzar**si**	
(io)	**mi**	alzo
(tu)	**ti**	alzi
(lui/lei/Lei)	**si**	alza
(noi)	**ci**	alziamo
(voi)	**vi**	alzate
(loro)	**si**	alzano

The reflexive verbs are always accompanied by a reflexive pronoun. In the infinitive, as in the case of **alzarsi**, for example, the reflexive pronoun is attached to the shortened infinitive, which has lost the **-e**: **alzare ▶ alzarsi**.

alzarsi – *to arise, get up*

mettersi qc –
to put something on
lavarsi – *to wash*
(oneself)
pulirsi – *to clean up,*
wash (oneself)
vestirsi – *to get dressed*

▶ **The Personal**
Pronoun, p. 71

mettersi:	Che cosa **ti metti**?
lavarsi:	**Ti lavi** prima tu?
pulirsi:	**Mi pulisco** i denti.
vestirsi:	Perché non **ti vesti**?

As soon as a reflexive verb is conjugated, the reflexive pronoun must be placed before the verb. The verb itself is conjugated like any other nonreflexive verb ending in **-are**, **-ere**, or **-ire**.

The position of the reflexive pronoun follows the same rules as those for other pronouns.

2. Irregular Forms

If a verb is regular in its nonreflexive form, it remains regular in its reflexive form as well.

tenersi –
to hold on, hold fast
sedersi – *to sit down,*
take a seat

		tenersi		sedersi
(io)	mi	**tengo**	mi	**siedo**
(tu)	ti	**tieni**	ti	**siedi**
(lui/lei/Lei)	si	**tiene**	si	**siede**
(noi)	ci	teniamo	ci	sediamo
(voi)	vi	tenete	vi	sedete
(loro)	si	**tengono**	si	**siedono**

The Reflexive Verbs in the Compound Tenses

Mia moglie ed io **ci siamo conosciuti** grazie a Internet.	Fabio si trasferì in Germania perché **si era innamorato** di una ragazza tedesca.	Appena **ti sarai separato** da Anna verrò ad abitare da te.
①	②	③

1. My wife and I got acquainted thanks to the Internet. 2. Fabio moved to Germany because he had fallen in love with a German girl. 3. As soon as you have separated from Anna, I'll move in with you.

The formation of the compound tenses—the present perfect, past perfect, and future perfect—is quite simple with reflexive verbs. They are always formed with the auxiliary verb **essere**.

Here we provide an example: the verb **lavarsi** in the present perfect and past perfect:

	Present Perfect		Past Perfect	
(io)	mi **sono** lavat**o, -a**	mi	**ero**	lavat**o, -a**
(tu)	ti **sei** lavat**o, -a**	ti	**eri**	lavat**o, -a**
(lui/lei/Lei)	si **è** lavat**o, -a**	si	**era**	lavat**o, -a**
(noi)	ci **siamo** lavat**i, -e**	ci	**eravamo**	lavat**i, -e**
(voi)	vi **siete** lavat**i, -e**	vi	**eravate**	lavat**i, -e**
(loro)	si **sono** lavat**i, -e**	si	**erano**	lavat**i, -e**

The past participle agrees in number and gender with the subject.

If the reflexive verb is used with **dovere**, **potere**, or **volere**, then there are two possibilities with regard to the compound tenses:

(io)	**mi**	**sono**	**dovuto, -a**	lavare
(tu)	**ti**	**sei**	**dovuto, -a**	lavare
(lui/lei/Lei)	**si**	**è**	**dovuto, -a**	lavare
(noi)	**ci**	**siamo**	**dovuti, -e**	lavare
(voi)	**vi**	**siete**	**dovuti, -e**	lavare
(loro)	**si**	**sono**	**dovuti, -e**	lavare

You can use the auxiliary verb **essere**. Then the reflexive pronoun precedes the auxiliary verb.

(io)	**ho**	**dovuto**	lavar**mi**
(tu)	**hai**	**dovuto**	lavar**ti**
(lui/lei/Lei)	**ha**	**dovuto**	lavar**si**
(noi)	**abbiamo**	**dovuto**	lavar**ci**
(voi)	**avete**	**dovuto**	lavar**vi**
(loro)	**hanno**	**dovuto**	lavar**si**

You can also use **avere** as the auxiliary verb, however. In this case, the reflexive pronoun must be attached to the shortened infinitive, minus the **-e**.

The Reflexive Verbs

1. Complete the text, using the verbs supplied in the present tense. Add the appropriate personal endings. *

a) La mattina mio marito ed io (svegliarsi) _____ alle sei. b) Lui (alzarsi) _____ subito e (preparare) _____ la colazione. c) Io invece (alzarsi) _____ _____ quando tutto è pronto. d) Dopo la colazione Fabio (lavarsi) _____ , (farsi) _____ la barba e (prepararsi) _____ per andare in ufficio. e) Quando lui è uscito, io posso (lavarsi) _____ , (vestirsi) _____ e (occuparsi) _____ poi tranquillamente della casa. f) Verso le nove (mettersi) _____ _____ a lavorare. g) Durante il giorno Fabio ed io (vedersi) _____ raramente. h) A mezzogiorno io (farsi) _____ un panino e Fabio (andare) _____ a mangiare da sua madre. i) La sera, dopo cena, Fabio ed io (uscire) _____ con degli amici oppure (sedersi) _____ _____ davanti al televisore.

2. Put the sentences below in the present perfect. **

a) Sai che Carlo si sposa? _____

trasferirsi – *to move (residence)*

b) I vicini devono trasferirsi a Parma. _____

iscriversi – *to enroll*

c) Elena, ti informi tu per il treno? _____

addormentarsi – *to fall asleep*

d) Pia e Pietro si incontrano spesso. _____

annoiarsi – *to be bored*

e) Oggi Lucia può riposarsi un po'. _____

f) Luca vuole iscriversi a medicina. _____

g) Perché se ne va, Elena? _____

h) Mia figlia non si diverte con noi. _____

i) Luca non può addormentarsi. _____

j) Al mare Luca si annoia molto. _____

k) Rosa non vuole mettersi la gonna. _____

Impersonal Verbs and Expressions

È **bello** essere in vacanza, vero? ①

Quando non **piove** e non **fa** troppo **caldo**, sì. ②

E quando non **bisogna** alzarsi presto per fare una gita da qualche parte. ③

1. It's nice to be on vacation, isn't it? 2. When it's not raining and isn't too hot, yes.
3. And when you don't have to get up early to take a trip somewhere.

> Impersonal verbs and expressions do not have a definite subject.

The impersonal verbs include the following:

Oggi **piove/nevica/grandina.** **Fa bel/brutto tempo.** **Fa caldo/freddo/fresco.**	Verbs and expressions that describe the weather.
Basta fare attenzione. **Bisogna** pagare subito. **Conviene** dire la verità. Con questo tempo **è meglio** rimanere a casa. Ma **è necessario** partire tanto presto? Non mi **piace** giocare a golf. **Sembra** strano, ma è vero. Con lui non **serve** parlare. **Ci vuole** molto per convincermi.	Verbs and expressions that generally are rendered in English with *it*, *it is*, *one*, or *you*, such as **basta** (*it's enough*), **bisogna** (*it's necessary, one must*), **conviene** (*it's advisable*), **è meglio** (*il's better*), **è necessario** (*it's necessary*), **piace** (*... like, it pleases*), **sembra** (*it seems*), **serve** (*it's useful, it helps*), **ci vuole poco / molto** (*there's not much / a lot to it*).

È bastato poco per convincerlo. Non **è servito** a niente parlare con lui. Mi **è sembrato** che tutto andasse bene.	Impersonal verbs and expressions generally form the compound tenses with the auxiliary verb **essere.**

nevicare – *to snow*
grandinare – *to hail*
fa caldo – *it's warm, it's hot*
freddo – *cold*
fresco – *nippy, cool*

convincere qu – *to convince someone*

Ha fatto bel tempo. **Ha fatto** un po' **fresco.** Quest'estate **ha fatto caldo.**	Atmospheric phenomena that are expressed with **fare**, however, form the compound tenses with **avere.**
Ieri **è/ha** piovuto tutto il giorno. Quest'anno non **è/ha nevicato** molto.	Otherwise, when talking about the weather you have a choice between **essere** and **avere.**
Secondo te **basteranno i soldi?** **I soldi** non **sono bastati.**	Many impersonal verbs and expressions can also be used personally.
Qui **succedono** tante **cose** strane. **Sono successi** molti **incidenti.**	In this case the verb agrees in number and gender with the subject.
Vi **piacciono gli spaghetti?** **La serata** non mi **è piaciuta.**	
Ci vogliono pochi **minuti** per fare il caffè. **C'è voluta** molta **forza** per aprire la porta.	
C'è poco **posto** per le macchine. **Ci sono** pochi **parcheggi.**	The Italian equivalent of English *there is / are* is **c'è**, if the subject is in the singular ...
+ Cosa c'è da mangiare, oggi? **~ Ci sono le tagliatelle** alla bolognese.	... and **ci sono**, if it is in the plural.

The following expressions are used personally in Italian:

Sto bene.	*I'm fine.*
Ho freddo/caldo.	*I'm cold / hot.*
Riesco ad arrivare in tempo.	*I'm able to arrive on time.*
Sono lieto/contento di vederti.	*I'm glad to see you.*

1. Put the words in **bold** in the present perfect. **

a) Oggi **fa bel tempo**, però **fa un po' fresco**.

   _____

b) Da noi **nevica** e **fa molto freddo**.

   _____

c) Qui **fa caldo** e il posto mi piace molto; purtroppo i soldi **non bastano**
   per rimanere ancora alcuni giorni.

   _____

d) Quest'estate **piove** molto qui al Nord.

   _____

2. Fill in the blanks in the dialogues, using the appropriate verb
or expression. ***

a) ~ Secondo te _____ un'ora per preparare le lasagne?

   + Mah, dipende. Se le compri già preparate _____ anche venti
     minuti. Se però le vuoi preparare tu _____ anche più di
     un'ora.

b) + Ma a voi _____ fare campeggio?

   ~ Moltissimo, perché, a te no?

   + No, io preferisco la vacanza rilassante, dove non _____
     fare niente, assolutamente niente.

c) + Che cosa _____ da mangiare, oggi?

   ~ Dunque, _____ gli gnocchi e delle fettine di vitello. Ai
     bambini _____ gli gnocchi?

   + Ma certo, moltissimo!

d) + Ho letto che per mantenersi in forma _____ almeno
     30 minuti di esercizio fisico al giorno.

   ~ Accidenti, non è poco!

   + D'accordo, però _____ che _____ una
     passeggiata a ritmo veloce.

ci sono

sembra

basta

piace

basti

ci vogliono

ci vuole

piacciono

bisogna

bastano

c'è

mantenersi in forma –
to keep in shape
l'esercizio fisico –
physical exercise

The Infinitive
The Present Infinitive

> Stamattina sono uscito senza **fare** colazione. Adesso sono proprio contento di **mangiare** un bel piatto di spaghetti!

This morning I left without eating breakfast. Now I'm really glad to eat a big plate of spaghetti!

1. Forms

compr**are** vend**ere** part**ire**	Italian has three forms of the infinitive: infinitives ending in **-are**, **-ere**, and **-ire**.
distr**arre** prop**orre** cond**urre**	In a very few cases, the infinitive ends in **-arre**, **-orre**, or **-urre**.

distrarre – to distract, sidetrack
proporre – to propose, suggest
condurre – to conduct, lead, guide

2. Infinitive + Personal Pronoun

Temo di **farti** male. Sono contenta di **vedervi**. Vengono a **prendermi** alle otto.	The personal pronouns are attached to the infinitive, minus its final **-e**.
Non vorrei **distrarti**. Avrei una soluzione da **proporvi**. Cercherò di **impormi**.	With verbs ending in **-arre**, **-orre**, and **-urre**, the final **-re** of the infinitive is dropped.

imporsi –
to assert oneself

Use

Quite often Italian uses an infinitive where English would use a gerund, the *–ing* form, especially with certain prepositions. The preposition precedes the infinitive. Sometimes the infinitive follows the conjugated verb directly, with no preposition.

The infinitive occurs without a preposition ...

Giovanna **deve rimanere** a casa.
Posso aprire la finestra?

■ ... after **dovere**, **potere**, **volere**, and **sapere**, ...

Rita non **ama spendere** troppo.
Desidererei partire presto.
Ti **ho sentito telefonare**.

■ ... after a number of other verbs, such as **amare**, **desiderare**,
preferire, **sentire**, and **vedere**, ...

È facile criticare gli altri.
È meglio chiudere la porta.
Basta fare attenzione.

■ ... and after impersonal verbs and expressions, such as **è facile**,
è meglio, **basta**, **bisogna**, **mi/ti ... piace**.

▶ **Impersonal Verbs and Expressions**, p. 165

After **mi/ti . . . dispiace**, **mi/ti . . . pare**, and **mi/ti . . . sembra**,
however, the infinitive is attached by using **di**.

Mi dispiace di non poter venire.
Mi pare di essere dimagrita.
Mi sembra di stare meglio.

Frequently the infinitive is preceded by **a**, for example, after ...

Mi sono abituata ad alzarmi presto.
Non **riesco ad aprire** la porta.
Tanta gente **si diverte a navigare** su Internet.

■ ... the verbs **abituarsi a**, **divertirsi a**, **fermarsi a**, **riuscire a**,
servire a, etc., ...

If the preposition
a is followed by a
word that begins
with a vowel, the
preposition **a** often
becomes **ad**. The **d**
is present to make
pronunciation easier.

Vado a fare la spesa.
I'm going to do the (grocery) shopping.
Perché Luigi non **rimane a dormire**?
Why doesn't Luigi stay here to sleep?
Passo a salutarti.
I'm coming by to say hello.
Veniamo a trovarvi stasera.
We're coming to visit you this evening.

■ ... after verbs of motion and of remaining, such as **andare a**,
correre a, **passare a**, **rimanere a**, **(re)stare a**, **venire a**, ...

Cominciamo a lavorare presto.
Continui a studiare il tedesco?
Ha iniziato a scrivere poesie.
Forse **mi metto a fare** jogging.

▌ ... after verbs of beginning and continuing, such as
cominciare a, **continuare a**, **iniziare a**, **mettersi a**, ...

Non **sono abituato a stare** solo.
Non **è adatta a fare** l'insegnante.
È bravo a suonare il piano.
Siamo obbligati a cambiar casa.

▌ ... and frequently after **essere** + adjective, as with **essere abituato
a**, **essere adatto a**, **essere bravo a**, **essere obbligato a**, etc.

The infinitive follows the preposition **di** ...

Finisco di lavorare verso le sette.
Non **smette di piovere**.

▌ ... with verbs of completing an action, such as **finire di**,
smettere di, ...

Ho bisogno di stare solo.
Hai ragione di difenderti.
Non **ho tempo di fare** la spesa.

▌ ... often with **avere** + noun: **aver bisogno di**, **aver ragione di**,
aver tempo di, **aver voglia di**, etc., ...

Siamo contenti di vederti.
Sono felice di essere qui.
Sei stufo di stare in casa?

▌ ... often with **essere** + adjective: **essere contento di**, **essere felice
di**, **essere stanco di**, **essere stufo di**, **essere triste di**, etc. ...

Aspettiamo di poter partire.
Cercherò di arrivare in tempo.
Credo di stare meglio.
Gli **ho promesso di telefonargli.**
Ricordati di comprare la frutta!

▌ ... and with a number of other verbs, such as **aspettare di**, **cercare
di**, **credere di**, **decidere di**, **dimenticare di**, **promettere di**,
ricordarsi di, **sperare di**, **temere di**, etc.

la poesia – *the poem*
mettersi a fare qc –
*to start to do / doing
something*
adatto – *suitable,
appropriate*
essere obbligato –
to be obliged
smettere – *to stop, cease*
aver ragione – *to be
right*
sono stufo – *I'm fed
up / tired*
promettere – *to promise*

The infinitive follows the preposition **da** to identify and qualify ...

Che cosa c'è **da mangiare?**
Vorrei **qualcosa da bere**.

... with **che cosa?**, **qualcosa**, **niente**, **molto** and **poco** ...

Non ho **tempo da perdere**.
Abbiamo **una proposta da farvi**.

... and with nouns.

la proposta – *the suggestion*
disdire – *to cancel*

In addition, the infinitive occurs ...

Sono qui **per scusarmi**.
Il dottor Renzi ha telefonato **per disdire** l'appuntamento.

... after the preposition **per** (*in order to*), ...

Invece di studiare è uscito con Pia.
Telefonami **prima di partire**!
È uscito **senza salutare**.

... after **invece di** (*instead of*), **prima di** (*before*), and **senza** (*without*) ...

Sono io **a non volere** il telefonino. (= Sono io che non voglio il ...)

... and after the preposition **a** in place of a relative clause.

> An infinitive becomes a noun if it is accompanied by the definite article **il**, **lo**, or **l'**, as in this example:
> **Il mangiare** era ottimo. *(The meal was excellent.)*

The Perfect Infinitive

Dopo **aver mangiato** abbiamo fatto una passeggiata.
①

Penso di **essere dimagrito**.
②

1. After we had eaten we took a walk. 2. I think I have lost weight.

Formation

Penso di **aver(e) detto** tutto.
Crede di **aver(e) fatto** il necessario.
Pensiamo di **esser(e) partiti** in tempo.

The perfect infinitive is formed with the infinitive of **avere** or **essere** (the ending **-e** may be omitted) and the past participle of the main verb in question.

> Carlo teme di **esser(e) stato** poco gentile.
> Eva è contenta di **esser(e) venuta** con noi.
> I **genitori** temono di **esser(e) partiti** tardi.
> **A Pia e Rosa** dispiace di **esser(e) arrivate** tardi.

If the perfect infinitive is conjugated with **essere**, then the past participle agrees in number and gender with the subject.

Perfect Infinitive + Personal Pronouns

Unstressed personal pronouns are attached to **esser-** or to **aver-**.

▶ The Position of the Unstressed Object Pronouns, p. 71

> Dopo **essermi** lavata i capelli sono uscita.
> Dopo **esserci** riposati un po' siamo andati a mangiare.
> Ho telefonato a Enzo. Credo di **avergli** fatto piacere.
> Chissà dove sono le chiavi. Pensavo di **averle** messe nella borsetta e invece lì non ci sono.

Use

> A Chiara dispiace di **essersi arrabbiata**.
> Penso di non **aver chiuso** la finestra del soggiorno.

The perfect infinitive is used to denote an event or process that has already taken place …

insultarsi – *to abuse / insult each other*

> Dopo **aver fatto** la spesa sono tornata a casa.
> Dopo **essersi insultati** hanno fatto la pace.

… or that took place before another event or process.

1. Add the prepositions **a**, **da**, or **di** where necessary. **

a) Vado _____ comprare il giornale.

b) Carlo ha molto _____ fare, non può _____ occuparsi dei bambini.

c) In agosto è meglio _____ prenotare il posto in treno.

d) Siamo stufi _____ sentire le vostre discussioni.

e) Hai qualcosa di fresco _____ bere?

f) Spesso basta _____ scusarsi gentilmente.

g) Monica è uscita senza _____ ringraziare.

h) Con i miei genitori non serve _____ discutere.

i) Non riesco _____ capire Pietro.

j) Siamo felici _____ rivederti.

k) Sandro è bravissimo _____ riparare la macchina.

l) Ho dimenticato _____ chiudere la porta a chiave.

m) Ci dispiace _____ non poter venire al matrimonio.

n) A che ora venite _____ prenderci?

2. Replace the present infinitive with the perfect infinitive. *

a) Siamo contenti **di incontrarvi.** _____

b) Mi dispiace **di litigare** con te. _____

c) Mi sembra **di lavorare** abbastanza. _____

d) Eva è contenta **di andare** a teatro. _____

3. Replace the sentence element in **bold** with an object pronoun. **

a) Non vorrei incontrare **i vicini.** _____

b) Dovresti telefonare **a Pietro.** _____

c) Sono felice di rivedere **i miei.** _____

d) Hai promesso di scrivere **a Pia.** _____

e) Mi pare di aver già visto **il film.** _____

lo

le

gli

li

li

The Present Participle

No, sono scivolata **facendo** la doccia.

Cos'è successo? Ti sei fatta male **sciando?**

1. What's happened? Did you hurt yourself while skiing? 2. No, I slipped while taking a shower.

Formation

The present participle is formed as follows:

and**are**:	**andando**	with verbs ending in **-are**, by attaching the ending **-ando** to the verb stem.
prend**ere**:	**prendendo**	with verbs ending in **-ere** and **-ire**, by attaching the ending **-endo** to the verb stem.
dorm**ire**:	**dormendo**	
fin**ire**:	**finendo**	
bere:	**bevendo**	A few verbs have an irregular present participle. With these verbs, the ending **-endo** is attached to the imperfect stem.
dire:	**dicendo**	
fare:	**facendo**	
trarre:	**traendo**	**Trarre**, **porre**, and **produrre** serve as models for forming the present participle of the other verbs ending in **-arre**, **-orre**, and **-urre**.
porre:	**ponendo**	
produrre:	**producendo**	

Stare + Present Participle

Ma dov'è Mario?

Sta facendo la doccia.

1. But where is Mario? 2. He's taking a shower.

1. Formation

(io)	**sto**	**scrivendo**	With **stare** + present participle,
(tu)	**stai**	**leggendo**	**stare** is conjugated with the
(lui/lei/Lei)	**sta**	**dormendo**	usual personal endings. The
(noi)	**stiamo**	**lavorando**	present participle is that of the
(voi)	**state**	**uscendo**	verb indicating the action being
(loro)	**stanno**	**mangiando**	described.

2. Position of the Personal Pronouns

+ Hai già risposto a Rita? ~ **Le** sto scrivendo adesso. Io torno a casa, **mi** sto annoiando.	The unstressed personal pronouns and the reflexive pronouns usually are placed before **stare**.

Use

+ Cosa **state facendo**?
~ **Stiamo guardando** le foto delle vacanze.

You can use **stare** + present participle to describe an action that is in progress.

+ Cosa **stavi facendo** ieri quando ho telefonato?
~ **Stavo lavorando** in giardino.

The action described may also be in the past. In this case, use the forms of the imperfect tense for **stare**.

+ Sai dov'è Pietro?
~ Credo che **stia cercando** qualcosa in cantina.
Non sapevo che tu **stessi studiando** il tedesco.

After a verb that requires the subjunctive, **stare** is in the present subjunctive or in the imperfect subjunctive.

The Present Participle as a Substitute for Dependent Clauses

Gianni ed io ci siamo conosciuti **chattando su Internet**. ①	**Prendendo il treno delle 7.55** siete a Roma alle 12.20. ②

1. Gianni and I met while chatting on the Internet. 2. If you take the 7:55 train, you'll be in Rome at 12:20.

The present participle can be used instead of dependent clauses if the actions of the main clause and the dependent clause occur simultaneously and have the same subject:

Viaggiando in treno incontro tanta gente simpatica.
(= **Quando viaggio** in treno ...)
When I travel by train, I meet a lot of nice people.

The present participle can replace dependent clauses that are introduced by **quando**, ...

Sono caduto **scendendo** le scale.
(= ... **mentre scendevo** le scale.)
I fell while going down the stairs.

... dependent clauses that are introduced by **mentre**, ...

Mangiando di meno dimagrisci.
(= **Se mangi** di meno ...)
If you eat less, you'll lose weight.

... dependent clauses that express a condition, ...

Essendo in ritardo, prendiamo un taxi.
(= **Siccome siamo** in ritardo ...)
Since we're running late, let's take a taxi.

... dependent clauses that indicate a cause ...

Pur conoscendo bene l'inglese, non capisco questo testo.
(= **Anche se conosco** bene ...)
Although I know English well, I don't understand this text.

... and dependent clauses that are introduced by **anche se** can be replaced with **pur** + present participle.

Position of the Personal Pronouns

Unstressed personal pronouns and reflexive pronouns are simply attached to the present participle.

Telefonando**gli** adesso lo disturbi.
If you phone him now, you'll disturb him.
Offendendo**mi** non ottieni niente.
By insulting me you won't gain anything.

The Present Participle

1. Answer the questions by putting the verbs supplied in the appropriate tense of the progressive form **stare** + present participle. **

a) Ma cosa fate?   giocare a carte

_____

b) Sai dov'è Franca?   vestirsi per uscire

_____

c) Dove sono i bambini?   guardare la televisione

_____

d) Che cosa facevate ieri alle sette?   cenare

_____

e) Ti ho telefonato, ma tu non c'eri.   fare la spesa

_____

f) Ma perché non risponde, Carlo?   ascoltare la musica.

_____

2. Replace the present participle with the dependent clause called for in each case. ***

a) Leggendo la lettera Maria piangeva.

<u>Mentre</u> _____

b) Passando per il centro farai più in fretta.

_____

c) Non avendo il tuo indirizzo elettronico ti ho mandato una lettera.

_____

d) Ho cambiato opinione su di te vedendoti giocare con tuo figlio.

_____

e) Pur avendo fretta Carla si è fermata a guardare le vetrine.

_____

f) Organizzandoti bene riuscirai a fare molte cose.

_____

g) Ho incontrato Piero uscendo dal cinema.

_____

l'indirizzo elettronico – *the e-mail address*
aver fretta – *to be in a hurry*

177

The Passive Voice

«La Repubblica» **viene letta da** molta gente.
①

«Il nome della rosa» **è stato tradotto** in molte lingue.
②

---

1. La Repubblica *is read by many people.* *2.* The Name of the Rose *has been translated into many languages.*

Active and Passive Sentences

An active sentence with a direct object can be changed into a passive sentence:

Active sentence: **I turisti** visitano **il duomo.**
The tourists visit the cathedral.

Passive sentence: **Il duomo** è/viene visitato **dai turisti.**
The cathedral is visited by the tourists.

In the passive sentence, the originator of the action can remain unmentioned:

Questa villa **è stata costruita** nel 1924.
I clienti **vengono trattati** bene.

If the originator of the action is mentioned, then the preposition **da** is used as a connector:

Questa villa è stata costruita **da un famoso architetto francese.**
I clienti vengono trattati bene **dal personale.**

The Simple Tenses

1. The Present Tense

(io)	**sono/vengo invitato, -a**
(tu)	**sei/vieni invitato, -a**
(lui/lei/Lei)	**è/viene invitato, -a**
(noi)	**siamo/veniamo invitati, -e**
(voi)	**siete/venite invitati, -e**
(loro)	**sono/vengono invitati, -e**

The present passive is formed with the present tense of **essere** or **venire** and the past participle of the main verb. The participle must agree in number and gender with the subject.

2. The Other Simple Tenses

Imperfect:	Il duomo	**era/veniva visitato.**
Future:	La mostra	**sarà/verrà visitata.**
Preterit:	I musei	**furono/vennero visitati.**
Conditional:	Le città	**sarebbero/verrebbero visitate.**

The other simple tenses are formed with the corresponding tense of **essere** or **venire** and the past participle of the main verb.

The passive voice with **essere** often tends to express a state or condition; the passive with **venire** always expresses an event or process. If you want to stress the event, then form the passive with **venire**:

La finestra **viene chiusa**.	*The window is [being] closed.*
Carla **viene invitata**.	*Carla is [being] invited.*

If, however, you want to describe a state or condition, use **essere**:

La finestra **è chiusa**.	*The window is closed.*
Carla **è invitata**.	*Carla is invited.*

3. Periphrastic Passive

If the originator is not mentioned, it is possible in Italian to use a circumlocution, that is, to express the passive in a roundabout or periphrastic way. You can choose among the following constructions:

Qui **si vende** frutta fresca.	*Fresh fruit is sold here.*

■ **si** (*one*) + verb in the 3rd person singular with a singular object.

Non **si accettano** carte di credito.	*Credit cards are not accepted.*

■ **si** (*one*) + verb in the 3rd person plural with a plural object.

Qui **costruiscono** un grande centro commerciale.	*A large shopping center is being built here.*

■ the 3rd person plural of the verb.

The Compound Tenses

La casa **è stata costruita** due anni fa.
①

La storia **era stata pubblicata** subito.
②

Credo che il film **sia stato lodato**.
③

Senza di te non **sarei** mai **stato invitato**.
④

---

1. The house was built two years ago. 2. The story was published immediately.
3. I think that the film was praised. 4. Without you I never would have been invited.

In the passive voice, you can form the compound tenses only with **essere** and the past participle of the main verb. **Essere** is put in the required tense.

1. The Present Perfect

(io)	sono	stato, -a	invitato, -a
(tu)	sei	stato, -a	invitato, -a
(lui/lei/Lei)	è	stato, -a	invitato, -a
(noi)	siamo	stati, -e	invitati, -e
(voi)	siete	stati, -e	invitati, -e
(loro)	sono	stati, -e	invitati, -e

2. The Other Compound Tenses

Past perfect:	(io)	ero	stato, -a	invitato, -a
Present perfect subjunctive:	(io)	sia	stato, -a	invitato, -a
Past perfect subjunctive:	(io)	fossi	stato, -a	invitato, -a
Conditional perfect:	(io)	sarei	stato, -a	invitato, -a

1. Which of the following sentences are passive sentences, and which are active sentences? Enter the corresponding letters in the appropriate boxes. **

a) Il viaggio verrà organizzato dall'Istituto italiano di cultura.

b) Il documentario è stato realizzato dalla televisione tedesca.

c) Nostro figlio viene a trovarci spesso.

d) Questa villa venne costruita nel 1925.

e) Ieri è venuto Claudio con la sua ragazza.

f) Il professor Salvi è stato da noi alcune settimane fa.

g) Credo che Claudio sia venuto in treno.

h) Sembra che questo quadro sia stato dipinto da Dalì.

Active sentences: ☐ ☐ ☐ ☐   Passive sentences: ☐ ☐ ☐ ☐

2. Put each sentence in the tenses given, as well as in the conditional and the subjunctive. *

a) Present: <u>I turisti vengono accolti molto bene.</u>

b) Imperfect: _____

c) Conditional: _____

d) Present Perfect: _____

d) Present subjunctive: <u>Credo che</u>_____

3. Fill in the blanks with the passive voice in the tense required. **

a) L'anno prossimo (costruire) _____ un

nuovo centro commerciale vicino alla stazione.

b) Il mese scorso (inaugurare) _____

la mostra di Mirò.

c) Ogni anno a Salsomaggiore (eleggere)_____

Miss Italia.

d) I Bronzi di Riace (trovare)_____ nel 1972.

il centro commerciale –
the shopping center
inaugurare – *to open,*
inaugurate
eleggere – *to elect,*
choose

The Impersonal Form *si*

The English impersonal *one* is rendered in Italian with **si**.

Quando **si viaggia** in macchina, **si hanno** spesso troppi bagagli.

When you're [one is] traveling by car, you often have [one often has] too much luggage.

Use

The use of **si**, unfortunately, is somewhat complicated.

In questo albergo **si sta** bene.
Se **si continua** per questa strada **si arriva** in centro.

After **si**, the verb is in the 3rd person singular

Da qui **si ha una bellissima vista** su tutta la città.
A casa nostra **si beve poca birra.**

After **si**, the verb is in the 3rd person singular if it is followed by a direct object in the singular.

Come **si preparano le lasagne** verdi?
Qui **si mangiano delle ottime trenette** al pesto.

After **si**, the verb is in the 3rd person plural if it refers to a direct object in the plural.

Chissà se **ci si metterà** d'accordo.
In inverno **ci si ammala** facilmente.

In conjunction with a reflexive verb, this form results: **ci si** + verb.

Quando **si è malati** si dovrebbe stare a casa.
Quando **si diventa padri** si cambia; **si diventa** più **pazienti.**

With **si** + **è** or **diventa**, the following adjective / noun is in the masculine plural.

Chissà cosa fa Carlo; non **lo si** vede più.
Who knows what Carlo is doing; one no longer sees him.

In conjunction with an unstressed personal pronoun, **si** is placed second.

Non **se ne** parla più.
It is no longer spoken of.

In conjunction with **ne**, **si** becomes **se** and is placed first.

Si in the Compound Tenses

All'invito **si è mangiato** bene e **si sono fatti** discorsi interessanti.

At the party, people ate well and had interesting conversations.

With the impersonal **si**, the compound tenses always are formed with **essere**. The variability of the past participle depends on three criteria:

Si è partiti presto e **si è arrivati** verso le sei.
Durante il viaggio **ci si è fermati** solo due volte.

verso – *toward*
durante – *during*

If the verb in the personal form is conjugated with **essere** (for example, **sono partito** and **mi sono fermato**), then the past participle in the impersonal form ends in **-i**.

Durante le vacanze **si è giocato** a tennis.
Si è mangiato molto bene, ma **si è** anche **pagato** molto.

If the verb in the personal form is conjugated with **avere** (**ho giocato**, **ho mangiato**), then the past participle ends in **-o**.

Si è bevuto un ottimo prosecco.
Si è fatta una lunga passeggiata.
Si sono comprati alcuni souvenir.
Si sono fatte alcune fotografie.

If the impersonal verb is followed by a direct object (here: **prosecco**, **passeggiata**, **souvenir**, **fotografie**), then **essere** and the past participle agree in number and gender with this object.

183

Other Ways to Express the Impersonal *One*

Se **uno è prudente** non succede niente.
If you're [one is] careful, nothing will happen.

The impersonal *one* can be expressed with **uno** (*one*), ...

Bisogna stare attenti.
It's necessary to be careful. / One has to be careful.

... with **bisogna** + infinitive, ...

Se non **vuoi** avere problemi **devi** stare calmo.
If you don't want to have problems, you have to stay calm.

... with the 2nd person singular (*you*), ...

Stanno restaurando il duomo.
They're restoring the cathedral.

... or with the 3rd person plural.

1. What is typically Italian? Write it by filling in the impersonal form **si**
and the appropriate verb form. **

a) (bere) _____ il caffè in piedi.

b) (incontrarsi) _____ in piazza.

c) Tra amici (salutarsi) _____ con un abbraccio o un

bacio.

d) A tavola (usare) _____ lo stuzzicadenti.

e) (parcheggiare) _____ in doppia fila.

f) (consumare) _____ molte verdure.

g) (preparare) _____ molti sughi freschi.

h) (usare) _____ poco la panna e il burro.

lo stuzzicadenti –
the toothpick

la fila – *the file,*
rank, row

2. Fill in the blanks in the questions using the impersonal form **si** and
the appropriate form of the present tense. **

a) Come (prepara) _____ gli spaghetti alle vongole?

b) Dove (mangiare) _____ bene senza pagare troppo?

c) Dove (comprare) _____ i migliori grissini?

d) Come (festeggiare) _____ da voi il Natale?

e) Dove (trovare) _____ dei prodotti biologici?

f) A che ora (andare) _____ a cena, da voi?

3. In the following sentences, mark the correct verb form and fill in the
missing endings. **

a) Quando si è/sono giovan_____ non si pensa/pensano alla vecchiaia.

b) Nel nostro quartiere si è/sono costruit_____ troppo.

c) Nel centro storico si è/sono restaurat_____ parecchi vecchi edifici.

d) Quando si è/sono brill_____ non si dovrebbe/dovrebbero guidare.

e) Al vernissage si è/sono vist_____ tanta gente dello spettacolo.

f) Se si è/sono timid_____ si diventa/diventano ross_____ facilmente.

la vecchiaia –
the old age

brillo – *tipsy*

timido – *shy, timid*
gente dello spettacolo –
show business people

Negation
Negation with *no*

Vuoi anche tu un caffè?
①

No, io **no**.
②

Perché **no**?
③

Ne ho appena
bevuto uno.
④

1. Do you want [a cup of] coffee too? 2. No, I don't. 3. Why not? 4. I just drank one.

+ Vuoi una birra? ~ **No** grazie, sto bene così. Allora, venite sì o **no**?	**No** stands alone or occurs in sentences or parts of sentences without a verb, or also at the end of the sentence.
+ Viene anche Pietro? ~ Credo/Penso/Spero **di no**.	After **credere**, **dire**, **pensare**, and **sperare**, **no** is linked with **di**.
No, grazie.	**No** means *no* in English.
Io sto bene, lui **no**. Perché **no**?	At the end of the sentence, it generally means *not*.
Allora, ti decidi di telefonare **sì o no**?	In the expression **sì o no**, however, it means *no*.

Si is also linked with **di**:
Credo/Penso/ Spero di sì.

Negation with *non*

Sta lavorando Michele?
①

No, **non** sta lavorando.
②

Perché **non** lavora?
③

Perché **non** ne ha voglia.
④

1. Is Michele working? 2. No, he's not working. 3. Why isn't he working?
4. Because he has no wish to.

Michele **non** lavora molto *Michele doesn't work much.*	**Non** is rendered in English as *not* ...
Non ha voglia di lavorare. *He has no wish to work.*	... or as *no*.

Non cannot stand alone. It is found:

Stasera **non esco**. Oggi **non ho fatto** colazione. Pia **non è uscita**.	before the conjugated verb or before the auxiliary verb in compound tenses.
+ Dov'è il mio passaporto? ~ **Non lo** so, **non l'ho** visto.	before the pronoun in the combination unstressed personal pronoun + verb.
+ Ti è piaciuto il film? ~ **No, non** mi è piaciuto.	together with **no** in order to intensify negative responses.

Multiple Negations

Non capisco **niente**. ①	Pietro **non** racconta **mai niente**. ②

1. I understand nothing. / I don't understand anything. 2. Pietro never describes anything.

1. The Elements of Negation

The following negations consist of several elements of negation. Here are some ways of translating them into English:

Non legge	**ancora**.	▶ not yet
Non legge	**affatto**.	▶ not at all
Non legge	**mai**.	▶ never
Non legge	**mica**.	▶ not (at all)
Non vede	**nessuno**.	▶ not anyone, no one
Non legge	**niente/nulla**.	▶ nothing
Non legge	**neanche/nemmeno/** **neppure**.	▶ not even
Non legge	**né** riviste **né** libri.	▶ neither … nor
Non legge	**più**.	▶ no more, not anymore

Mica is a colloquial expression.

The elements of negation can also be combined. They do not always appear as negations in an English translation, however.

Non ti telefonerò **mai più**.	I will never telephone you again.
Non ti presterò **mai più niente**.	I will never lend you anything again.
Non presterò **mai più niente a nessuno**.	I will never again lend anything to anyone.

2. The Position of Elements of Negation

Pierino **non** cammina **ancora**. **Non** siamo **affatto** stanchi. **Non** andiamo **mai** a teatro. **Non** è **mica** un bambino! Qui **non** conosco **nessuno**. Per Natale **non** le regalo **niente**. **Non** le regalo **neanche** un libro. A Pia **non** piace **né** il mare **né** la montagna. Carlo **non** va **più** a scuola.	When several elements of negation appear in a negation, **non** precedes the conjugated verb or the unstressed personal pronoun. The particles of negation usually follow the conjugated verb.

The elements of negation occupy these positions:

Non compro **niente**.	They enclose the conjugated verb.
Non posso comprare **niente**.	They enclose the conjugated verb and the infinitive.
Non ho comprato **niente**.	They enclose the auxiliary verb and the past participle in the compound tenses.
Non sto comprando **niente**.	They enclose **stare** + present participle.
Non viene comprato **niente**. **Non** è stato comprato **niente**.	In the passive voice, they enclose the conjugated form of **venire** or **essere** and the past participle.

If the predicate consists of several verb elements, then the second element of negation in **non … ancora**, **non … mai**, **non … mica**, and **non più** occupies a different position. The second element of negation is found:

Non posso **ancora** partire.	between the conjugated verb and the infinitive.
Non sono **ancora** partito. **Non** ho **ancora** mangiato.	between the auxiliary verb and the past participle in the compound tenses.
Non sto **ancora** partendo.	between **stare** and the present participle.

Non viene **ancora** venduto. **Non** è **ancora** stato venduto.	between the conjugated form of **venire** or **essere** and the past participle, in the passive voice.

Mai, **nemmeno/neanche/neppure**, **niente/nulla**, **né ... né**, and **nessuno** can also appear at the beginning of the sentence. In this case, they are used without **non** and carry special weight. This use is not very common, however.

Mai ti lascerò solo! **Nessuno** sarà migliore di noi! **Nemmeno** noi lasciava entrare! **Niente** lo convince!	*Never will I leave you alone!* *No one will be better than we!* *Not even us did he allow to enter.* *Nothing convinces him!*

Negation

1. Complete the dialogues with **no** or **non**. If necessary, add the preposition **di**. **

a) + Avete visto il nuovo videoclip degli Avion Travel?

~ Io sì, loro due _____ so.

b) + Tu ascolti la musica jazz?

~ Normalmente _____ . E tu l'ascolti?

+ _____ , la musica jazz proprio _____ l'ascolto mai.

c) + Hai preso la medicina, oggi?

~_____ , oggi _____ l'ho ancora presa.

d) + Secondo te è troppo tardi per telefonare al dottor Panzini?

~ Penso _____ .

disturbare – to disturb
ingrassare – to gain weight

+ _____ lo disturbo, allora.

~ _____ , _____ credo.

e) + Vuoi una pasta?

~ Grazie, ma a quest'ora _____ mangio niente.

+ _____ vuoi ingrassare, vero?

~ Ma _____ ! _____ la prendo perché stasera sono invitata

a cena e se prendo una pasta adesso, stasera _____ ho

appetito.

2. Who is Silvia? Put the words in the correct order, and you will learn more about her. **

a) Silvia – è – simpatica – molto – non

_____

b) molto – non – è –nemmeno – carina

_____

c) invita – nessuno – mai – non

_____

d) esce – non – la sera – mai

_____

e) di – interessa – niente – si – non

_____

f) così – telefona – le – nessuno – e – va – a – nessuno – trovarla

_____

_____

3. Translate the following sentences dealing with eating and drinking. ***

a) I didn't eat much today.

_____

b) Sonia eats neither meat nor fish.

_____

c) Stefania doesn't eat dessert. She doesn't even eat fruit.

_____

_____

d) The children haven't eaten breakfast yet.

_____

e) I don't eat much for breakfast.

_____

f) In the evenings I never eat.

_____

g) Stefano doesn't want to drink any more wine in the evenings.

_____

h) We've never eaten polenta before.

_____

i) We're not eating yet.

_____

Word Order
The Declarative Sentence

> I miei genitori hanno
> una nuova macchina.
> ①

> Ieri hanno fatto una
> gita in montagna.
> ②

---

1. My parents have a new car. 2. Yesterday they took a trip to the mountains.

1. The Declarative Sentence with No Mention of Place and Time

Word order in a normal declarative sentence is as follows:

Subject	Predicate	Objects
Carlo	ha comprato	dei fiori.
Luciana	ha regalato	una cravatta a suo marito.

If a direct object and an indirect object occur in a sentence, then the direct object precedes the indirect one:

Subject	Predicate	Direct Object	Indirect Object
Marco	fa	l'insegnante.	
Marco	ha studiato	lingue.	
Marco	insegna	l'italiano	agli stranieri.
Marco	scrive		ai suoi amici.

> In Italian, the auxiliary verb and the participle must not be separated:
> Marco **ha studiato** lingue.
> *Marco has studied languages.*

If the direct object or the indirect object is replaced by an unstressed pronoun, then this pronoun precedes the predicate:

> Marco insegna **l'italiano agli stranieri**.
>
> Marco **lo** insegna agli stranieri.   Marco **gli** insegna l'italiano.

Even if both objects are replaced by an unstressed pronoun, these pronouns precede the predicate:

> Marco **glielo** insegna da due anni.

> ▶ The Position of the Unstressed Object Pronouns, p. 71

2. The Declarative Sentence with Mention of Place and Time

If information about time and place appears in a sentence, then this order generally prevails:

Oggi ho un appuntamento.	expressions of time at the beginning of the sentence.
Ho un appuntamento **al bar**.	expressions of place at the end of the sentence.
Oggi ho un appuntamento **al bar**.	This also holds true when both place and time are stated in a sentence.
Ho un appuntamento **al bar, oggi**.	Expressions of time and place can also occur at the end of the sentence, usually in this order: place – time. In this case, the time expression is emphasized.

l'appuntamento –
the appointment, date, engagement

The Dependent Clause

Anche se avrò molto lavoro, domenica prossima voglio fare una gita al mare.	**Siccome mio marito non mangia le cipolle**, non posso mai fare il fegato alla veneziana.
①	②

1. Even though I'll have a lot of work, I want to take a trip to the ocean next Sunday.
2. Since my husband doesn't eat onions, I can never make "fegato alla veneziana" [liver and onions, Venetian style].

In Italian, the dependent clause uses the same word order as the main clause:

Main Clause:		Subject	Predicate	Object
		Rosa	compra	un dolce
Dependent Clause:	Conjunction	Subject	Predicate	Object
	perché	**suo marito**	**ha invitato**	**degli amici.**

Be sure to place the predicate before the object in the dependent clause as well.

!

The Interrogative Sentence

In Italian, as in English, you can ask a question with or without a question word.

1. Mama, when will Santa Claus come? 2. The day after tomorrow. 3. And will he bring me a lot of presents?

The Interrogative Sentence Without a Question Word

Il tuo collega abita fuori città? ①

Lavora nel tuo ufficio, il signor Renzi? ②

1. Does your colleague live outside of town? 2. Does Mr. Renzi work in your office?

With a question that contains no question word, you have the option to place the subject either first or last in the sentence.

Subject	Predicate	Complement
Carla	si è sposata	in chiesa?

In an interrogative sentence without a question word, the word order may be the same as in a declarative sentence. The question is expressed merely by raising the voice.

Predicate	Complement	Subject
Si è sposata	in chiesa,	Carla?

In an interrogative sentence without a question word, the subject may, however, be placed at the end of the sentence.

If the subject is expressed only in the personal ending of the verb, the word order in a question remains the same as in a declarative sentence:

Declarative sentence:	Si è sposata in chiesa.	*She got married in church.*
Interrogative sentence:	Si è sposata in chiesa?	*Did she get married in church? She got married in church?*

The Interrogative Sentence with a Question Word

① **Quando** è tornato Gianni?

② **Dove** hai comprato il computer?

---

1. When did Gianni return? 2. Where did you buy the computer?

1. Word Order

① **Chi** c'era all'invito?

② Al matrimonio **chi** c'era?

---

1. Who all came to the party? 2. Who all was at the wedding?

> If a question contains a question word, you usually have two possibilities with regard to word order.

Most interrogative sentences that contain a question word follow this word order: question word – predicate – subject and / or complement.

Question Word	Predicate	Subject/Complement/Indication of Time and Place
Come	stai?	
Chi	viene	stasera?
Dove	hai messo	il giornale?
Cosa	hai detto	a Franca?
Perché	è partito	Gianni?

> **Tip!** With a question using **perché**, you have three options for word order:
> **Perché Pia** è triste?
> **Perché** è triste **Pia**?
> **Pia perché** è triste?

Perché **Gianni** è partito? Perché **Carla** si è sposata a Berlino?	With a question containing **perché**, the subject also can precede the predicate.
Tuo marito come sta? **Gianni** perché è partito? **Stasera** chi viene? **A Franca** cosa hai detto?	With most questions that contain a subject and / or a complement, these elements also can be placed at the beginning of the sentence. This lends them emphasis.
Il giornale quando **lo** leggi? **La spesa** chi **la** fa? **La carne** come **la** prepari? **Gli occhiali** dove **li** hai messi? **Le tue amiche** quando **le** inviti?	If the complement is a direct object, then it has to be referred to again by adding the appropriate unstressed object pronoun.

2. Invariable Question Words

These question words are invariable in form. Their meaning, however, changes in connection with a preposition and depending on the following verb.

> Con chi sei uscito? ①

> Chi hai incontrato ieri? ②

> A chi hai telefonato? ③

1. With whom did you go out? 2. Whom did you meet yesterday? 3. Whom did you telephone?

Chi

Chi è quel signore? **Chi** hai invitato?	**Chi** means *who* or *whom*.

In connection with prepositions, **chi** usually is translated as:

A chi hai scritto?	– *whom / to whom*
Con chi esci?	– *with whom*
Di chi parlate?	– *about whom*
Per chi è il caffè?	– *for whom*

Use **di chi è / sono** to ask about the owner of an object:

Di chi sono questi guanti?	*To whom do these gloves belong?*

Che cosa

Che cos'è questo? **Che cosa** succede?	**Che cosa** means *what*. It is used to ask about things, facts, and circumstances.

In colloquial speech, **che cosa** often is shortened to **cosa** or **che**:
Cosa c'è da bere?
Che fai?

In connection with prepositions, **che cosa** is translated as:

A che cosa pensi?	– *about what*
Con che cosa si pulisce?	– *with what*
Di che cosa parlate?	– *about what, of what*

Che

pulire – *to polish, clean*
la taglia – *the dress size*

Che tipo è il nuovo direttore? **Che** taglia ha, signora?	**Che** means *what*, *which* and precedes a noun.
Che ora è? **Che** tempo fa?	Use **che** to inquire about the time and the weather.
A che ora parte il treno?	Use a **che** to ask about a point in time.

Come

Come si arriva al Duomo? **Come** stai? **Come** ti chiami?	**Come** means *how*.

Dove

Dove sono i bambini? **Dove** andate? **Di dove** sei? **Da dove** vieni a quest'ora?	**Dove** means *where*. With **andare** it means *(to) where, where to*. Use **di dove** to ask about someone's place of birth / hometown. **Da dove** means *from where, where from*.

Quando

Quando vai in vacanza?	**Quando** means *when*.

In connection with prepositions, **quando** means:

Da quando sei tornato? **Fino a/fin quando** rimani?	– *how long* (used to ask how much time has elapsed since an action started) – *until when*

Perché

+ **Perché** sei qui? ~ **Perché** ti voglio vedere.	**Perché** means *why*. In the response, **perché** means *because*.

3. Variable Question Words

Quali film di Antonioni hai visto?

①

Quale ti è piaciuto di più?

②

There are two variable question words: **quale** and **quanto**.

1. Which films of Antonioni's have you seen? 2. Which did you like best?

Quale – quali

Singular	Use **quale** to ask about a person or thing as part of a certain group or quantity. It is translated as *which*.
Quale pullover preferisci? **Quale** rivista leggi?	

The Interrogative Sentence

Tip!

Whether you ask your question with **quale** or **quali** depends on the grammatical number of the noun you are inquiring about.

Plural	Use **quali** to ask about several persons or things. It is translated as *which*.
Quali libri hai letto? **Quali** sono le Sue valigie?	

In connection with prepositions, **quale** and **quali** mean:

Con quale treno arrivi? **Con quale** amica viaggi? **Per quale** collega è il vino?	– *with which* – *with which* – *for which*
A quale dei tuoi amici hai prestato la macchina?	Use **a quale** to ask about a person who is the indirect object in an Italian sentence.
A quali vicini mandi una cartolina?	Use **a quali** to ask about several persons who are the indirect object.
Qual è il tuo indirizzo? **Qual era** il vostro albergo?	**Quale** is shortened to **qual** before **è** and **era**.

In colloquial speech, **quale** and **quali** before a noun are often replaced by **che**:
A quale / **A che** nome? *In what name?*

Quanto – quanta – quanti – quante

	masculine	feminine
Singular	**Quanto** vino vuoi?	**Quanta** gente c'era?
Plural	**Quanti** figli hai?	**Quante** lingue sai?

Quanto agrees in number and gender with the noun it modifies. It is used to inquire about:

Quanto costa questo vestito? **Quanto costano** le scarpe verdi?	price (*how much*),
Quanto (tempo) rimani qui? **Quanti anni** hai?	duration (*how long*), age (*how old*).

In connection with prepositions, these forms of **quanto** are used:

Con quanti amici vai in vacanza? **Per quante** persone è la cena? **A quanta** gente hai dato l'indirizzo? **Di quanti** soldi disponete?	– *with how many* – *for how many* – *(to) how many* – *(of) how many*

disporre di – *to have the use of, dispose of, have available*

1. These sentences tell about a certain Claudia. You will learn something about her by combining the elements in each item to form a declarative sentence. **

a) 28 anni – Claudia – ha

_____

b) sposata – è – non – perché – l'uomo giusto – ha – trovato – non – ancora

_____

_____

c) è – innamorata – per il momento – neanche – non

_____

d) quasi mai – in casa – la sera – è – non

_____

e) va – il sabato – in discoteca – spesso

_____

f) fa – niente – la domenica – non

_____

g) una passeggiata – fa – nemmeno – non

_____

h) un appartamento – da qualche mese – sta cercando – in città

_____

i) abitare – più – fuori città – vuole – non – anche se – meno caro – è

_____

_____

2. Now, using the following words, ask Claudia a few questions. **

a) vai – la sera – dove ?

_____

b) tutta la domenica – fai – a casa – che cosa?

_____

c) vuoi – fuori città – non – abitare – perché – più?

_____

Word Order

3. Complete the following questions by adding the appropriate interrogative pronouns. Three interrogative pronouns will be left over. **

A chi – Quando – Che – Come – Da dove – Dove – Perché – Quanto – Quanti – Qual è – Da quanto tempo – Di dove

a) _____ ti chiami?

b) _____ sei?

c) _____ abiti?

d) _____ anni hai?

e) _____ lavoro fai?

f) _____ sei qui a Roma?

g) _____ il tuo numero di telefono?

rivedersi – *to meet again, see each other again*

h) _____ possiamo rivederci?

i) _____ non vuoi rispondermi?

4. Translate the following questions. ***

a) May I ask you something?

_____

b) How much do these shoes cost?

_____

c) Which bus goes to the train station?

_____

d) What time is it?

_____

e) At what time does the film begin?

_____

f) Do you like the United States?

_____

g) What is the weather like in your country?

_____

The Relative Clause

Come si chiama la collega **che ha telefonato ieri?**
①

Marta.
②

③
È la collega **con cui sei stato a Milano?**

No, Marta è la collega **il cui marito ha costruito il nuovo centro commerciale.**
④

Italian usually does not use a comma before a relative clause.

---

1. What's the name of the colleague who telephoned yesterday? 2. Marta. 3. Is she the colleague with whom you were in Milan? 4. No, Marta is the colleague whose husband built the new shopping center.

Relative clauses are introduced by relative pronouns. The relative pronoun generally is placed directly after the noun it modifies. Most relative clauses are not joined to the main clause by a comma.
Only relative clauses whose information is unimportant for understanding the main clause are separated by commas, as here:

> Ieri ho incontrato Maria, **che non vedevo da tempo.**
> *Yesterday I ran into Maria, whom I haven't seen for a long time.*
> Marta, **che amava tanto la sua vita da single,** si è sposata un mese fa.
> *Marta, who loved her life as a single person so much, got married a month ago.*

The Relative Clause with *che*

Ho visto il film **che** mi hai consigliato. A me però non piacciono i film **che** finiscono male.
①

Hai già letto il libro **che** ti ho regalato?
②

---

1. I saw the film that you recommended to me. But I don't like films that end badly.
2. Have you already read the book that I gave you as a present?

Most relative clauses are introduced by the relative pronoun **che**. **Che** is invariable.

Under no circumstances can you use **chi** as the subject.

C'è un signore **che** vuole parlare con te.
Quanto costa la borsetta nera **che** è in vetrina?

Che can serve as the subject, with these meanings:
that, which

Le pesche **che** ho comprato al mercato sono dolcissime.
Questo è il cd **che** mi ha regalato Piero.

Che can also be the object, with the same meanings:
that, which

Tip! Always memorize verbs together with their complement! Then you will know which relative pronoun to use. For example:
**aiutare qu ▶ che
dare a qu ▶ a cui
parlare di qu ▶ di cui**

The Relative Clause with *cui*

È Mario il collega **a cui** hai venduto la macchina? ①

No, Mario è il collega **di cui** ti ho parlato ieri. ②

1. Is Mario the colleague to whom you sold the car? 2. No, Mario is the colleague about whom I talked to you yesterday.

When **in cui** refers to a location, you can replace it with **dove**:
Roma è una città **dove/in cui** mi piacerebbe vivere.

Chi sono i ragazzi **con cui** esci ogni sera?
Come si chiama il film **di cui** mi hai parlato ieri sera?
Roma è una città **in cui** mi piacerebbe vivere.
Carla è l'amica **(a) cui** mando sempre gli auguri di Natale.

Cui is invariable and is used in connection with a preposition.
Cui cannot stand alone.
Only the preposition **a** can be omitted.

The Relative Clause with *il quale, la quale, i quali, le quali*

È Mario il collega **al quale** hai venduto la macchina? ①

No, Mario è il collega **del quale** ti ho parlato ieri. ②

1. Is Mario the colleague to whom you sold the car? 2. No, Mario is the colleague about whom I talked to you yesterday.

Il quale, **la quale**, **i quali**, and **le quali** can stand in for **cui**.

il quale: È un programma **con il quale/con cui** si lavora molto bene.
È quello l'uomo **del quale/di cui** si è innamorata Chiara?

i quali: La Francia e la Svizzera sono paesi **nei quali/in cui** si vive bene.

la quale: La ditta **per la quale/per cui** lavoro è tedesca.
Ecco la casa **nella quale/in cui** ho abitato tanti anni.
le quali: Rosa e Pia sono le amiche **con le quali/con cui** sono
andata in Inghilterra.

la ditta – the company

Il quale, **la quale**, **i quali**, and **le quali** agree in number and gender with
the noun they modify.
Remember that the prepositions **a**, **da**, **di**, **in**, and **su** combine with the
definite article of **il / la quale** and **i / le quali**.

The Relative Clause with *chi*

Chi scrive molto ha bisogno
del computer.
①

Non aprire la porta **a chi**
non conosci!
②

Chi can be used
alone or with a
preposition.

1. *Anyone who writes a lot needs the computer.* 2. *Don't open the door to someone (whom) you don't know!*

Chi desidera partecipare alla gita lo dica al receptionist. **Chi** tornerà dopo mezzanotte troverà la porta chiusa. Non presto la macchina **a chi** non conosco. Io esco solo **con chi** mi piace. Ho saputo **per chi** lavora Enzo.	**Chi** is used only in a general sense and cannot refer to a specific person. **Chi** means *who, whoever, anyone who, someone who.* Depending on the verb, **a chi** means *to anyone whom,* etc. **Con chi** means *with whomever,* etc., and **per chi**, *for whom,* etc.

il receptionist – the receptionist

The Relative Clause with *quello che, ciò che*

Pago solo **ciò che** ho mangiato
e bevuto veramente.
①

È vero **quello che**
raccontano gli altri?
②

1. *I'm paying only for what I actually ate and drank.* 2. *Is it true what the others say?*

Ciò che vorrei sapere, è la tua opinione sul nuovo governo. È tutto **quello che** sappiamo.	**Quello che** and **ciò che** are invariable and have the same meaning. They usually are translated as *what* or *that.*

l'opinione – the opinion
il governo – the government

ereditare – to inherit

Ho pensato **a quello che** mi hai detto ieri. Ha vissuto **con ciò che** aveva ereditato da suo zio.	**Quello che** and **ciò che** are also used with prepositions. Here, **a quello che** means *about what* and **con ciò che** means *with what*.

The Relative Clause with *il che*

Stamattina ha telefonato il dott. Renzi, **il che** mi ha fatto molto piacere.
①

Carla vuole perdere dieci chili, **il che** non sarà facile.
②

---

1. This morning Dr. Renzi phoned, which made me very happy. 2. Carla wants to lose 10 kilos, which will not be easy.

Tip! Instead of **il che**, you also can say **e ciò** or **ciò che**: Ha scritto Rita, **il che/ ciò che/ e ciò** è raro.

Il che is invariable. It refers to the entire preceding clause or to the statement contained in it, and it usually is translated as *which*.

The Relative Clause with *il cui, la cui, i cui, le cui*

La prima città italiana **il cui** centro storico è stato chiuso al traffico è Bologna.
①

Visconti, **i cui** film sono conosciuti nel mondo intero, era un uomo molto affascinante.
②

---

1. The first Italian city whose historic center was closed to traffic is Bologna. 2. Visconti, whose films are known worldwide, was a very fascinating man.

Il cui, **la cui**, **i cui**, and **le cui** agree in number and gender with the following noun. They are rendered in English with *whose*.

attirare – to attract
valere – to be worth
la fortuna – the fortune
l'artista – the artist
privo di – devoid of, free from

il cui: Bologna è la prima città italiana **il cui centro storico** è stato chiuso al traffico.
la cui: La Sardegna è una regione **la cui bellezza** attira molti turisti.
i cui: Van Gogh, **i cui quadri** valgono una fortuna, è morto povero.
le cui: Heinz Spoerli è un artista **le cui coreografie** non sono prive di ironia.

Il cui, **la cui**, **i cui**, and **le cui** are also used with prepositions.

La ditta **dei cui** prodotti sto parlando si trova nel Friuli.

1. Fill in the blanks in the questions, using the relative pronouns supplied. *

a) C'è una città tedesca _____ Le piacerebbe vivere?

b) Ci sono persone _____ non telefona volentieri?

c) Ci sono cose _____ Lei non potrebbe mai mangiare?

d) Conosce una persona _____ può parlare di tutto?

e) Ci sono animali _____ ha particolarmente paura?

f) C'è uno scrittore _____ Le piace particolarmente?

che
con cui
a cui
che
in cui
di cui

2. Match the two columns to form complete sentences. *

a) Chi è la ragazza

b) Non è facile vivere con qualcuno

c) Ecco i libri

d) Mi stai raccontando delle cose

e) C'è una cosa

f) Bravo, hai fatto un esame

1. che pensa solo al lavoro.

2. della quale abbiamo tutti bisogno.

3. con la quale ti ho visto ieri?

4. del quale puoi essere contento.

5. dei quali ti ho parlato.

6. alle quali non posso credere

3. Fill in the blanks in the passage below, using the appropriate relative pronouns. ***

a) Ragazzi, vi prego di non fare confusione perché visitiamo ora la chiesa di S. Vitale _____ è molto antica. b) La chiesa _____ ci troviamo è stata costruita nel VI secolo. c) Fate attenzione soprattutto ai mosaici _____ abbiamo parlato a scuola e _____ siamo venuti. d) I colori _____ gli artisti hanno usato sono bellissimi. e) Spero che ricordiate la lezione _____ abbiamo parlato di questi capolavori. f) I mosaici _____ dovrete poi scrivere le vostre impressioni, rappresentano l'imperatore Giustiniano e l'imperatrice Teodora. g) Quando avrete finito la visita, uscite dalla chiesa e ritornate nel piazzale _____ siamo venuti.

la confusione – *the confusion, pandemonium*
il colore – *the color*
il capolavoro – *the masterpiece*
l'impressione – *the impression*
l'imperatore – *the emperor*

The Relative Clause

4. Translate the sentences below. ***

a) You have to say what you know.

_____

b) The book that you gave me is very interesting.

_____

c) I no longer know what I wanted to say.

_____

d) Yesterday Enrico phoned me, which made me very happy.

_____

e) Anyone who is tired can stay at home.

_____

f) Anyone who doesn't like classical music can go to the disco.

_____

g) On Sunday we saw the film about which you told us.

_____

h) What is the name of the boy whose mother does yoga with you?

_____

i) Is that the coat for which you paid 500 euros?

_____

5. And in conclusion, a little guessing game. What is being described in each case?

a) È qualcosa da cui esce l'acqua.   la f _____

b) È qualcosa con cui si fa il vino.   l'u _____

c) È un oggetto in cui si mettono i soldi.   il p _____

d) È una cosa con cui si paga senza soldi.   la c _____

e) È un oggetto per cui si può spendere molto. il q _____

f) È una cosa davanti a cui ci si deve fermare. il s _____

The Conditional Sentence

Se dimagrisco, mi **compro** un bikini. ①

Se **fossi** più alta e più snella, **potrei fare** la modella. ②

1. If I lose weight, I'll buy myself a bikini. 2. If I were taller and thinner, I could work as a model.

There are real and unreal conditional sentences. They consist of a main clause and a dependent clause. The dependent clause, in this case also called the **se** clause, expresses a condition. The resulting consequence is contained in the main clause.

> The main clause can also precede the **se** clause:
> **Mi compro** un bikini, **se demagrisco**.
> **Potrei fare** la modella, **se fossi** più alta e più snella.

The Real Conditional Clause

Se mi accompagni, mi **fai** piacere. ①	Se sai l'inglese, **troverai** facilmente lavoro. ②	Se non **stai** bene, **dimmelo.** ③

1. If you come with me, I'll be glad. 2. If you know English, you will easily find work.
3. If you don't feel well, tell me.

The real conditional sentence is used when you start with a possible condition and draw from it a conclusion that can be fulfilled.

Sequence of Tenses in the Real Conditional Sentence

se clause	main clause
Se mi **accompagni,**	mi **fai** piacere.
Se **sai** l'inglese,	**trovi/troverai** facilmente lavoro.
Se non **stai** bene,	**dimmelo.**

In the **se** clause, the present tense is used, and in the main clause:

▶ the present tense, if the consequence occurs simultaneously.
▶ the present tense or the simple future, if the consequence will occur in the future.
▶ the imperative, if a command or demand follows.

The Unreal Conditional Sentence

Se conoscessi la verità, te la **direi**.	**Se fossimo partiti** prima, adesso **saremmo** già a casa.	**Se ti fossi messo** il cappotto, **non ti saresti ammalato**.
①	②	③

1. If I knew the truth, I would tell it to you. 2. If we had left earlier, we would already be at home. 3. If you had worn the coat, you would not have gotten sick.

The unreal conditional sentence is used when you set out from an unlikely or impossible condition and draw an improbable or unfulfillable conclusion from it.

Sequence of Tenses in the Unreal Conditional Sentence

se clause	main clause
Se conoscessi la verità,	te la **direi** / te l'**avrei detta**.
Se fossi più snella,	**metterei** il bikini.
Se tu facessi un po' di sport,	**staresti** meglio.

If the unlikely or impossible condition refers to the present time, then the imperfect subjunctive is used in the **se** clause and in the main clause:

▸ the conditional, if the consequence would occur in the present time.
▸ the conditional perfect, if the consequence would have occurred in the past.

se clause	main clause
Se fossimo partiti prima,	adesso **saremmo** già a casa.
Se tu avessi letto il giornale,	adesso **saresti** informato.
Se ti fossi messo il cappotto,	non **ti saresti ammalato.**
Se aveste fatto attenzione,	non **sarebbe successo** niente.

If the condition refers to the past, then the past perfect subjunctive is used in the **se** clause and in the main clause:

▸ the conditional, if the consequence would occur in the present.
▸ the conditional perfect, if the consequence would have occurred in the past.

In colloquial speech, the imperfect often is used in unreal conditional sentences in the past:
Se ti mettevi il cappotto, non **ti ammalavi.**

1. Can you identify the unreal conditional sentences? Mark them. *

a) ☐ Non ti avrei mai detto la verità, se avessi saputo quanto ti saresti arrabbiato.

b) ☐ Se non troviamo un taxi, dobbiamo tornare a piedi.

c) ☐ Se non avessi partecipato al torneo di tennis, non ti avrei mai conosciuto.

    partecipare – to participate
il raffreddore – the head cold, common cold

d) ☐ Non avresti il raffreddore se ti fossi messo il cappello.

e) ☐ Appena saremo a casa ti manderemo una e-mail.

f) ☐ Che ne dite, andiamo al lago se domenica fa bel tempo?

g) ☐ Saremmo felici se tu potessi venire con noi.

h) ☐ Andrei io a fare la spesa se non dovessi andare dal medico.

i) ☐ Se mi aspettate vengo con voi.

2. Complete the sentences by putting the verbs in parentheses in the present tense or in the imperfect subjunctive. Use the same person found in the main clause in each case. **

a) Se (arrivare) _____ prima dell'una, potete mangiare con noi.

b) Cercherei un altro lavoro se (essere) _____ più giovane.

c) Se (venire) _____ con noi in piscina, non ti annoierai.

d) Eva sarebbe più snella se (rinunciare) _____ ai dolci.

    rinunciare – to renounce, give up

e) Se (prendere) _____ un taxi, arriviamo in tempo.

f) Avresti più tempo per leggere se (guardare) _____ meno la televisione.

g) Lino non ti telefonerebbe tutti i giorni se non ti (amare) _____ _____.

h) Non saresti tanto stanca, se (dormire) _____ di più.

i) Se non ti vedo tutti i giorni, non (essere) _____ contento.

j) Cambiereste vita se (potere) _____ ?

k) Dovete dirlo se (volere) _____ andare a teatro.

In Italian, the subjunctive is used only rarely in indirect discourse.

Indirect Discourse

① Sandro **dice che sta meglio.**

② Sandro **disse che stava meglio.**

1. Sandro says that he feels better. 2. Sandro said that he felt better.

Indirect discourse is introduced by a verb of speaking or writing and **che**. These verbs (verbi dicendi) include, for example, **dire**, **promettere**, **raccontare**, **rispondere**, **spiegare**, and **scrivere**. The tense of this verb determines the sequence of tenses in the indirect discourse.

Indirect Discourse with the Main Clause in the Present, Future, or Present Perfect

① Che cosa dice Cinzia?

② **Dice che è** contenta, **che ha trovato** lavoro e **che dovrà trasferirsi** in Belgio.

1. What does Cinzia say? 2. She says that she's glad that she found work and that she will have to move to Belgium.

Direct discourse:	
Cinzia: „**Sono** contenta."	present
„**Ho trovato** lavoro."	present perfect
„**Dovrò** trasferirmi in Belgio."	simple future

Indirect discourse:	
Cinzia **dice/dirà/ha detto**	
che è contenta.	present
che ha trovato lavoro.	present perfect
che dovrà trasferirsi in Belgio.	simple future

If the verb of saying or writing is in the present tense or the future, then the indirect discourse uses the same tense as the direct discourse.
If the verb of saying or writing is in the present perfect, then the indirect discourse uses the same tense as the direct discourse, if the statement in the dependent clause is still valid. The present perfect, in this case, is regarded as a tense of the present time.

1. The Present Perfect as a Tense of the Present

The present perfect is considered to be a tense of the present if the statement in the dependent clause still has validity, that is, if nothing new has occurred in the meantime:

> Cinzia **ha detto** che adesso **è contenta.**
> *Cinzia said that she is happy now.*

> Cinzia **ha detto** che **ha trovato** lavoro. Comincerà domani.
> *Cinzia said that she found work. She will start tomorrow.*

> Quando mio padre è andato in pensione, **ha detto** che **farà** un viaggio attraverso l'Australia. Ieri è andato in un'agenzia di viaggio.
> *When my father retired, he said that he would take a trip through Australia. Yesterday he went to a travel agency.*

2. The Present Perfect as a Tense of the Past

The present perfect is considered to be one of the tenses of the past if the statement in the dependent clause no longer is valid, because something new has occurred in the meantime. Thus the statement in the dependent clause is viewed as part of the past:

> Cinzia **ha detto** che ieri **era contenta.** Adesso purtroppo non lo è più.
> *Cinzia said that she was happy yesterday. Now, she unfortunately is so no longer.*

> Cinzia **ha detto** che **aveva trovato** lavoro. Adesso però è di nuovo disoccupata.
> *Cinzia said that she had found work. Now, however, she is unemployed again.*

> Quando mio padre è andato in pensione, **ha detto** che **avrebbe fatto** un viaggio attraverso l'Australia. Purtroppo ha dovuto rinunciarvi per motivi di salute.
> *When my father retired, he said he would take a trip through Australia. Unfortunately he had to give it up for health reasons.*

As you see, in this case the tenses in the dependent clause follow the rules of indirect discourse with the main clause in a past form.

Indirect Discourse with the Main Clause in a Past Form

Ti ricordi cosa aveva detto Cinzia?
①

Certo, **aveva detto che era contenta**, **che aveva trovato** lavoro e **che avrebbe dovuto trasferirsi** in Belgio.
②

1. Do you remember what Cinzia had said? 2. Certainly. She had said that she was happy that she had found work and that she would have to move to Belgium.

The forms of the past tense include the imperfect, the present perfect, the preterit, and the past perfect.

Direct discourse:	
Cinzia: „**Sono** contenta."	present
„**Ho trovato** lavoro."	present perfect
„**Dovrò** trasferirmi in Belgio."	simple future

Indirect discourse:	
Cinzia **diceva/ha detto/disse/aveva detto**	
che era contenta.	imperfect
che aveva trovato lavoro.	past perfect
che avrebbe dovuto trasferirsi...	conditional perfect

If the verb of speaking or writing is in one of the past tenses, then most of the tenses change in the indirect discourse.
With the present perfect, in this case the statement in the dependent clause belongs to the past and is no longer valid in the present.

In the dependent clause, the following tenses change:

Lelio: „Mi **piace** la Germania." Lelio diceva/ha detto/disse/aveva detto che gli **piaceva** la Germania.	
The **present tense** becomes	the **imperfect.**

Lelio: „**Ho** già **visitato** varie città." Lelio diceva/ha detto/disse/aveva detto che **aveva** già **visitato** varie città.	
The **present perfect** becomes	the **past perfect.**

Lelio: „Quest'anno **andrò** a Berlino."
Lelio diceva/ha detto/disse/aveva detto che quell'anno **sarebbe andato** a Berlino.

The **simple future** becomes   the **conditional perfect**.

Lelio: „Mi **piacerebbe** vivere ad Amburgo."
Lelio diceva/ha detto/disse/aveva detto che gli **sarebbe piaciuto** vivere ad Amburgo.

The **conditional** becomes   the **conditional perfect.**

The following tenses remain the same:

Lelio: „Quando **ero** piccolo mi **sarebbe piaciuto** vivere a Monaco."
Lelio diceva/ha detto/disse/aveva detto che quando **era** piccolo gli **sarebbe piaciuto** vivere a Monaco.

The **imperfect** remains the **imperfect**, and the **conditional perfect** remains the **conditional perfect**.

Lelio: „**Ero stato** a Monaco con i miei genitori."
Lelio diceva/ha detto/disse/aveva detto che **era stato** a Monaco con i suoi genitori.

The **past perfect** remains the **past perfect.**

The Indirect Question

Sandro **chiede se vogliamo un aperitivo.** ①

Lara **ha domandato quanto vino deve comprare.** ②

---

1. Sandra is asking whether we want an aperitif. 2. Lara asked how much wine she should buy.

An indirect question is introduced by **chiedere**, **domandare**, or **voler sapere**, followed by **se** or an interrogative pronoun or adverb, such as **(che) cosa**, **come**, **dove**, **quando**, **quanto**, etc.

Sequence of Tenses in an Indirect Question

The same rules apply to the sequence of tenses for both an indirect question and indirect discourse. The distinction made in the case of the present perfect in indirect discourse between still-valid and no-longer-valid statements in the dependent clause no longer applies, however. In an indirect question, you can use either sequence of tenses equally well.

The verb introducing the question in the present, future, or present perfect

disturbare – *to disturb*

Lalla: „**Posso** disturbarti?"	present
„Cosa **hai comprato?**"	present perfect
„Quando **partirai?**"	simple future
Lalla, mi **chiede/chiederà/ha chiesto**	
se **può** disturbarmi.	present
cosa **ho comprato.**	present perfect
quando **partirò.**	simple future

If the verb introducing the question is in the present tense, simple future, or present perfect, then use in the indirect question the same tense as in the direct question.

The verb introducing the question in a past tense form

Lalla: „**Posso** disturbarti?"	present
„Cosa **hai comprato?**"	present perfect
„Quando **partirai?**"	simple future

Lalla mi **chiedeva/ha chiesto/chiese/aveva chiesto**	
se **poteva** disturbarmi.	imperfect
cosa **avevo comprato.**	past perfect
quando **sarei partito.**	conditional perfect

If the verb introducing the question is in one of the past tenses—present perfect, preterit, past perfect—then the tenses in the dependent clause of the indirect question change as they do in the dependent clause of indirect discourse, that is:

– the **present** becomes   the **imperfect**,
– the **present perfect** changes to   the **past perfect**,
– and the **simple future** becomes   the **conditional perfect**.

Lalla mi **chiedeva/ha chiesto/chiese/aveva chiesto**	
se **potesse** disturbarmi.	imperfect subjunctive
cosa **avessi comprato.**	past perfect subjunctive

In literary Italian, the imperfect is replaced by the imperfect subjunctive, and the past perfect is replaced by the past perfect subjunctive.

The Indirect Command

① I genitori **mi dicono** di fare attenzione.	② Mio padre **mi pregò di** non tornare a casa troppo tardi.	③ L'insegnante **ci** raccomanderà di lavorare di più.

1. My parents tell me to pay attention. 2. My father asked me not to come home too late.
3. The teacher will advise us to work more.

The indirect command is quite easy. It is introduced by **dire**, **pregare**, **ordinare**, or **raccomandare**, followed by **di** + infinitive, or by **di** + **non** + infinitive in a negative command.

Sequence of Tenses in the Indirect Command

Direct command:

Eros: „**Ascoltami**, per favore!"

Indirect command:

Eros mi **dice/dirà/ha detto di ascoltarlo.**
Eros mi **diceva/ha detto/disse/aveva detto di ascoltarlo.**

In an indirect command with **di** + (**non**) + infinitive, the tense of the introducing verb has no influence on the dependent clause. The verb in the dependent clause always remains in the infinitive form.

Changes When Converting to Indirect Discourse

In indirect speech, both Italian and English adapt certain elements to the new perspective:

Carlo: „Ezio, **vieni** da **me domani** sera? **Ti** presenterò **mia** sorella.

Ezio: „Carlo mi chiede se **vado** da **lui** domani sera. **Mi** presenterà **sua** sorella."

Ezio: „Carlo mi chiese se **andavo** da **lui l'indomani** sera. Mi avrebbe presentato **sua** sorella."

l'indomani sera – on the following evening

Changing from direct to indirect discourse not only affects the tense of the verbs, but also the pronouns and expressions of time and place. In many cases, **venire** becomes **andare**.

Indirect Discourse

1. Match the direct commands with their indirect equivalents. ******

a) Carlo: „State attenti!"

b) Carlo: „Aiutami!"

c) Carlo: „Sta' attento!"

d) Carlo: „Aiutatemi!"

1. Carlo ci ha detto di aiutarlo.

2. Carlo mi ha detto di aiutarlo.

3. Carlo ci ha detto di stare attenti.

4. Carlo mi ha detto di stare attento.

a) ☐   b) ☐   c) ☐   d) ☐

2. Report what Claudio is saying by changing the sentences into indirect discourse. ******

a) Ho conosciuto una ragazza molto interessante. b) Mi sono innamorato di lei. c) Ci vediamo tutti i giorni. d) Quando non ci vediamo ci telefoniamo. e) Chissà se un giorno ci sposeremo? f) A me, comunque, piacerebbe vivere con lei.

a) Claudio racconta che

_____.

b) Dice che

_____.

c) E che

_____.

d) Dice anche che

_____.

e) Claudio si chiede se

_____.

f) Alla fine dice che

_____.

3. Several years after the fact you still remember what Claudio told you, and you relate it to a friend. *******

a) Claudio aveva raccontato che

_____.

b) Aveva detto che

_____.

c) E che

_____.

d) Aveva anche detto che

_____.

e) Claudio si era chiesto se

_____.

f) Alla fine aveva detto che

_____.

4. Furio, along with his wife, visited the family in Italy. How would you express the statements, questions, and commands in his account of the visit in direct discourse? ***

a) Mio padre ci ha detto che era contento di rivederci.

_____

b) La mamma ci ha chiesto se volevamo un caffè.

_____

c) La nonna voleva sapere se avevamo fatto buon viaggio.

_____

d) Il nonno invece ha domandato quanto tempo saremmo rimasti.

_____

e) La mia sorella maggiore ci ha detto di non partire troppo presto.

_____

f) Anche la mia sorellina ci ha pregato di rimanere almeno due settimane.

_____

g) Mio fratello ha chiesto se avevamo voglia di andare al mare con lui.

_____

h) E poi ha detto che gli sarebbe piaciuto partire con noi per la Germania.

_____

The use of prepositions is not easy. Most of them have several functions. Two or more can also perform the same function, however.

Prepositions

Se desidera qualcosa **di** leggero, **a** mezzogiorno c'è il menu **di** lavoro. ①

② Oppure abbiamo come specialità **del** giorno il fegato **alla** veneziana e come primo il risotto **ai** funghi porcini.

1. If you want something light, there is the businessman's special at midday. 2. Or, as the specialty of the day, we have liver and onions Venetian style, and, as a first course, risotto with porcini.

▶ **The Definite Article**, p. 12

A, **da**, **di**, **in**, and **su** can be combined with the definite article, as here: **a** + **la** ▶ **alla**, **di** + **i** ▶ **dei**.

The Preposition *a*

A is used:

Ho scritto **a** Gianna. Che cosa regaliamo **al** nonno?	to indicate the indirect object.
Prima siamo andati **a** Napoli, poi **a** Capri. Ci vediamo **al** bar? Mi piace mangiare **al** ristorante. Vengo a prenderti **alla** stazione.	to indicate place and direction with cities, small towns, and small islands, as well as numerous other statements of location and direction.
Accanto **al** cinema c'è un bar. Abito vicino **all'**ospedale.	together with numerous prepositions of place.
Il prossimo paese è **a** 20 chilometri.	to indicate distance.
Il risotto **ai** funghi porcini è ottimo. Vado in ufficio **a** piedi.	to indicate manner.
Ho comprato un vestito **a** righe. Sul lago ci sono molte barche **a** vela. Io non porto le scarpe **a** tacco alto.	to form compound nouns in which the second noun states a characteristic of the first noun.
Sei riuscito **a** leggere il giornale? Carlo si è preparato **all'**esame.	after certain verbs.

a piedi – *on foot*
a righe – *striped*
la barca a vela –
the sailboat
il tacco –
the (shoe) heel
l'esame – *the exam*

A Natale e **a** Pasqua andiamo al mare. Ci vediamo **alle** quattro. Mi sono sposata **a** vent'anni.	as an expression of time and in connection with **anno** or **anni** to indicate age, in the meaning *at the age of ... years.*
Ci vediamo due volte **all'** anno. Il prezzo della camera è di 65 euro **al** giorno e **a** persona.	to indicate frequency, and in the sense of *pro.*

The Preposition *con*

Con is used:

Chi gioca a carte **con** me?	in the meaning *with.*
Ezio lavora **con** grande serietà. Vi incontro **con** piacere.	to indicate manner.
Con questo chiasso io non dormo. **Con** questo tempo si sta in casa.	in the meaning *with* or *in* when a condition or state is being described.

la serietà – *the seriousness*
il chiasso – *the noise, uproar*
lodare – *to praise*
la conferenza – *the address, lecture*

The Preposition *da*

Da is used:

Questo film è lodato **dalla** critica. La conferenza verrà tenuta **dal** dott. Renzi.	in the passive voice, to state the originator of the action.
Saremo **da** voi alle sette. Alle due devo essere **dal** medico.	to indicate place and direction when speaking of people.
Torno **dall**'ufficio verso le sette. Ho saputo **dalla** radio che ha vinto la Germania.	to indicate place of departure and origin.
Per andare a Torino passiamo **dal** Gran San Bernardo. I ladri sono passati **dalla** finestra.	in connection with **passare** in the meaning *through*, *across.*
Ci mancano i bicchieri **da** cognac. La camera **da** letto è bella grande. Hai visto i miei occhiali **da** sole? Devo comprare delle scarpe **da** tennis.	to form compound nouns in which the second noun states the purpose for which the first is used.

When origin refers to someone's hometown, use the preposition **di**:
Sono **di** Napoli.
I come from Naples.

il ladro – *the thief*
il bicchiere da cognac – *the glass of cognac*
gli occhiali da sole – *the (pair of) sunglasses*
le scarpe da tennis – *the tennis shoes*

Quella ragazza **dagli** occhi azzurri mi piace. Carlo è un ragazzo **dalla** volontà di ferro.	to indicate a physical or character-related feature in persons.
Abito in una villetta **dalle** persiane azzurre. Vorrei cambiare un biglietto **da** 500 euro.	to mention an external or value-related feature in things.
C'è gente che piange **dalla** gioia. Sto tremando **dal** freddo.	to state the cause.
Sono sposata **da** quattro anni.	in the meaning *for (a length of time)*.
La lezione è **dalle** otto **alle** nove. Ho lavorato **dalla** mattina **alla** sera.	in connection with **a** to indicate a segment of time.
Da bambino ero molto timido. **Da** studente dormivo molto.	with regard to persons, in the meaning *as*.
Il direttore mi tratta **da** amico. Si comporta **da** vero gentiluomo.	with regard to behaviors, in the meaning *as, like*.

azzurro – *sky-blue, azure*
la volontà di ferro –
the iron will
la persiana –
the (window) shutter
la gioia – *the joy*
trattare – *to treat*
comportarsi – *to behave*
il gentiluomo –
the gentleman

The Preposition *di*

Di is used:

La casa **dei** nonni è nel centro. Questa è la camera **di** Emma.	to indicate belonging and possession.
Dov'è la chiave **della** macchina? Il professore **d'**inglese è giovane.	to form compound nouns.
Mi dia un chilo **di** pere, per favore.	in statements of quantity.
Per il pranzo di Natale preparo qualcosa **di** speciale. Non dice niente **di** interessante.	in connection with **qualcosa** or **niente** to mean *something / nothing* + noun.
Pia è **di** Pisa, il marito è **di** Parma. Lei è **del** Sud, lui **del** Nord.	to indicate origin, in the sense of hometown.
Ho un figlio **di** vent'anni. Ho bevuto un vino **di** quindici anni.	to state someone's age.

la pera – *the pear*

Lavoro **di** notte e dormo **di** giorno. **D'**estate non mi piace viaggiare.	to give the time of day and the season.
Ho ricevuto un orologio **d'**oro. Leo ha messo una giacca **di** pelle.	to indicate the material of which something is made.
Noi mangiamo **prima dell'**una. **A sinistra della** chiesa c'è il cimitero.	in connection with certain prepositions of time and place.
Ricordati **di** telefonare al medico! Non ho voglia **di** uscire, stasera.	after certain verbs and expressions.

> The seasons can also be given with **in**: d'estate/**in** estate d'autunno/**in** autunno d'inverno/**in** inverno

l'oro – *the gold*
la pelle – *the leather*
il cimitero – *the cemetery*
emigrare – *to emigrate*
il parente – *the relative*
il bosco – *the forest, woods*

The Preposition *in*

In is used:

Tanti italiani sono emigrati **in** America e **in** Australia. Abbiamo dei parenti **in** Francia. Quest'estate andremo **in** Sicilia. Mi piace il bosco **in** autunno.	to indicate place and direction with continents, countries, and regions, as well as in numerous other indications of location and direction.
In ufficio ci vado **in** bicicletta; non ci vado mai **in** macchina.	to state the method of locomotion with means of transportation.
In agosto saremo al mare. **In** primavera può ancora nevicare.	with months and seasons.
Mi sono sposata **nel** 1986. **Nel** '900 ci sono state due guerre mondiali.	to refer to year dates, centuries, and epochs.
Questo piatto si fa **in** pochi minuti. **In** dieci minuti sono in ufficio.	in the temporal meaning *in*, *within*.
Il menu è scritto **in** italiano, **in** tedesco e **in** inglese.	to indicate the language in which something is expressed.

> With months, the use of **a** has also become common: **In/A luglio** non ci siamo.

la guerra mondiale – *the world war*
il piatto – *the dish, plate (food)*

The Preposition *per*

Per is used:

+ **Per** chi è l'aranciata? ~ **Per** la bambina.	to render *for*.
Ti telefono **per** scusarmi.	to render *in order to*.
Sono a Roma **per** motivi di lavoro. La ringrazio **per** il Suo aiuto.	to state a reason.
Il traghetto **per** Olbia è già partito. Quando partite **per** Londra? Prima di continuare **per** la Sicilia ci fermiamo un po' a Napoli.	in connection with means of transportation or with verbs like **partire** and **continuare** to indicate destination.
Ho camminato **per** la campagna. Ha viaggiato **per** tutta l'Europa.	with **camminare** and **viaggiare** in the meaning *through / across*.
Le mando la conferma **per** fax.	to indicate means.
Ho camminato **per** ore e ore. Ha piovuto **per** tutta la notte.	to state duration.
La carne è **per** domani. **Per** le otto la cena sarà pronta.	to indicate a point in time.

l'aiuto – *the help*
il traghetto – *the ferry*
la conferma –
the confirmation

The Preposition *su*

Su is used:

Siamo saliti **sull'**Etna. **Sull'**autostrada c'è molto traffico. La mia camera dà **sul** giardino.	to indicate place and direction.
È una donna **sui** cinquant'anni. Abbiamo speso **sui** 1000 euro. Toni pesa **sugli** ottanta chili.	as an approximate indication of age, price, and size.
Ho visto un documentario **su** Roma. La conferenza è **sui** giovani. Hai letto l'articolo **sulle** scimmie?	to say what is being talked about or written about.
Su, vieni! *Let's go, come on!* **Su,** svelto! *Let's go, hurry up!* **Su** con il morale! *Head up!*	in colloquial speech, to express commands.

dare su – *to overlook, to look out on*
la conferenza –
the address, lecture
i giovani – *the young people, the youth*
la scimmia – *the monkey, ape*

1. Fill in the blanks with the prepositions supplied below. **

a – al – da – da – dal – del – della
delle – di – in – in – in – sui – sulla

a) Che tempo! Piove _____ stamattina.

b) _____ Torino _____ Ivrea ci vuole circa mezz'ora, _____ treno.

c) Il programma «Onda verde» informa _____ situazione _____
traffico.

il traffico – the traffic

d) Fufi è il cane _____ signora che sta _____ terzo piano.

e) La professoressa _____ tedesco è una signora _____
quarantacinque anni.

f) Oggi mia moglie tornerà _____ lavoro prima _____ sette.

g) Quest'estate andremo _____ Spagna. Ci andremo _____ aereo.

2. A tourist group somewhere in Italy. You will learn how the individuals
in the group spend the last day of vacation when you fill in the blanks
with **a**, **da**, or **in**, adding the definite article where necessary. **

a) Irene è _____ parrucchiere, perché stasera va _____ ristorante con suo marito. b) Hans vorrebbe andare _____ museo,
ma invece deve andare _____ medico, poveretto. c) Susanne è
andata _____ città, perché vuole fare le ultime fotografie e poi
deve anche andare _____ posta, perché vuole assolutamente
mandare un pacchetto _____ suo nipote _____ Austria.
d) Carina è _____ albergo e fa le valigie, mentre suo marito è ancora
_____ letto. e) Brigitte e Rainer non sono insieme. Lei è andata
_____ centro a fare gli ultimi acquisti, lui ha preferito andare
_____ cinema. f) Horst è andato _____ Paolo ed Elena, una
coppia che ha conosciuto _____ discoteca. g) Christiane è andata
_____ bar di fronte _____ albergo e si gode le ultime ore
di vacanza mangiando un gelato. h) Domani saranno di nuovo tutti
insieme _____ bus che li riporterà _____ Düsseldorf.

poveretto! – poor fellow!

la coppia – the couple
godersi qc – to enjoy
something

Numbers

The Cardinal Numbers

From 11 to 16, the tens are at the end of the word (un**dici**, do**dici**, ...), but from 17 to 19 they come first (**dici**assette, **dici**otto, **dici**annove).

0	zero	18	diciotto	50	cinquanta
1	uno	19	diciannove	60	sessanta
2	due	20	venti	70	settanta
3	tre	21	ventuno	80	ottanta
4	quattro	22	ventidue	90	novanta
5	cinque	23	ventitré	100	cento
6	sei	24	ventiquattro	101	centouno
7	sette	25	venticinque	108	centootto
8	otto	26	ventisei	200	duecento
9	nove	27	ventisette	360	trecento-
10	dieci	28	ventotto		sessanta
11	undici	29	ventinove	1 000	mille
12	dodici	30	trenta	2 000	duemila
13	tredici	31	trentuno	3 100	tremilacento
14	quattordici	32	trentadue	1 000 000	un milione
15	quindici	33	trentatré	2 000 000	due milioni
16	sedici	38	trentotto	1 000 000 000	un miliardo
17	diciassette	40	quaranta	2 000 000 000	due miliardi

Tip!

Sessanta (60) and **settanta** (70) are often confused. Remember that **settanta** is related to **sette** (7).

Have you noticed that almost all the cardinal numbers are invariable? The only variable ones are **mille**, **milione**, and **miliardo**.

Use

la fortuna – *the luck, (good) fortune*
il numero vincente – *the winning number*
lo spumante – *the sparkling wine*

Il tredici mi porta fortuna.
Il numero vincente è **il ventotto.**

As nouns, the cardinal numbers are masculine.

Io prendo **un** tè, Gianni prende **una** birra, Emma **un'**aranciata e Lucio **uno** spumante.

When **uno** comes before a noun, then it behaves like the indefinite article, ...

Sergio ha ventu**n** anni.
Fino a Natale ci sono quarantu**n** giorni.
Il libro ha novantu**n** pagine.

... and with tens that are linked with **uno**, the -o at the end of the number generally is omitted.

1.000.000	un milione **di** macchine
4.000.000.000	quattro miliardi **di** persone

■ After **milione** and **miliardo**, the noun is linked with **di**.

3.530.000 €	tre milioni cinquecentotrentamila euro

■ The **di** is omitted, however, when **miliardo** or **milione** is followed by hundreds, tens, or ones.

The Date

① Il compleanno di Marcello è il **1º** (primo) aprile, vero?

② No, il **1º** aprile è l'onomastico. Il compleanno è il **27** (ventisette) marzo.

1. Marcello's birthday is April 1, isn't it? 2. No, April 1 is his name day. His birthday is March 27.

> Note the use of the definite article in giving the date.

Pasqua è il **23** (ventitré) aprile.
Oggi è il **31** (trentun) luglio.
Il **15** (quindici) marzo è il compleanno di Lea.

■ The date is stated with the definite article **il** and the <u>cardinal numbers</u>.

Il **1º** (primo) maggio i negozi sono chiusi.
Il **1º** (primo) agosto parto per Parigi.

■ Only with the first day of the month is it necessary to use the ordinal number.

Parma, **2 gennaio 2001**   Parma, **02/01**   Parma, **02. 01.**
(due gennaio duemilauno)

■ In letters, the **il** is omitted in the date, with both day and year.

Nel 1933 c'è stato un inverno freddissimo.
Per il passaggio **dal** 1999 **al** 2000 ci sono stati grandi festeggiamenti.

il passaggio –
the passage, transition
il festeggiamento –
the celebration

■ Otherwise, year dates are used with the definite article.

Il **1968** (millenovecentosessantotto) è stato un anno importante.
Leo è nato nel **1986** (millenovecentoottantasei).

■ Year dates are read like normal cardinal numbers.

Statements of Quantity

> Mi dia **mezzo chilo di** tortellini con il ripieno di zucca e **tre etti di** parmigiano grattugiato, per favore.

Give me half a kilo of tortellini with pumpkin filling and 300 grams of grated Parmesan, please.

> The unit of measurement "100 grams" has a special name in Italian: **un etto**.

100 g:	un etto **di** parmigiano
250 g:	due etti e mezzo **di** burro
1 kg:	un chilo **di** mele
2,5 kg:	due chili e mezzo **di** patate

The preposition **di** must be used between the quantity and the following noun.

1/2 kg:	**mezzo** chilo **d'**uva
1/2 l:	**mezzo** litro **di** vino

When **mezzo** stands alone, the indefinite article **un** is omitted.

Telling Time

> **Che ora è,**
> **per favore?** ①

> ② **Sono le cinque**
> **meno un quarto.**

1. What time is it, please? 2. It's quarter to five.

Che or**a è?**
Che or**e sono?**

To ask what time it is, you can use the singular with **è** or the plural with **sono**.

 È mezzogiorno

 È mezzanotte.

 È l'una.

 Sono le due.

In the case of noon and midnight, use **è** to state the time. To say it is one o'clock, use **è** + **l'**, but otherwise use **sono** + **le**.

Sono le due
e dieci.

 Sono le due
e un quarto.

 Sono le due
e mezza.

 Sono le due
e trentacinque.

■ Generally, from the full hour to the thirty-ninth minute, hours and minutes are connected with **e**. *Quarter after* is **e un quarto**, and the half hour is given as **e mezza**.

 Sono le tre
meno venti.

 Sono le tre
meno un quarto.

 Sono le tre
meno cinque.

■ From the fortieth minute on, Italians usually subtract from the next hour by using **meno**. *Quarter to / till* is **meno un quarto**.

Parto alle otto **del mattino** e arrivo alle tre **del pomeriggio**.
Parto alle tre **di notte** e arrivo alle otto **di sera**.

■ Time is given with the cardinal numbers from 1 to 12. The time of day is added with expressions such as **del mattino**, **del pomeriggio**, **di sera**, and **di notte**.

+ **A** che ora venite? ~ **Alle** otto e mezza.

■ You can use the preposition **a** to state a time or to ask the time.

`18:44`   Il treno parte alle **18.44** (diciotto e quarantaquattro).

`21:15`   C'è un Intercity alle **21.15** (ventuno e quindici).

■ For official statements of time, the hours and minutes are counted as on a digital clock, using the 24-hour, 60-minute system.

a che ora ...? – *at what time ... ?*
alle otto e mezza – *at eight thirty.*

The Ordinal Numbers

La nostra casa ha tre piani. Al **primo** piano c'è un commercialista, al **secondo** ci siamo noi e al **terzo** ci abita una famiglia con due bambini.

Our building has three floors. On the first floor is a tax consultant, we are on the second, and on the third lives a family with two children.

1º	primo	From 1 to 10, the ordinal numbers have irregular forms.
2º	secondo	
3º	terzo	
4º	quarto	
5º	quinto	
6º	sesto	
7º	settimo	
8º	ottavo	
9º	nono	
10º	decimo	
11º	undicesimo	From 11 on, form ordinal numbers by replacing the final vowel with **-esimo**, as here:
12º	dodicesimo	**vent(i) + esimo ▶ ventesimo.**
20º	ventesimo	
24º	ventiquattresimo	
25º	venticinquesimo	
23º	ventit**re**esimo	Numbers that are combined with **tre** or **sei** retain the final vowel.
33º	trentat**re**esimo	
46º	quarantas**ei**esimo	
66º	sessantas**ei**esimo	

Use

1º piano:	il **primo** piano
2ª classe:	la **seconda** classe

Scendiamo alla **terza** fermata.
Le **prime** file sono già occupate.

When the ordinal numbers modify a noun, they precede that noun and agree with it in number and gender.

| Carlo V | (Carlo **quinto**) |
| Giovanni XXIII | (Giovanni **ventitreesimo**) |

With kings and popes, the Roman numerals are not written as ordinal numbers, but they are read as such nonetheless.

il IV secolo a. C. (il **quarto** secolo avanti Cristo)
il II secolo d. C. (il **secondo** secolo dopo Cristo)
il XXI secolo (il **ventunesimo** secolo)

The same applies in the case of centuries.

avanti Cristo –
before Christ, b.c.
dopo Cristo –
after Christ, a.d.

From the thirteenth to twentieth centuries, in addition to the option with the ordinal number, there are two other possibilities in common use:

13th century:	**il '200 / il Duecento**
14th century:	**il '300 / il Trecento**
19th century:	**l' 800 / l'Ottocento**
20th century:	**il '900 / il Novecento**

Numbers

1. Write the numbers in numerals or in letters, as called for. *

a) 16   _____

b) 67   _____

c) _____   settantasei

d) _____   centotredici

e) 119   _____

f) _____   milleduecentododici

g) 2217   _____

h) _____   undicimilatrecentoquindici

i) _____   quindicimilaquattrocentoquattordici

j) 1.619.788   _____

_____

2. Write the numbers indicated as words. *

a) Ho (4) _____ figli. b) Nicola ha (7) _____

anni e frequenta la (2ª) _____ elementare.

c) Daniela ha (10) _____ anni ed è in (5ª) _____

elementare. d) Matteo ha già (16) _____ anni e fa la

(3ª) _____ liceo, mentre Simona, la più grande è al (4⁰)

_____ anno di ingegneria, anche se ha già (28)

_____ anni.

3. Translate this shopping list into Italian. Write down the quantities in words. **

a) ½ kg spinach   _____

b) 1 kg apples   _____

c) 2 ½ kg grapes   _____

d) 1 bottle olive oil   _____

e) 250 g Parmesan   _____

f) 300 g raw (cured) ham _____

Conjunctions

② No, no, vengo con voi, **anche se** dovrei ancora studiare.

① Vieni anche tu in pizzeria **o** preferisci tornare a casa?

1. Are you coming to the pizzeria too, or do you prefer to go home? 2. No, no, I'm coming with you, even though I should study some more.

Coordinating Conjunctions

① Hai comprato il giornale?

② Sì, **ma** non l'ho ancora letto.

1. Did you buy the newspaper? 2. Yes, but I haven't read it yet.

Coordinating conjunctions link two elements of equal value, such as nouns, adjectives, and main clauses. These conjunctions include:

Luca **e** Giorgio sono fratelli.	**e** *(and)*,
Ho comprato il giornale, **ma/però** non l'ho ancora letto.	**ma/però** *(but)*,
Vuoi un caffè **o/oppure** un tè?	**o/oppure** *(or)*,
A Pia regalo **o** un libro **o** un disco.	**o ... o** *(either ... or)*,
Oggi non fa **né** caldo **né** freddo.	**né ... né** *(neither ... nor)*,
Se mi inviti tu, **allora** vengo.	**allora** *(then)*,
Allora, dov'è il problema?	**allora** *(so)*,
Lucio è un tipo molto socievole, **infatti** è simpatico a tutti.	**infatti** *(in fact, indeed)*.

il disco – *the record*
socievole – *sociable*

il pranzo – *the noon meal, lunch*

Piove, **e tuttavia** non fa freddo.	**(e) tuttavia** *(however, but, still)*,
Simona non c'è, **perciò/quindi/dunque** prepari tu il pranzo.	**perciò/quindi/dunque** *(therefore, so, hence)*.

Subordinating Conjunctions

Quando mi vede gira la testa.①	Sandro cammina **come se** avesse bevuto un po' troppo.②

1. When he sees me, he turns his head. 2. Sandro walks as if he had drunk a little too much.

Subordinating conjunctions introduce a dependent clause.

1. Conjunctions That Require the Indicative

dimmelo! – *tell (it to) me!*
stare con qu – *to be with someone*
andare/venire a trovare qu – *to (pay a) visit to someone*

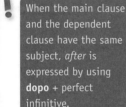

When the main clause and the dependent clause have the same subject, *after* is expressed by using **dopo** + perfect infinitive.
Dopo essere stata in banca/**Dopo aver fatto** la spesa, sono andata a casa.

triste – *sad*
mettersi a – *to start to*
piangere – *to cry*

Quando avrai finito, dimmelo!	**quando** *(when, once)*
Quando esco con te non mi annoio.	**quando** *(whenever, every time)*
Quando mi ha visto si è girato.	**quando** *(when)*
Da quando sta con te è più calmo.	**da quando** *(since)*
Appena sarò libero, verrò a trovarti.	**appena** *(as soon as)*
Leo è arrivato **dopo che** eri uscito.	**dopo che** *(after)*
Potete stare qui **finché** volete.	**finché** *(as long as)*
Aspettateci **finché non** arriviamo.	**finché non** *(until)*
Mentre andavo a scuola, ho incontrato Furio.	**mentre** *(while)*
Non esco **perché** ho mal di testa.	**perché** *(because)*
Siccome/Dato che/Visto che è il tuo compleanno, andiamo a Roma.	**siccome/dato che/visto che** *(since, as)*
Il film piace, **anche se** è difficile.	**anche se** *(although)*
La storia è **così/tanto/talmente** triste **che** ci si mette a piangere.	**così/talmente/tanto ... che** *(so ..., that)*

C'era **un tale** vento **che** si faceva fatica a camminare.	**un tale ... che** (*such a, ... that*)	fare fatica – *to struggle, have trouble*
Sto male **di modo che/in modo che/per cui** non posso partecipare alla riunione.	**di modo che/in modo che/per cui** (*so that*).	partecipare a – *to participate in* la riunione – *the meeting, gathering*

parlare piano – *to speak slowly*
nascondere – *to hide, conceal*
il cioccolatino – *the (piece of) chocolate*

2. Conjunctions That Require the Subjunctive

Parla piano, **di modo che/in modo che** tutti ti capiscano.

di modo che/in modo che (*so that*), when the subordinate clause contains something wished for.

Ho nascosto i cioccolatini **affinché/perché** Giorgio non li mangi.

affinché/perché (*so that*),

Benché/Malgrado/Nonostante/Sebbene dorma poco, non sono stanco.

benché/malgrado/nonostante/sebbene (*although*),

Ho preparato il dessert **prima che** arrivassero gli ospiti.

prima che (*before*),

Ti presto la macchina **purché/a condizione che/a patto che** tu sia a casa prima di mezzanotte.

purché/a condizione che/a patto che (*providing, provided that*),

Ti portiamo noi all'aeroporto, **a meno che non** lo faccia Giorgio.

a meno che non (*unless*),

Luca si comporta **come se** fosse lui il padrone di casa.

come se (*as if*),

Siamo usciti **senza che** gli altri se ne siano accorti.

senza che (*without*).

> When the main clause and the subordinate clause have the same subject, you should express *before* with **prima di** + infinitive: **Prima di uscire** mi trucco.

prestare qc a qu – *to loan something to someone*
il padrone di casa – *the man / master of the house*
accorgersi di qc – *to notice something*

3. Conjunctions That Require the Indicative in Certain Cases and the Subjunctive in Others

Che

Sappiamo **che siete** arrivati ieri sera.

▪ **che** *(that)* + indicative, when the subordinate clause is introduced by a verb that expresses a certainty, such as **sapere**.

Carlo dice **che** non **ha** tempo.

▪ **che** *(that)* + indicative, when the main clause introduces indirect discourse.

▸ **Indirect Discourse**, p. 210

Con questo tempo non penso **che si possa** partire in macchina.

▪ **che** *(that)* + subjunctive, when the subordinate clause is introduced by a verb that expresses doubts, such as **non pensare**.

▸ **The Subjunctive**, p. 146

Se

Non so **se** il ristorante **sia** aperto anche la domenica.

▪ **se** *(if, whether)* + subjunctive, when the subordinate clause is introduced by a verb that expresses uncertainty, such as **non sapere**.

la mostra –
the exhibition, show

Se abbiamo tempo andiamo a vedere la mostra del Perugino.

▪ **se** *(if, in case)* + indicative in real conditional sentences.

Se avessimo tempo andremmo a vedere la mostra del Perugino.

▸ **The Conditional Sentence**, p. 208

▪ **se** *(if, in case)* + subjunctive in unreal conditional sentences.

1. Subjunctive or indicative? Mark the correct verb form in each pair. **

a) Non ti ho scritto perché non avevo / avessi il tuo indirizzo.

b) Vi abbiamo telefonato, affinché siete / siate informati.

c) L'ingegner Rossi è sempre molto gentile quando mi telefona / telefoni.

d) Vorrei vedervi prima che partite / partiate.

e) Anche se ho studiato / abbia studiato molto, l'esame non è andato bene.

f) Vi accompagno io alla stazione se volete / voleste.

g) Roberto guida come se è / fosse un campione di formula 1.

h) Ho fatto la spesa dopo che eri uscito / tu fossi uscito.

i) Vado io a prendere la nonna, a meno che non vuoi / voglia andarci tu.

l'indirizzo – *the address*
l'esame – *the exam*
il campione –
the champion
la formula 1–
Formula 1

2. Complete the sentences below using the conjunctions provided. **

a) _____ il vino mi piaccia, non ne bevo più di un bicchiere.

b) Sono tornato a casa _____ avevo dimenticato il biglietto.

c) Il negozio era ancora chiuso _____ erano già le 10.

d) _____ avrò fatto l'esame partirò per il Canada.

e) La lettera è arrivata _____ eri uscito.

f) Mio padre ci ha lasciato andare in Australia _____ gli telefonassimo almeno tre volte alla settimana.

g) Abbiamo incontrato i Mazza _____ andavamo a teatro.

dopo che
anche se
mentre
benché
a patto che
perché
appena

3. Among the conjunctions provided, you will find one that can replace the conjunction used in each sentence. Write them down. ***

a) Carlo continua a fumare, <u>sebbene</u> gli faccia male. _____

b) <u>Visto che</u> è domenica, rimango a letto più a lungo. _____

c) C'era tanto traffico, <u>di modo che</u> ho perso il treno. _____

d) Ti do le chiavi di casa <u>perché</u> tu ti senta più libero. _____

e) Ti compro il telefonino <u>purché</u> tu non lo usi a scuola. _____

appena
affinché
per cui
anche se
a patto che
nonostante
siccome
senza che

235

Prefixes and Suffixes That Alter Meaning

Hai ragione; ma lo sai che il direttore ogni tanto sragiona. ... Adesso però ci beviamo un bicchier**ino** e non ne parliamo più.
②

Ma che giornat**accia**, oggi!
①

With the help of prefixes and suffixes, you can change the meaning of a noun, an adjective, or a verb.

1. What a terrible day today! 2. You're right, but you know that the boss talks a lot of nonsense at times ... But now let's drink a little glass (of grappa) and not talk about it anymore.

Suffixes for Nouns and Adjectives

Che bel ve-stit**ino**!
①

Ti piace? L'ho trovato da «Moda Eva». Hanno delle cos**ette** abbastanza carine e per niente care.
②

1. What a pretty dress! 2. Do you like it? I found it at "Moda Eva." They have really cute things and they're not expensive at all.

Italian has a great many suffixes that add a certain note to the basic meaning of a noun or an adjective. There are diminutive forms, augmentative forms, forms that convey belittlement, and pejorative forms.

1. The Diminutive Forms *-ino*, *-ina*, *-etto*, *-etta*, *-uccio*, *-uccia*

il ragazzo	il ragazz**ino**	*the little boy*
la ragazza	la ragazz**ina**	*the young girl*
l'uccello	l'uccell**ino**	*the tiny bird*
bello, -a	bell**ino,-a**	*rather pretty, nice*
brutto, -a	brutt**ino, -a**	*relatively ugly*
giallo	giall**ino, -a**	*yellowish*
piccolo, -a	piccol**ino, -a**	*rather small*

The most commonly used diminutive form is the ending **-no** / **-ina**. When suffixed to an adjective, it conveys a lesser degree of the adjective's root meaning.

il pacco	il pacch**etto**	*the little package*
la cosa	la cos**etta**	*the small thing*
il lavoro	il lavor**etto**	*the small, insignificant act*
il gioco	il gioch**etto**	*the little game, the trifle*
fresco, -a	fresch**etto**, -a	*rather cool*

The ending **-etto / -etta** is also very popular. Depending on the word to which this suffix is linked, and in the context in which the new word formation appears, it can lend a diminutive sense or be slightly disparaging.

la casa	▸	la cas**etta**	▸	la cas**ettina**
la cosa	▸	la cos**etta**	▸	la cos**ettina**
la villa	▸	la vill**etta**	▸	la vill**ettina**
il pacco	▸	il pacch**etto**	▸	il pacch**ettino**
il libro	▸	il libr**etto**	▸	il libr**ettino**

The endings **-etto** and **-ino** can also be combined. This intensifies, or further diminutes, the diminutive.

la bocca	la bocc**uccia**	*the pretty little mouth*
il letto	il lett**uccio**	*the cute little bed*
il caldo	il cald**uccio**	*the cozy warmth*
la cosa	la cos**uccia**	*the small, modest thing*
la casa	la cas**uccia**	*the small, modest house*
l'avvocato	l'avvocat**uccio**	*the unimportant lawyer*
l'attore	l'attor**uccio**	*the insignificant actor*
il medico	il medic**uccio**	*the mediocre doctor*
caro	car**uccio**	*really rather expensive*
debole	debol**uccio**	*really rather weak*
lontano	lontan**uccio**	*relatively distant*

The suffix **-uccio / -uccia** is basically a diminutive form. However, depending on the word and the context, it can also add a note of belittlement. In designations of persons and occupations it can even take on a derogatory meaning.

2. The Derogatory Form -accio, -accia

il ragazzo	il ragazz**accio**	*the ragamuffin, street urchin*
la donna	la donn**accia**	*the slut, the hooker*
il film	il film**accio**	*the miserable film*
il giornale	il giornal**accio**	*the bad newspaper*
il tempo	il temp**accio**	*the wretched weather*
la parola	la parol**accia**	*the curse word*

The suffix **-accio** / **-accia** lends a pejorative and derogatory sense.

3. The Augmentative Form -one, -ona

il libro	il libr**one**	*the big, fat book*
il bacio	il baci**one**	*the gigantic kiss*
la donna	il donn**one**	*the huge, fat woman*
	la donn**ona**	
la nuvola	il nuvol**one**	*the enormous cloud*
	la nuvol**ona**	
la borsa	il bors**one**	*the big handbag*
	la bors**ona**	

What English expresses with the adjectives *big*, *huge*, *enormous*, and the like, Italian conveys by using the suffix **-one** or **-ona**. The masculine ending **-one** is also attached to a feminine noun. The newly created word is then masculine in gender and is preferred to the feminine version ending in **-ona**.

4. Lexicalized Derivations

There are words that originally were formed with the help of suffixes but now have become full-fledged terms, in which the "suffixes" are not always interpreted as conveying meaning. For example:

le manette	(la mano)	*the handcuffs*
l'ombrellone	(l'ombrello)	*the umbrella*
la lampadina	(la lampada)	*the light bulb*
il padrino	(il padre)	*the godfather*
la madrina	(la madre)	*the godmother*
gli orecchini	(l'orecchio)	*the earrings*

It is usage that determines why a word tends to be combined with one suffix rather than another. For non-native speakers it is always advisable to stick to existing word formations.

Prefixes for Nouns and Adjectives

> La **dis**occupazione è più alta nel sud che nel nord del Paese.
> ①
>
> La **stra**grande maggioranza degli italiani è contro la guerra.
> ②

---

1. Unemployment is higher in the south of the country than in the north. 2. The overwhelming majority of Italians are against the war.

1. The Prefixes *dis-, in-, im-, s-*

l'interesse	**il dis**interesse	*the disinterest*
l'attenzione	**la dis**attenzione	*the inattention*
occupato	**dis**occupato	*unemployed, jobless*
abitato	**dis**abitato	*uninhabited*
la capacità	**l'in**capacità	*the incapacity*
la possibilità	**l'im**possibilità	*the impossibility*
naturale	**in**naturale	*unnatural*
morale	**im**morale	*immoral*
il vantaggio	**lo s**vantaggio	*the disadvantage*
contento	**s**contento	*discontent*

The prefixes **dis-**, **in-**, **im-**, and **s-** reverse the meaning of the original word. If a word begins with **b**, **p**, or **m**, **in-** is replaced by **im-**.

2. The Prefixes *arci-* and *stra-*

il vescovo	**l'arci**vescovo	*the archbishop*
il duca	**l'arci**duca	*the archduke*
noto	**arci**noto	*well-known everywhere*
contento	**arci**contento	*overjoyed*
ricco	**stra**ricco	*loaded, extremely wealthy*
pieno	**stra**pieno	*completely sloshed*
carico	**stra**carico	*overloaded, overcrowded*
cotto	**stra**cotto	*boiled to shreds*

Before a noun, **arci-** means *arch-*, but before an adjective the prefix **arci-** intensifies the root meaning to a much greater degree. Similarly, **stra-** conveys a very high degree of a property or quality. The use of **arci-** and **stra-** with adjectives is usually restricted to colloquial speech.

Prefixes for Verbs

Mi **dis**piace molto che non ci possiamo **ri**vedere prima di Pasqua.

I'm very sorry that we can't see each other again before Easter.

1. The Prefix *ri-*

> Don't confuse **risposarsi** (*to marry again*) with **riposarsi** (*to lie down, rest*).

sposarsi	**ri**sposarsi	*to marry again*
cominciare	**ri**cominciare	*to start again*
dare	**ri**dare	*to give back*
avere	**ri**avere	*to get back, have again*

The prefix **ri-** is very frequently used. It can express the repetition of an action or the meaning *back*.

2. The Prefixes *dis-*, *s-*, and *de-*

> **Tip!** Verbs with a prefix are conjugated the same way as the original verb in question.

dire	**dis**dire	*to cancel*
fare	**dis**fare	*to take apart*
approvare	**dis**approvare	*to disapprove*
caricare	**s**caricare	*to unload*
consigliare	**s**consigliare	*to advise against*
parlare	**s**parlare	*to say mean things*
ragionare	**s**ragionare	*to talk nonsense*
colorare	**de**colorare	*to bleach*
comporre	**de**comporre	*to decompose*

The prefixes **dis-**, **s-**, and **de-** reverse the meaning of the original verb. Depending on the verbs, the prefix **s-** can add a negative connotation, as with **sparlare** and **sragionare**. The prefix **de-** is very popular in more recent word formations.

3. The Prefix *stra-*

fare	**stra**fare	*to do too much, exaggerate*
vincere	**stra**vincere	*to win by a mile*
cuocere	**stra**cuocere	*to overcook*
pagare	**stra**pagare	*to overpay*
parlare	**stra**parlare	*to fantasize, talk wildly*

By using **stra-** as a prefix, the meaning of the original verb is greatly intensified.

Prefixes and Suffixes That Alter Meaning

1. Can you identify the original verb in the following list of verbs?
Write down each one. *

a) _____ ricostruire

b) _____ disinvitare

c) _____ disinnamorarsi

d) _____ deconcentrare

e) _____ sbloccare

f) _____ straperdere

g) _____ rimettere

h) _____ spiovere

i) _____ rivendere

k) _____ deformare

2. Match the Italian words with the English equivalents. **

schiudere – rivisitare – la disattenzione – la riscoperta
lo strapotere – disimparare – struccarsi – strabere – lo stradone
stragrande – la stradina – stravolere – il disaccordo – la stradaccia

a) to want too much

_____

b) to visit again

_____

c) gigantic

_____

d) the disunity

_____

e) the little street

_____

f) the inattention

_____

g) to remove one's makeup

_____

h) the bad street

_____

i) the wide street

_____

j) the rediscovery

_____

k) to drink too much

_____

l) to forget

_____

m) the omnipotence

_____

n) to (half) open

_____

Prefixes and Suffixes That Alter Meaning

3. The twin sisters Silvia and Rosa are two entirely different personalities. Complete the description of the twins by filling in the opposites of the words in **bold**. Use the prefixes **dis-**, **in-**, and **s-**. ***

a) Silvia è una ragazza **onesta**, Rosa invece tende ad essere _____ _____.

b) La camera di Silvia è molto **ordinata**, mentre quella della sorella è sempre _____.

c) Rosa è una persona piuttosto **sicura** di sé; Silvia purtroppo si sente spesso _____.

d) Passare la serata con degli amici per Silvia è una cosa molto **piacevole**, per Rosa invece fa parte delle cose che trova _____.

e) Rosa vorrebbe diventare una persona molto **conosciuta**, a Silvia non importa di rimanere del tutto _____.

f) A scuola Silvia era molto **attenta**, Rosa era spesso _____.

g) Quando escono insieme Rosa è sempre **elegante**, mentre Silvia si veste spesso in modo piuttosto _____.

4. Replace the words in **bold** below with a single word that means the same. Use the endings **-one**, **-ino**, **-etto**, and **-accio**. ***

a) Secondo me Rosa ha un **brutto carattere** _____.

b) L'anno prossimo il mio **fratello più piccolo** _____ andrà all'asilo.

l'asilo – *the kindergarten*
il mazzo di fiori – *the bouquet of flowers*
la prima – *the premiere*

c) Non voglio che tu dica delle **brutte parole** _____.

d) Ho comprato un **piccolo mazzo** _____ di fiori per Roberta.

e) La prima dell'*Aida* è stata un **grande successo** _____.

f) Sembra che faccia bene fare una **breve passeggiata** _____ _____ dopo aver mangiato.

g) I nonni ti hanno mandato un **piccolo pacco** _____.

h) Se parti senza salutare farai una **gran brutta figura** _____ _____.

Answers

Article (pp. 16 – 17)

1. **masculine singular:**
un caffè – uno spumante – l'aceto –
il gelato – lo zucchero
masculine plural:
gli spaghetti – i panini
feminine singular:
la città – un'aranciata – l'uva –
una birra – un'insalata
feminine plural:
le uova – le mele

2. al/a+il – alle/a+le – dei/di+i –
delle/di +le – alle/a+le – all'/a+l' –
nel/in+il – dal/da+il – della/di+la –
del/di+il – dalla/da+la

3. un libro/il libro – uno scialle/lo
scialle – una borsetta/la borsetta –
un'agenda/l'agenda – un pigiama/il
pigiama, un abbonamento/l'abbonamento – una sciarpa/la sciarpa –
una camicia/la camicia

4. a) –
b) le
c) la, il, il
d) il, i, gli
e) la, il, la
f) il, l', il, lo

Noun (pp. 26 – 27)

1. **il** vestito – i vestiti, il cinema – i
cinema, il ristorante – i ristoranti, il
caffè – i caffè
lo specchio – gli specchi, lo
sciopero – gli scioperi, lo zio – gli
zii, lo sport – gli sport
l'ufficio – gli uffici, l'arancia – le
arance, l'albergo – gli alberghi,
l'uovo – le uova

la valigia – le valigie, la radio – le
radio, la stazione – le stazioni, la
città – le città

2. a) la, collega
b) figlie
c) una ragazza, amiche, medico,
madre
d) una bambina
e) l'attrice

3. a) gli uffici informazioni
b) i marciapiedi
c) le madri modello
d) i libri di cucina
e) le camere da letto
f) i pianoforti
g) gli asciugamani
h) gli anni record

4. a) il foglio
b) la banca
c) la fine
d) la capitale
e) la porta
f) il capitale

5. a) la professoressa
b) l'autrice
c) l'insegnante
d) la moglie
e) la donna
f) la lavoratrice
g) l'impiegata
h) la farmacista
i) la tedesca
j) la studentessa
k) la psicologa
l) la parrucchiera

> With nouns such as
> **l'aceto**, **l'olio**, **l'uva**,
> **l'insalata**, the
> definite article
> gives no clue as to
> the noun's gender.
> In such cases, you
> can tell the gender
> of the noun from its
> ending.

> Languages are
> always masculine
> in gender.

> **Tip!** Always
> memorize a noun
> together with its
> indefinite article. That
> way you are learning
> the gender at the
> same time, as here:
> **un** amico, **un'**amica,
> **un** elefante, **un'**idea

masculine nouns		feminine nouns	
il computer	il fax	la e-mail/la mail	la chat
Internet	il monitor	la home-page	la web-cam
lo scanner	il modem		
il software	l'hardware		
il mouse	il display		
il file	il CD-Rom		
il laptop	l'hacker		
l'SMS	l'euro		

Adjective (pp. 37–38)

1. a) lunghi, corti
   b) italiana, francese
   c) tranquille, attive
   d) bianco, rosso
   e) moderni, antichi
   f) stretti, larghi
   g) rossi, viola
   h) bianchi, verdi

2. bello:
   a) bella
   b) belle
   c) bei
   d) bel
   e) bell'
   f) bello
   g) begli

   buono:
   a) buon
   b) buona
   c) buono
   d) buoni
   e) belle
   f) buona
   g) buoni

3. a) di   d) che
   b) che   e) del
   c) che   f) che

4. b) Ha incontrato alcune persone molto interessanti.
   c) Ho visto un ottimo film francese.
   d) Ho rotto il bel vaso antico di mia nonna.
   e) Ho passato una serata molto divertente con alcuni vecchi amici.
   f) Ho fatto una lunga telefonata con un caro amico d'infanzia.
   g) Ho fatto una breve passeggiata nel bosco.
   h) Ho comprato un motorino blu.

5. a) Emma è la mia migliore amica.
   b) È più giovane di me e molto carina.
   c) È un'ottima traduttrice.
   d) Ha tre sorelle maggiori, Rita, Maria e Lucia.
   e) Emma però è la più grande di tutte.

Adverb (pp. 45–46)

1. a) normalmente
   b) raramente
   c) leggermente
   d) felicemente
   e) follemente
   f) male
   g) violentemente
   h) direttamente

2. a) facile
   b) facilmente
   c) difficile
   d) naturalmente, bene, buon, puntuale, regolarmente

3. a) I clienti sono appena arrivati.
   b) Il film non è ancora cominciato.
   c) Carlo suona anche il pianoforte.
      Anche Carlo suona il pianoforte.
   d) Non riesco a finire il lavoro per venerdì, purtroppo.
      Purtroppo non riesco a finire il lavoro per venerdì.
   e) Sandra è uscita tardi.
   f) Cerca di non stancarti tanto.
   g) Sono già partiti gli ospiti?
   h) Dovresti rispondere subito.
   i) Ines non vuole mai uscire il sabato sera.

4. a) peggio, malissimo
   b) meglio, benissimo
   c) meno, pochissimo
   d) più, moltissimo
   e) più tardi, tardissimo
   f) più rapidamente, molto rapidamente

Possessive Pronoun (pp. 52–53)

1. a) i miei   d) il nostro
   b) la tua   e) le vostre
   c) i suoi   f) i loro

2. a) il suo   d) le sue
   b) suo, la loro e) i loro
   c) le loro   f) la loro, il loro

3. mio, la mia, mia, la mia, i miei, la mia, mio
   i tuoi, la tua, il tuo, la tua, le tue, la tua
   suo, la sua, i suoi, suo, le sue, il suo

4. a) mia, la mia
   b) i miei, i suoi, i miei
   c) mio, il mio
   d) mia, il suo, sua, la mia, il suo
   e) i miei, i tuoi, i miei
   f) mio, il tuo, il mio

5. a) a casa mia
   b) da parte nostra, di mio padre
   c) è colpa tua
   d) in camera sua, suo cugino

Kinship Terms

masculine		feminine	
il padre	lo zio	la madre	la zia
il figlio	il cugino	la figlia	la cugina
il fratello	il suocero	la sorella	la suocera
il nonno	il genero	la nonna	la nuora
il nipote	la nipote		

Special Features of Kinship Terms

il nipote	*nephew, grandson* la nipote *niece, granddaughter*
i figli	*sons, children*
i fratelli	*brothers, siblings*
i nonni	*grandfathers, grandparents*
gli zii	*uncles, aunts and uncles*
i suoceri	*fathers-in-law, parents-in-law*
i nipoti	*grandsons, nephews, grandchildren, nieces and nephews*

> The following words are not considered to be kinship terms:
> **il ragazzo/la ragazza**
> **l'amico/l'amica**
> **il compagno/ la compagna** (*partner, m. and f.*),
> **la famiglia**

> **Tip!** Note the way *friend* is translated: It is **amico / amica** for a chum, but **ragazzo / ragazza** for an intimate relationship.

Demonstrative Pronoun (p. 57)

1.
a) quell'
b) quella
c) quei
d) quell'
e) quello
f) quel
g) quegli

2.
a) questa, quella, quella
b) quel
c) quei, quello
d) quest'
e) questi, quelli, quelli
f) quegli, quelli, quelli, quelli

Indefinite Pronoun (p. 64)

1.
a) ogni
b) ognuno
c) qualche
d) qualsiasi
e) tutti gli
f) troppa
g) nessuno
h) niente

2.
a) nessun
b) nessun
c) nessuno
d) nessuno
e) nessuna
f) nessuna
g) nessuno
h) nessun'
i) nessun
j) nessun'
k) nessuno
l) nessuna

Personal Pronoun (pp. 76 – 78)

1. io, voi
io, loro, Ci, Ci
tu
ci, ci, io, lei

2.
a) Le
b) La
c) Le
d) Le
e) La
f) Le

3.
a) 3)
b) 5)
c) 4)
d) 8)
e) 2)
f) 7)
g) 1)
h) 6)

4.
a) ci
b) li
c) La
d) Gli
e) Ne
f) le
g) le
h) lo
i) Ne
j) gli
k) le
l) ne

5.
a) Quando vieni a prenderci?
b) Posso telefonarLe stasera?
c) Ne posso assaggiare un po'?
d) Dobbiamo vederci stasera.
e) Carlo si deve trasferire a Roma.
f) Vorrei scusarmi per ieri sera.
g) Al cinema non voglio andarci.
h) Vi vorrei presentare un mio collega.
i) Purtroppo non ti so spiegare niente.

6.
a) Mi scuso.
b) La posso aiutare/posso aiutarLa, signora Nuti?
c) Gli telefono domani.
d) Vi mando una mail/e-mail.
e) La ringrazio, signor Carli.
f) L'aspetto, signora Lanzi.

7.
a) glielo
b) me li
c) ce lo, ve lo
d) glieli

> **Tip!** Don't forget that the forms of **suo** are used to refer to <u>one</u> owner or possessor. For more than one, use **loro**.

Present Tense (pp. 88 – 89)

1. io: bevo
   tu: leggi, tieni
   lui/lei/Lei: è, vuole, parte
   noi: mangiamo
   voi: cercate
   loro: dicono
2. **avere:** ho, hai, ha, abbiamo, avete, hanno
   dare: do, dai, dà, diamo, date, danno
   essere: sono, sei, è, siamo, siete, sono
   sapere: so, sai, sa, sappiamo, sapete, sanno
3. andiamo, vado, va, vanno, fate, andate
   rimaniamo
4. a) rimango, rimanere
   b) spengono, spegnere
   c) salgono, salire
   d) tiene, tenere
   e) tengono, tenere
   f) piacciono, piacere
   g) vogliono, volere
   h) scelgono, scegliere
   i) produce, produrre
5. a) vado
   b) stanno
   c) dormo, faccio, vado
   d) incontro
   e) rimaniamo, giochiamo, chiacchieriamo, andiamo, facciamo
   f) decidiamo
   g) sono, preferisco, leggo, guardo
   h) esco, devo

Present Perfect (pp. 96 – 97)

1. **lavorare:** ho/ hai/ ha/ abbiamo/ avete/ hanno lavorato
   partire: sono/ sei/ è partito, -a siamo/ siete/ sono partiti,-e
   capire: ho/ hai/ ha/ abbiamo/ avete/ hanno capito
   sapere: ho/ hai/ ha/ abbiamo/ avete/ hanno saputo
2. a) risposto, mosso, visto
   b) rotto, dovuto, deciso, messo
   c) venuto, promesso, vissuto, rimasto

3. a) comprato, comprati
   b) fatto, fatta, trovato
   c) prese, comprate
4. a) ho conosciuto, ho aperto, ho disdetto
   b) sono stato/-a, ho prodotto, ho bevuto, ho chiesto
   c) ho discusso, ho offerto, ho letto, sono nato/-a
5. a) Pia è andata in città.
   b) Pia ha comprato ...
   c) Le scarpe sono costate molto.
   d) I soldi non sono bastati.
   e) Ha dovuto pagare con la ...
   f) Paola e Maria sono uscite ...
   g) Rosa e Enzo sono andati al bar.
   h) Gino e Elena hanno mangiato ...
   i) Orazio è andato al cinema.
   j) Il film è cominciato alle 7. 30 ed è finito alle 8.
   k) Il film gli è piaciuto.
   l) .... Orazio è dovuto tornare ...
   m) Ha fatto molto caldo.
   n) Chiara non è voluta uscire.

Imperfect (p. 104)

1. **stare:** stavo, stavi, stava, stavamo, stavate, stavano
   sapere: sapevo, sapevi, sapeva, sapevamo, sapevate, sapevano
   partire: partivo, partivi, partiva, partivamo, partivate, partivano
   capire: capivo, capivi, capiva, capivamo, capivate, capivano
2. a) avevo, piacevano
   b) compravo, tornavo, ascoltavo
   c) erano, studiavo, ero
3. a) ero
   b) piaceva
   c) detestavo, era
   d) è arrivato
   e) era, piaceva, ho cominciato, sono diventata

Preterit (pp. 110 – 111)

1. **pagare:** pagai, pagasti, pagò, pagammo, pagaste, pagarono

dovere: dovetti, dovesti, dovette, dovemmo, doveste, dovettero

dormire: dormii, dormisti, dormì, dormimmo, dormiste, dormirono

2. nacque – nascere, studiò – studiare, si laureò – laurearsi, cominciò – cominciare, tradusse – tradurre, venne – venire, scrisse – scrivere, fu – essere, pubblicò – pubblicare, arrivò – arrivare, si tolse – togliersi

3. a) chiese, discusse
   b) chiusero, conobbe
   c) crebbi, ebbe
   d) corse, furono
   e) persi, successero
   f) presero, si accorsero
   g) misero, scese
   h) piovve, videro
   i) lessi, vinsi
   j) vollero, venne

4. faceva, disegnava, realizzava, prese, cominciò, tornava, riempiva, andava, si trasferì, iniziò, comprò, aprì, investì, aveva, si mise, nacque

Past Perfect (pp. 114 – 115)

1. a) era tornata
   b) erano tornati
   c) era tornato
   d) erano tornate

2. a) era uscita, aveva preso
   b) avevano litigato
   c) era caduta, si era fatta male
   d) aveva lavorato
   e) aveva lavati, aveva rotto
   f) aveva trovato

3. **Present perfect:**
   ha ritrovato, è ritornato, ha riconosciuto, è morto
   Imperfect:
   aveva, mancavano, sopportava, stava
   Past perfect:
   era scappato, aveva vissuto
   Preterit:
   sparì

4. a) è stata
   b) ha perso
   c) era successo, correva
   d) è arrivata, aveva sentito
   e) è andata, faceva, ha rubato

f) andava, è rimasta, aveva dimenticato
g) tornava, ha visto, è caduta
h) aveva comprato, si è rotta

Future (p. 120)

1. a) vedrò   i) dovremo
   b) avrai   j) starete
   c) vorrà   k) lascerò
   d) rimarremo   l) saprai
   e) vivranno   m) mangerà
   f) otterrò   n) faremo
   g) berrai   o) pagheranno
   h) cercherà

2. a) andrai, potrò
   b) andremo, faremo
   c) passeranno, verrà, passerà, saranno
   d) saremo, potrete

Future Perfect (p. 123)

1. a) sarò arrivata
   b) avrà smesso
   c) avrai fatto
   d) saranno arrivati
   e) mi sarò rimesso, -a

2. a) avrò finito (finirò), partirò
   b) tornerai, avremo mangiato
   c) sarai stato, parlerai
   d) presterò, avrò letto
   e) rientreranno, sarà andato (andrà)

3. a) avrà dormito
   b) sarà uscita, avrà preso
   c) avrà mangiato
   d) avrà lavorato
   e) avrà fatto

Conditional (pp. 128 – 129)

1. | Conditional | Infinitive |
   |---|---|
   | sarebbe | essere |
   | verreste | venire |
   | darei | dare |
   | berremmo | bere |
   | dovrebbero | dovere |
   | terrei | tenere |
   | sapresti | sapere |
   | vivrei | vivere |
   | vedresti | vedere |
   | rimarrebbero | rimanere |
   | andrei | andare |
   | avrei | avere |

Tip! Remember that reflexive verbs form all the compound tenses with the auxiliary verb **essere.**

Tip! The past perfect formed with **avere** changes according to the same rules as the present perfect, when a direct object pronoun (**lo**, **la**, **li**, **le**) or **ne** precedes the auxiliary verb **avere.**

2. a) realizzerei, prenderei, partirei
b) servirebbero, potrei, potremmo
c) farebbero
d) spenderei, metterei, darei

3. a) Accompagneresti tu ...?
b) Mi farebbe vedere ...?
c) Mi potrebbe fare ...?
d) Ci fareste vedere...?
e) Potrei provare ...?
f) Ci porterebbe ...?
g) Ci aiutereste a fare ...?
h) Potrebbe dirmi ...?
i) Mi passeresti il pane ...?
j) Letizia, faresti un caffè ...?
k) Signora, Le dispiacerebbe ...?

Conditional Perfect (p. 132)

1. a) sarei venuto, -a
b) avrebbe fatto
c) saremmo voluti partire
d) avrebbe preferito
e) avremmo aiutato
f) avresti dovuto dirmi, avrei preparato

2. a) avrebbe salvato
b) sarebbe sparita
c) sarebbero giunti
d) si sarebbero opposti

Imperative (pp. 140 – 141)

1. tu: a, e, f, h, i **Lei:** b, c, d, g, j

2. a) Mi aiuti,...!
b) Stia ...!
c) Guardi...!
d) ..., mi ascolti!
e) Ci aspetti!
f) Non si preoccupi!
g) Venga ...!
h) Risponda Lei, ...!
i) Sia gentile e mi faccia ...!

3. a) Non guardare!
b) Non ci aspetti!
c) Non prendete ...!
d) Non telefonarmi ...!
e) Non si fermi!
f) Non venga ...!
g) Non usciamo ...!
h) Non andartene!
i) Non lasciatemi/Non mi lasciate!
j) Non passi ...!
k) Non prendere ...!

4. a) Scusi, entri pure, dica
b) Senta, faccia pure

5. a) Mi telefoni, per favore!
b) Lasci un messaggio, per favore!
c) Aspetti un momento, per ...!
d) Si accomodi/si sieda, per ...!
e) Scusi il ritardo!
f) Prenda la prima strada a destra!

Subjunctive (pp. 157 – 159)

1. a) faccia
b) vada
c) abbia cambiato, stia
d) dovesse
e) fosse

2.

Present subjunctive	**Imperfect subjunctive**
a) parli	parlassi
b) cerchi	cercassi
c) cresca	crescesse
d) viviamo	vivessimo
e) partiate	partiste
f) finiscano	finissero
g) sappia	sapessi
h) possa	potessi
i) debba	dovesse
j) vogliamo	volessimo
k) vadano	andassero
l) sia	fossi
m) abbia	avessi

3. a) sia
b) ha
c) abbia letto
d) succeda
e) puoi
f) sa
g) possano

4. a) stessi
b) fosse uscito
c) sarebbero ritornati/ritornassero
d) fosse
e) avesse fatto
f) pagaste
g) avrei potuto/potessi
h) andasse

5. a) voglia
b) si sposino
c) si sia annoiato
d) abbiano divorziato
e) andiate
f) abbia detto
g) possiate
h) faccia

Tip! For the verbs with a regular imperative, memorize a familiar singular imperative form for each conjugation group, for example:
scusare ▶ scusa!
rispondere ▶ rispondi!
sentire ▶ senti!

Using these forms, you can obtain the imperative for the **Lei** form. The endings are the opposite ones in each case:

TU	LEI
scusa!	scusi!
rispondi!	risponda!
senti!	senta!

i) sia piaciuto
j) telefoniate

6. a) facessi, faccia
  b) esca, rimanessi
  c) prenda, andassi
  d) si riunisse, suonasse
  e) restasse, stia

Reflexive Verbs (p. 164)

1. a) ci svegliamo
  b) si alza, prepara
  c) mi alzo
  d) si lava, si fa, si prepara
  e) lavarmi, vestirmi, occuparmi
  f) mi metto
  g) ci vediamo
  h) mi faccio, va
  i) usciamo, ci sediamo

2. a) si è sposato
  b) hanno dovuto trasferirsi/si sono dovuti trasferire
  c) ti sei informata
  d) si sono incontrati
  e) ha potuto riposarsi/si è potuta riposare
  f) ha voluto iscriversi/si è voluto iscrivere
  g) se n'è andata
  h) non si è divertita
  i) non ha potuto addormentarsi/ non si è potuto addormentare
  j) si è annoiato
  k) non ha voluto mettersi/non si è voluta mettere

The Verb **andarsene** *to go away*

Present tense:	(io) me ne vado, (tu) te ne vai, (lui/lei/Lei) se ne va (noi) ce ne andiamo, (voi) ve ne andate, (loro) se ne vanno
Present perfect:	(io) me ne sono andato,-a; (tu) te ne sei andato, -a; (lui/lei/Lei) se n'è andato, -a; (noi) ce ne siamo andati, -e; (voi) ve ne siete andati, -e; (loro) se ne sono andati, -e

Impersonal Verbs (p. 167)

1. a) ha fatto bel tempo, ha fatto un po' fresco
  b) è/ha nevicato, ha fatto molto freddo
  c) ha fatto caldo, non sono bastati
  d) è/ha piovuto

2. a) basta, bastano, ci vuole
  b) piace, bisogna

c) c'è, ci sono, piacciono
d) ci vogliono, sembra, basti

Infinitive (p. 173)

1. a) a   h) –
  b) da, -   i) a
  c) –   j) di
  d) di   k) a
  e) da   l) di
  f) –   m) di
  g) –   n) a

2. a) di avervi incontrati ,-e
  b) di aver litigato
  c) di aver lavorato
  d) essere andata

3. a) Non vorrei incontrarli/Non li vorrei incontrare.
  b) Dovresti telefonargli/Gli dovresti telefonare.
  c) Sono felice di rivederli.
  d) Hai promesso di scriverle.
  e) Mi pare di averlo già visto.

Present Participle (p. 177)

1. a) Stiamo giocando a carte.
  b) Si sta vestendo per uscire.
  c) Stanno guardando la televisione.
  d) Stavamo cenando.
  e) Stavo facendo la spesa.
  f) Sta ascoltando la musica.

2. a) Mentre leggeva la lettera, Maria piangeva.
  b) Se passi per il centro farai …

c) Siccome non ho/ non avevo il tuo indirizzo elettronico, ti …
d) Ho cambiato opinione su di te quando ti ho visto giocare …
e) Anche se aveva fretta Carla …
f) Se ti organizzi bene, riuscirai …
g) Ho incontrato Piero mentre uscivo dal cinema.

Remember that **sembra** is followed by the subjunctive.

Don't forget! Reflexive verbs form the present perfect and the other compound tenses with the auxiliary verb **essere**.

Ho visto Chiara uscendo dal cinema. *I saw C. when I came out of the movie theater.* (same subject)

Ho visto C. uscire/ che usciva dal cinema. *I saw C. coming out of the movie theater / I saw C. when she came out of the movie theater.*

Passive Voice (p. 181)

1. Active sentences: c, e, f, g
Passive sentences: a, b, d, h
2. b) I turisti venivano accolti bene.
c) I turisti verrebbero accolti bene.
d) I turisti sono stati accolti bene.
e) Credo che ...vengano accolti ...
3. a) verrà costruito
b) è stata inaugurata
c) viene eletta
d) sono stati trovati/ vennero trovati

Impersonal Form *si* (p. 185)

1. a) si beve   e) si parcheggia
b) ci si incontra   f) si consumano
c) ci si saluta   g) si preparano
d) si usa   h) si usano
2. a) si preparano   d) si festeggia
b) si mangia   e) si trovano
c) si comprano   f) si va
3. a) si è giovani, si pensa
b) si è costruito
c) si sono restaurati
d) si è brilli, si dovrebbe
e) si è vista
f) si è timidi, si diventa

Negation (pp. 190–191)

1. a) non
b) no, no, non
c) no, non
d) di no, non, no, non
e) non, non, no, non, non
2. a) Silvia non è molto simpatica.
b) Non è nemmeno molto carina.
c) Non invita mai nessuno.
d) La sera non esce mai./Non esce mia la sera.
e) Non si interessa di niente.
f) Così nessuno le telefona e nessuno va a trovarla.
3. a) Oggi non ho mangiato molto.
b) Sonia non mangia né la carne né il pesce.
c) Stefania non mangia il dessert. Non prende nemmeno la /della frutta.
d) I bambini non hanno ancora fatto colazione.

e) A colazione non mangio molto.
f) La sera non mangio mai.
g) Stefano non vuole più bere vino, la sera.
h) Non abbiamo ancora mai mangiato la polenta.
i) Non stiamo ancora mangiando.

Word Order (pp. 199–200)

1. a) Claudia ha 28 anni.
b) Non è sposata, perché non ha ancora trovato l'uomo giusto.
c) Per il momento non è neanche innamorata./Non è neanche innamorata, per il momento.
d) La sera non è quasi mai in casa. Non è quasi mia in casa, la sera.
e) Il sabato va spesso in discoteca./ Va spesso in discoteca, il sabato.
f) La domenica non fa niente./ Non fa niente, la domenica.
g) Non fa nemmeno una passeggiata.
h) Da qualche mese sta cercando un appartamento in città.
i) Non vuole più abitare fuori città, anche se è meno caro.
2. a) La sera dove vai?/Dove vai la ...
b) Che cosa fai tutta la domenica a casa?
c) Perché non vuoi più abitare fuori città?
3. a) Come   f) Da quanto tempo
b) Di dove   g) Qual è
c) Dove   h) Quando
d) Quanti   i) Perché
e) Che
4. a) Posso chiederLe qualcosa?/ Le posso chiedere qualcosa?
b) Quanto costano queste scarpe?
c) Quale bus va alla stazione?
d) Che ora è?/Che ore sono?
e) A che ora comincia il film?
f) Le piace gli Stati Uniti?
g) Com'è il tempo da voi?

Relative Clause (pp. 205–206)

1. a) in cui   d) con cui
b) a cui   e) di cui
c) che   f) che

2. a) 3. d) 6.
b) 1. e) 2.
c) 5. f) 4.
3. a) che
b) in cui/nella quale
c) di cui/dei quali, per cui/
per i quali
d) che
e) in cui/nella quale
f) su cui/sui quali
g) da cui/dal quale
4. a) Dovete dire quello che/ciò che
sapete.
b) Il libro che mi hai regalato è
molto interessante.
c) Non so più quello che/ciò che
volevo dire.
d) Ieri mi ha telefonato Enrico, il
che/ e ciò/ ciò che mi ha fatto
molto piacere.
e) Chi è stanco può rimanere a
casa.
f) A chi non piace la musica
classica può andare in discoteca.
g) Domenica abbiamo visto il film
di cui/del quale ci hai parlato.
h) Come si chiama il ragazzo la cui
madre fa yoga con te?
i) È questo il cappotto per cui/per
il quale hai speso 500 euro?
5. a) la fontana e) il quadro
b) l'uva f) il semaforo
c) il portafoglio
d) la carta di credito

Conditional Sentence (p. 209)

1. Unreal conditional sentences:
a, c, d, g, h
2. a) arrivate
b) fossi
c) vieni
d) rinunciasse
e) prendiamo
f) guardassi
g) amasse
h) dormissi
i) sono
j) poteste
k) volete

Indirect Discourse (pp. 216 – 217)

1. a) 3. c) 4.
b) 2. d) 1.
2. a) ha conosciuto …
b) si è innamorato di lei.
c) si vedono tutti i giorni.
d) quando non si vedono si
telefonano.
e) Si chiede se un giorno si
sposeranno.
f) a lui, comunque, piacerebbe
vivere con lei.
3. a) aveva conosciuto
b) si era innamorato
c) si vedevano
d) quando non si vedevano, si
telefonavano
e) se un giorno si sarebbero sposati
f) a lui, comunque, sarebbe
piaciuto vivere con lei
4. a) Sono contento di rivedervi.
b) Volete un caffè?
c) Avete fatto buon viaggio?
d) Quanto tempo rimanete/
rimarrete?
e) Non partite troppo presto!
f) Rimanete almeno due
settimane!
g) Avete voglia di venire con me al
mare?
h) Mi piacerebbe partire con voi
per la Germania.

Prepositions (p. 223)

1. a) da
b) da, a, in
c) sulla, del
d) della, al
e) di, sui
f) dal, delle
g) in, in
2. a) dal, al
b) al, dal
c) in, alla, a, in
d) in, a
e) in, al
f) da, in
g) al, all'
h) nel, a

Tip! The subjunc-
tive is not used
following **dire che**
and **raccontare che**.

Tip! You can
avoid many mistakes
in the use of preposi-
tions by memorizing
three rules for state-
ments of place and
time:
▶ **andare/essere a +**
city / town,
▶ **andare/essere in +**
country / region,
▶ **andare/essere da +**
person

Answers

Tip!

Remember that **mille** can be used only for (one) thousand, that is, from 1,000 to 1,999. Starting with 2,000, *thousand* is expressed as **mila**: **duemila**, **tremila**, **quattromila, ...**

Numbers (p. 230)

1. a) sedici
   b) sessantasette
   c) 76
   d) 113
   e) centodiciannove
   f) 1212
   g) duemiladuecentodiciassette
   h) 11'315
   i) 15'414
   j) un milione seicentodiciannove-milasettecentoottantotto
2. a) quattro
   b) sette, seconda
   c) dieci, quinta
   d) sedici, terza, quarto, ventotto
3. a) mezzo chilo di spinaci
   b) un chilo di mele
   c) due chili e mezzo d'uva
   d) una bottiglia di olio d'oliva
   e) due etti e mezzo di parmigiano
   f) tre etti di prosciutto crudo

Times of Day	
Vengo ...	I'm coming ...
stamattina.	this morning.
oggi a mezzogiorno.	today at noon.
oggi pomeriggio.	this afternoon.
stasera	this evening.
domani mattina.	tomorrow morning.
domani pomeriggio.	tomorrow afternoon.
domani sera.	tomorrow evening.
domenica mattina	Sunday morning.
lunedì pomeriggio	Monday afternoon.
martedì sera.	Tuesday evening.
la mattina	in the mornings.
il/nel pomeriggio	in the afternoons.
la sera	in the evenings.

Conjunctions (p. 235)

1. a) avevo
   b) siate
   c) telefona
   d) partiate
   e) ho studiato
   f) volete
   g) fosse
   h) eri uscito
   i) voglia
2. a) Benché
   b) perché
   c) anche se
   d) appena
   e) dopo che
   f) a patto che
   g) mentre

3. a) nonostante
   b) Siccome
   c) per cui
   d) affinché
   e) a patto che

Prefixes and Suffixes That Alter Meaning (pp. 241–242)

1. a) costruire
   b) invitare
   c) innamorarsi
   d) concentrare
   e) bloccare
   f) perdere
   g) mettere
   h) piovere
   i) vendere
   k) formare
2. a) stravolere
   b) rivisitare
   c) stragrande
   d) il disaccordo
   e) la stradina
   f) la disattenzione
   g) struccarsi
   h) la stradaccia
   i) lo stradone
   j) la riscoperta
   k) strabere
   l) disimparare
   m) lo strapotere
   n) schiudere
3. a) disonesta
   b) disordinata
   c) insicura
   d) spiacevoli
   e) sconosciuta
   f) disattenta
   g) inelegante
4. a) caratteraccio
   b) fratellino
   c) parolacce
   d) mazzetto
   e) successone
   f) passeggiatina
   g) pacchetto
   h) figuraccia

Index

Index

458.2
421   Rovere-Fenati, Bea-
Rovere-   trice
fenati

         Mastering Italian
         grammar